# The Works of Stefan Ge

**UNC** | COLLEGE OF ARTS AND SCIENCES
Germanic and Slavic Languages and Literatures

From 1949 to 2004, UNC Press and the UNC Department of Germanic & Slavic Languages and Literatures published the UNC Studies in the Germanic Languages and Literatures series. Monographs, anthologies, and critical editions in the series covered an array of topics including medieval and modern literature, theater, linguistics, philology, onomastics, and the history of ideas. Through the generous support of the National Endowment for the Humanities and the Andrew W. Mellon Foundation, books in the series have been reissued in new paperback and open access digital editions. For a complete list of books visit www.uncpress.org.

# The Works of Stefan George

## Second Edition

TRANSLATED BY

OLGA MARX AND ERNST MORWITZ

UNC Studies in the Germanic Languages and Literatures
Number 78

Suggested citation: Marx, Olga, and Ernst Morwitz. *The Works of Stefan George: Second Edition*. Chapel Hill: University of North Carolina Press, 1974. DOI: https://doi.org/10.5149/9781469657875_Marx

Library of Congress Cataloging-in-Publication Data
Names: Marx, Olga and Morwitz, Ernst.
Title: The works of Stefan George / by Olga Marx and Ernst Morwitz.
Other titles: University of North Carolina Studies in the Germanic Languages and Literatures ; no. 78.
Description: Chapel Hill : University of North Carolina Press, [1974] Series: University of North Carolina Studies in the Germanic Languages and Literatures.
Identifiers: LCCN 73-16133 | ISBN 978-1-4696-5786-8 (pbk: alk. paper) | ISBN 978-1-4696-5787-5 (ebook)
Classification: LCC PT2613 .E47A25 1974 | DCC 831/ .8

Composed by
EKENÄS TRYCKERI AKTIEBOLAG
Ekenäs - Finland

# TRANSLATORS' NOTE

A first edition of this book was published in 1949 as Number 2 of the *University of North Carolina Studies in the Germanic Languages and Literatures,* with a subsidy from the North Carolina Center of the Carnegie Foundation for the Advancement of Teaching at the University of North Carolina. It was reprinted in 1966 by the AMS Press, Inc. of New York.

The present revised and enlarged edition has been edited after the death of Ernst Morwitz by Dietrich von Bothmer from the manuscripts and notes of the translators. Besides many changes in the poems, it contains additional translations intended to give a representative survey of Stefan George's earliest poems (which appeared in *The Primer*), of his dramatic sketches (Volume XVII of his Collected Works), and of his prose writings (*Days and Deeds*).

The translation, based on the final edition of Stefan George's poems (1927-1934), is an attempt to convey the language and the rhythm of the original and to facilitate the understanding of the difficult German text. Thus the rendering is, in itself, a synthetic commentary, such as Goethe recommends in the last paragraph of the chapter on translation in the notes to his *West-östlicher Divan.* It complements the analytical commentaries by Ernst Morwitz, *Kommentar zu dem Werk Stefan Georges* (München, Düsseldorf: Küpper, 1960; 2nd ed. 1969), and *Kommentar zu den Prosa-, Drama- und Jugenddichtungen Stefan Georges* (München, Düsseldorf: Küpper, 1962).

# CONTENTS

xxii

ODES

PILGRIMAGES

ALGABAL

Preface to the second edition of Odes, Pilgrimages, and Algabal

The author distributed the first printing of his poems which began to appear a decade ago, as a gift to his friends and patrons. This relieved him of all consideration for a public which, at that time, was particularly unwilling or unable to accept and enjoy poems as works of art. Now that painting and the decorative arts are on an upward trend and have awakened a new longing for beauty in many sections of our country, the author believes that, in response to increasing requests, he may abandon the shelter of his seclusion. ODES, PILGRIMAGES, AND ALGABAL introduce the series of his publications. Except for slight changes and additions and more punctuation marks, desirable at times though more often superfluous, they are given here in the form which orginally won them friends. And so is is to be hoped that a little of what was prophecied for these books may come true.

# ODES

## (1890)

To

Carl August Klein

The Trusted and True since the Days of our Youth

Berlin

MDCCCXC

## INSCRIPTION

BEFORE THE SPRING THIS SONG WAS TUNED BETWEEN
THE WHITE WALL AND THE RIVER EDGED WITH GREEN.
THIS YEAR I BRING MY DREAM IN GOLD AND BLUE
TO ALL MY PEOPLE'S SONS, THE YOUNG, THE NEW.

# INITIATION

The river calls! Where stately reeds unfurl
Their slender flags in gentle wind and hedge
The tender throng of ripples in their swirl
Of eagerness to bathe the mossy ledge,

Pause in your frantic vehemence, immersed
In vigorous, primeval scent unscored
By thought, with every alien breath dispersed
Fix your divining eyes upon award.

Do you discern the faint and rhythmic veer
Of leaves? The glow of glassy waters lance
The fragile wall of mist? And do you hear
The song the elves are singing to their dance?

The branches proffer in their angled frames
Star-cities in the regions of the blessed,
The flight of time erases wonted names
And Here and Now are images at best.

This is the hour! Down the goddess gleams,
Her gauzy veils the colour of the moon,
Her lids are lowered by the weight of dreams,
She leans to you and offers you her boon.

Her mouth is trembling closer to your cheeks,
So pure you seem to her, so ripe for bliss,
That now she does not shun your hand which seeks
To turn her lips to yours and to your kiss.


# IN THE PARK

The fountains rise as rubies, fall in pearls,
Which every lavish jet bestows upon
A carpet knit of green and silken curls

Where they disperse as soon as they are sown.
The poet, whom the birds serenely face,
In wide and shadowed arches dreams alone.

Who saw the dawning of that day of grace
Intensely knows — in strains of sweetness wound —
How flesh to flesh is groping for embrace.

The poet also hears the lure of sound,
And yet today he must not yield to spells,
Because his speech with spirits, holds him bound.

His hand must goad the pen — though it rebels.


## INVITATION

"Let us leave pavements and grime!"
How dear your offer sounded!
"There, where more light and elate
Thought and breath seem to chime
We shall enjoy the flower
And resurrection fête."


Gayly I fled from the rough
Clatter and tortuous maze.
Though I knew: Only love,
Newly from heaven blazed,
Pledges salvation below
And undying glow.


Feeling at ease as a child
You bear me with laughing glance,
Who closely cling to your side.
Does not the vista entrance!
How dawn-shimmers glint and breathe
Where shining villas wreathe!

Look! To the very peak,
Where through clefts in the stone
Little pine-trees leap,
Orchards tower in ranks,
Flashing waters flow
Beneath on fragrant banks.

Uphill without stopping we go.
"Follow!" you mockingly call.
Here at the summit I pause.
Downward again to the shore,
Swiftly! Branches of haws
Lend us their wings of snow.

Now for a while let us rest.
Dew on the grass, in haste
On we go, side by side!
You drove my anguish away,
Though feeling was never at tide
In hours of jubilant play.


AFTERNOON

Smoulder of sunrays guttering downward,
Down from the cloudless cupola of heaven,
Smoulder of sunrays in flashing assault.

The limpid southern air in noonday silence,
Tumult of throngs has died before the palace,
Died on flagstones glutted with radiance.
The soundless rampart and desolate terrace,
The walls in long battalions blindly loom
Like ovens afire with fuel of victims.
In the square of the courtyard, flanked by pillars,
Agile fountains falter in their arts.
Above the beds where shrubs have drooped and shrivelled,
Breath of blooms, half-withered, clings in layers.

12

Smoulder of sunrays guttering downward,
Down from the cloudless cupola of heaven.

He is lonely. They fall on his shoulders and hair
Ceaselessly, and he feels them with boundless delight,
For he fled from the chamber's fragrant coolness,
Seeking counter-blaze for destroying blazes,
Until faintness reprieves him. He yields and sinks
Down-sliding close to a column's base.

Smoulder of sunrays guttering downward.


AN ENCOUNTER

The longer shadows summoned milder glows,
The drooping body on which noon encroached
Was urging to the lips of fresher flows —
And then, between the pillars, you approached.

My glances drew me from the path I seek,
But brief and shy they only dared to yearn
On white, on velvet white of brow and cheek.
Unanswered they were driven to return.

And crazed with magic, mad to clasp, they trailed
The slender bow sweet limbs in walking curved,
And wet with longing, then, they fell and failed
Before into your own they boldly swerved.

Oh, that your whim restored you to my sight!
Let not a newer form obliterate
The past! It was my task through endless night
To conjure you devoutly, trait by trait.

In vain! A steady rain of bitter lye
Mists and obscures what painfully I scored.
It pales. How was your hair and how your eye?
It pales and trembles in a dying chord.

## LOVE FEASTS IN NEW TERRAINS

### I

The coals are glowing. Let the incense ooze!
And when the resins hiss and are dispelled
We cling in clouds where vapours fall and fuse,
And fervent wish and sweet desire weld.

Light up the sconces! Let the tapers shine!
The fumes hang heavy as in sacred naves,
And palm to palm, in silence we divine
A host of melodies that join to waves.

No tender breath! In choruses like these
Virginal down would mar the harmonies
Like curls produced by artifice and lies.

Cast other grains into the brazier, so
Our senses, caught in silver surge, may know
The woman, weary, wonderful, and wise.

### II

The sky-blue satin of the tent is traced
With golden symbols of the moon and stars,
And on a socle at the edge are placed
The malachite and alabaster jars.

A triple chain supports the copper globe
Which dims our shining brows with feeble rays,
An ample burnous serves us for a robe,
And let us not forget the myrtle sprays!

The draught will soon beget prophetic tone
We listen to on mats of plaited hair.
Before the hospodar — each gesture known —

The boy profoundly bows. As in a spring
Of magic, I am dawningly aware
Of early days when I was still a king.

14

# TRANSFORMATION

On twilit paths when shadows fall,
Over bridges and on toward tower and wall,
When lilted cadences call,

> In a golden chariot ferried
> On pearl-grey pinions, and carried
> Where scent of linden beguiles,
> Swing down to earth
> With gentle smiles
> And anodyne breath.

Under the mast of a ship which forges away
Over the glittering web of water and ray,
Entranced to be free of the bay,

> In a silver chariot ferried
> On chrysolite mirrors, and carried
> Where cinnabar vapour beguiles,
> Swing down to earth
> With joyful smiles
> And sensuous breath.

Jubilant dyes of the end, and the sun floated under,
Breakers snatch at the planks and tear them asunder,
And tempests rumble and thunder.

> In an iron chariot, ferried
> On clods of lava, and carried
> Where cinnabar vapour beguiles,
> Swing down to earth
> With savage smiles
> And smouldering breath.

## PARTING

The silver beeches linger hand in hand
Along the sands where crowding waves careen,
The yellow furrows verge on pasture-land,
A villa hides in gardens drenched with green.

Beside the morning-glory arbour, beams
Around his young and mournful forehead drew.
Belief in songs to come still fills his dreams,
His glances journey through the boundless blue.

Beyond, where clouds are shaped to shining peaks,
And ships advance with tall and carven prows
Or sleep surrendered to the bay, he seeks
The shores of wonder his desires rouse.

The eyes he loves are gazing fixed and wet,
He takes the gift of gods — a little shy,
A hint of sad adieu, a faint regret —
Without a thought of fame, without a sigh.

## SERENADE

Too long, too lavishly, your eyes — the blue
Of turquoise — shine for One. I wait in rue.
The stones are solaced by your garment's hem,
I scarcely by a dream.

In days of old the gods were not so cold!
When from the throng which rapture rendered bold,
A youth, in flames of holy fervour caught,
Forsook the sunny earth in adoration,
They prized the stainless sacrifice he brought,
And smiled and granted signs of commendation.

16

Am I beyond the age of offering?
Has honeyed lust for death annulled my right?
Did I not hear the fanfares soar, and sing
The shining ode of love's delight?

But if you deigned to let a shimmer sever
Your lashes, piercing me, then I should frown
Upon all hope of ecstasy forever,
Discard my psalter, having sung your grace,
I should reject the shadow of renown
And perish like the moth, without a trace.


SHORE


Oh, let us leave the meadows of the sea
Which — though they rear and strain in surly foam — sustain
Only the wild gulls in their dipping flight,
And lave the virgin heavens endlessly.
Too long we wore a mask before the light.

To emerald ponds with marsh and flowered trail,
Where grass, and vines, and leaves are rocked in tangled sheaves,
To shrines eternal evening sanctified!
The swans which from a distant inlet sail
In secret sheathed, are escort to the bride.

Delight has snatched us from the fallow fjords
— Where your lips are aglow, exotic petals flow —
And when like drifts of bloom your body sways,
Then all the stems begin to surge in chords
And turn to aloe, tea, and laurel sprays.

## LATE SUMMER

Voices from the terrace fading,
In the gardens gather sound.
Under platans' ample shading
Haughty beauties flounce around,
Pert in elegant allures,
On the arm of paramours
Closer clinging, and with sweet
Nods they greet.


Oh, the hoops that boast of rich
Children, agile in their wile,
Yielded to the airy style!
Questions idling on the tongue,
With the perfumes that bewitch
Swept along.


Drums are still and viols thrill.
Distant hoof-beats, riders amble
Slowly onward, careless ramble.
Flippant whispers flutter, rise
In surprise.


Gay and empty galantries
Foe to action's turbid seas.
Languid wisdom. Spas alone
Strike this tone.


Gondolas are gliding past,
Gentle rhythm, gentle lure,
Lap of oars on water cast
Mingle lightly to a sprightly
Pompadour.

## IN RETROSPECT

Once more I guess behind the curtain: scraps of mist the evening twines,
Behind the boughs of plane trees threaded through the grain in curious lines,
The realm my scepter yesterday still ruled, but now transformed and far,
A Tyrus, pond, and garden-frond in liquid tints of dew and tar.
Here beech-tops on the shore divide the airy villa from the street,
A clearing in the forest hums with flocks of deer on flitting feet.
O ships, parade of haughty swans! Your colours were a gift to me!
O you, that like a mother swelled my faith in my own songs, O sea!


## ON THE TERRACE

Before the boastful balustrade, the slopes
Effuse the skyey green of gliding glaze,
A web of trees and houses lit with hopes —
The goddess casts her shadow on the vase.


I hurry forward to the flaming wheel,
A flash! For us a chain of runic light,
On sudden pinnacles of grace we reel
And then are buried in abysmal night.


And now the tracks are blotted. I return.
The goddess casts her shadow on the vase.
If you were great enough and could discern...
My foolish transport scars me with its blaze.


Oh, triumph! It is you! In sunset flame
Of glances we exchanged I read my grief.
A herald of your self you staunchly came,
And our togetherness was proud and brief.

# ADDRESS

I never shall rejoice in cold esteem,
When you deny your flesh with regal pride
To common wenches and their brazen dream.
You held aloof from them and yet you sighed.

Your hands, indeed, must all in vain be wrung
For draught of solace from a higher sphere,
Oh, would that from a mother I were sprung
So I myself could bring it to you here!

Whether you begged or bade imperiously,
No double red would pour into my face.
I should surround you with a silken sea,
On sumptuous purple yield to your embrace.

But I can only soothe with phantom kiss,
A child of buoyant cloud and crystal air,
I cleave through chaos, sing your state of bliss,
And bear as I divine you also bear.


# PICTURES


# THE INFANTE

With shield and dagger under fallow frieze,
He stands in a dark oval rimmed with gold,
A pale and smiling child. His brother-twin
Was only briefly in this hall where then
No stranger gawked. The frosty mountain-breeze
Had proved a playmate who was more than bold.

But he himself will never grieve at all
That he was kept from growing old and grim
Like this or that one on the neighbouring wall,
For blessedness has been accorded him:

When glass pomegranates to the moon unclose
He is companioned by a shining elf,
And often follows, flying and in fall,
With her the fondly cherished silken ball
Which, coloured like the olive and the rose,
Is still agleam upon the oaken shelf.


FRA ANGELICO

Above the graceful headings of the story
— Eternal vigil over mortal plight,
The ruthless sire's message full of glory —
He worked the wonder of unfailing light.

The gold from holy chalices he took,
For yellow hair the stalks of ripened wheat,
The blue from women washing at the brook,
The pink from children colouring with slate.

The Lord in majesty's untarnished rays,
Beside him gentle singers of his praise
And victors over Gorgons, friends of Graces,

The bride with calm and childish bosom faces
Him meek, yet radiant as he reaches down
To set on her the first, the fairest crown.


THE GARDENS CLOSE

Early evening blurs the lawns, a cold
Drizzle dims the pond to greys,
And Dianas and Apollos fold
Radiant limbs in films of haze.

Faded leaves are whirling toward the tombs,
Dahlias, gillyflowers, roses,
Forced into a symphony of fumes
Yearn for sleep in downy mosses.

Through the gate the burning moons have fled.
What you hoped for — does it stand?
Can you still believe in what they said,
Pilgrim, with your staff in hand?

PILGRIMAGES

(1891)

TO THE POET

HUGO VON HOFMANNSTHAL

IN MEMORY

OF THE DAYS OF EAGER ENCHANTMENT

VIENNA

MDCCCXCI

*INSCRIPTION*

THEN I JOURNEYED FORTH
AND BECAME A STRANGER
AND I SOUGHT FOR SOME ONE
TO SHARE MY MOURNFULNESS
AND THERE WAS NO ONE.

# THE RECLUSE GOES FORTH

A lance of light does not deceive him now.
The winds that with a scourge of twisted hail
Had driven him away from every trail,
Are curved caressingly about his brow.

"O cell, from you I often seek release,
Your wall has never yielded me rewards
Like glints of red and blue on snowy swards.
How slumber numbs my senses in your peace."

And faintly dazed by flecks of changing gold,
Straight through the shining trees he makes his way,
And does not know the end will bring dismay.
He found the valley which he knew of old.

"They bend and sway with glaring crimson bows.
I dare the leap! But now — to whom to turn?
They made the long extinguished tinder burn,
I hate them, yet I blaze to clasp them close.

Why does my gaze explore the distant peak?
The arching stair, the figures saturate
With sun? They never falter in their gait.
To none of these my tongue shall ever speak.

To match my whim (already vengeance neared!)
I used to fashion stature, mouth, and eye.
Among the joyful rose my restless cry,
Is beauty always cheap? I asked and sneered.

But now my anguish hungers for a mien
Of sorrow, now a brow can strike me blind,
Lashes suffice to snare and sway my mind,
An arm entwined with rings of tourmaline."

How could he bear to leave this mournful site
Again, when blooms of frost are dew, to weave
The dance with scarlet women and believe
In careless revelry and loud delight?

Could he return once more to what he said
Farewell that day, still yearning for its fill,
To life with parchments, true and tried, until
Restoring dreams surround his lonely bed?


Stop your turning vanes, O mill,
So the heath may sleep at will.
Ponds await a thawing wind,
Rimmed with crystal lance on lance,
And the little trees are lined
Up like varnished woodwax plants.

On the blind and frozen tide
White-clad children softly glide
Homeward from communion, pray
Silently to God whom learning
Set aloof, while some essay
Pleas to Him who yields to yearning.

Did a whistle shrill below?
All the candles faintly flow.
Was it not like voices weeping?
Dark enchanters cast a spell,
Draw their brides into their keeping.
Ring, O bell, ring out, O bell!


While you listen to whispering flames,
Close to your knee is my cheek and claims
Only a breath of your warmth. But the mad

Tides of blood to my temples show
That where you go I must not go,
And bliss still leaves me chained and sad.

When in pity you smooth my hair
I am rewarded, and though I dare
Disaster, I court your sublimity

Like the devout who, in spite of their dread,
Daily at Angelus turn their head
To a Madonna of ebony.


Why do you squander
Tears on a she?
Foolish to ponder,
Wait and see

If in the valley
Snow has gone,
South wind will rally
Blooms on the lawn.

Will you be seeing
Her unveiled
Still before fleeing
June has paled?

Why do you squander
Tears on a she?
Foolish to ponder,
Wait and see!


All youth (or
So it seems to you)
Craves to be caught in flame.
But dawns and twilights flew,
When, in your presence I was poised and calm.

You speak! I
Almost start in fright!
Can I be wound
In so much zeal and light
By gay and childish laughter — empty sound!

And later
(Do not doubt I grieved!)
Gently your foot still fell,
Your finger gently weaved,
I spurned — and only then I praised you well.

O sister,
You dislike this strain?
When I depart,
Never to come again,
Let this enigma bind us heart to heart.


To ancient lands the vaulted passage calls,
Tapering shaft,
And light through which the long-drawn strophe falls.
And there I quaffed
Sun, when I fled the dragon's dripping claws.

A thorn impaled me at the garden gate.
Tearose, O yellow bloom,
Unflawed by white, aglow and saturate,
Strong and replete with doom.
Even a drop of dew would mar your state.

Too soon! I hanker after blandishment
First violets confer.
To seldom flowers in hothouse frames I bent,
And then, to float near her,
I loosened from my kerchief kindred scent.

# VISIONS

## I

When from the gondola she mounts the stair,
She trails her robe along the stones and suffers
— Accepting conquest with a haughty air —
The arm her escort, old and noble, proffers.

A gentle phrase cannot delight her ear,
In festal halls she sits devoid of feeling,
The only tale of joy she wants to hear
Comes from the tawny angels on the ceiling.

The swirls of heavy velvet, first of spoils
From cargoes never known before, enfold her,
She revels in the fumes of precious oils
Which traders from the Indies lately sold her.

Now to a wastrel lacking rank and name,
Within her curtained chamber she has spoken:
"Cry out upon the market place my shame,
I cower at your feet, abased and broken."

## II

Too long I lean against the gate and gaze
Through iron fretwork toward the lawn.
I hear a flute that yearns for far-aways,
In glossy laurel laughs a faun.

And when I meet you at the garnet tower,
You never have the grace to slow your tread,
You do not know my blessing for this hour
And how I mourn when it has fled.

The pledge I gave myself I now forswear!
We too are of an ancient race and should
I drop the shawl which hides my breast and hair
And then atone with early widowhood?

Ah, if he guessed the charms my lips invent:
— I guess them since my dreams revealed his face —
The oleanders drowning in their scent
And others soft as jessamine's embrace.

Too long I lean against the gate and gaze
Through iron fretwork toward the lawn.
I hear a flute that yearns for far-aways,
In glossy laurel laughs a faun.


## WARNING

You follow hordes that hail you to a throne
Of glaring yellow silk and massive gold,
From which a rain of blood has often rolled
While fires soared through seas of broken stone.

Now hallow every murder, every lust!
As mad as surf against the cliffs your mind
Exults in icy and destroying gust
And scorns the quiet well, the quiet wind.

They stammer their allegiance to your shoe,
The ravished women wail, and one is more
Distraught and shameless in her fear: Before
Your lordly eyes she tears her dress in two.

They bring you coral, diamonds, emeralds, pearls,
As if these were but common trumpery,
The priestess, whom her virgin mantle furls,
Cries: "Take me as your slave!" and bends her knee.

And lonely through a savage scene you move,
Your hair is fouled with offal from the street,
Your pride impatient to frequent the groove
Which sordid creatures plotted with their feet.

Is this, indeed, the land for which you warred?
Oh, disregard the voice that lured and lied!
And do not say that sorrow was your guide,
Nor cast aside the raiment of a lord!


The squares are forsaken and silent the song and the lute.
In frantic search I sped
Through palace and church and where dances and tilts are afoot.
How many tears I shed,
And still she fled from me!
Nor is she here, and yet I distinctly recall
How often these battlements beckoned, how turret and wall
Gave joyful prophecy.


I fly from the place where I never have tasted of bliss,
And roam through barren sand.
And uphill and downhill the thistles leave barbs in my flesh,
Like serpents the succulent creepers entwine the land.


Up over here I see
The mountain-top: an island of pastoral green,
A single Thuja tree,
And bushes along the ledge.
Below — as if primitive masters had painted the scene —
The meadows and cities are patterned with spire and bridge.
What new and varied goals!
The glory of evening melts into ochreous swirls.
The cup of a saffron surrenders its fragrance and furls,
And silver manna falls.


Sovereign dream I trusted at heart,
Oh, that your daughters were mates of my mirth
Stauncher than those I encountered on earth.

Long I watched them though I stood apart.

Glittering peacocks tempt through the night,
Spending the shudders we crave for delight,
Larks at dawn with their passionate cry,

Yet majestic as a cloudless sky.

Is the rejoicing in palpable tunes
Which in my mouth have resounded for moons,
A new incarnation and core?

Shall I find my true domains once more?


Silence despair!
Although you long
— But in vain — to possess,
Question and bear,
With conquering song
Master distress.

And so it was taught.
He patiently wrought,
Another year passed.
By south and by east
Deluded at last
He wearily ceased.

An oak overhead,
He shovelled a grave
For mantle and stave,
He felt they were dead.
For quests I prepare,
Unburdened by care.

The sluices broke,
Curbed waters rose higher.
He fought down a tear
And murmured: I fear
On this very oak
I must shatter my lyre.

Doff your mourning mien and vesture,
You are so immersed in grief,
Even if I brought relief
It would seem a mocking gesture.

Why, when all the rest are keeping
Trysts of gladness do you cling
To your pain, forever weeping
With the moon when fountains spring?

Though the storm may lurk and lower
And repeat a winter strain,
Many a rose is still in flower,
Far from ripened is the grain.

Does not faint desire flow
Out from fingers calm and frosty?
Sing the quests of long ago
Lest our sonant string grow rusty.


My early visions! With the dead you vanished,
I lack the strength to stay you in your flight,
From lands that are my birthright I am banished,
So now I taste a splendour tinged with blight.

By rumours of enchantment seized and shaken,
I see the herons, white and crimson, wheel
Across the valley's blue expanse and waken
The nearby lake that sleeps and shines like steel.

There, as in symmetry of chords she paces,
Her upward pointed finger lifts and takes
Her shrouding garment by its silken laces,
Which in the night she wove of willow flakes.

O subtle game: to guess through veils! Desires,
Spurred by my longing, whispered we were one,
But half-concealed in vines with bloomy spires,
Down to the nearby lake she glided on.

## BLESSING FOR NEW QUESTS

When hope still lured me to a distant zone,
In sleep that was not sleep I dreamed a bride,
And then the very hour I descried
You as her herald, I became your own.

When I renounced, when peace was almost won,
When flames of greed for her had slowly died,
Confess: Was destiny my proper guide,
Now that once more to mine your eyes are drawn?

I pace the nave and reach the middle throne,
On golden tripods myrrh and sandal smoke,
I sing as if an organ buoyed the tone.

For unction let me give my fiery blood.
Where shall I ever find my pilgrim's cloak
Again and where retrieve my pilgrim's hood?

Would that on mountain trails alone
And far away he bathed in sun,
And listened long to stream and leaf
Until they drowned the drone of grief.
Would he were steeled by stabbing wind
And then serenely sought his kind.

But in the wake of what curses and malice
Was he impelled to a marsh one night,
Where a resilient stalk seemed to buoy
Lightly a lily? Flutter of slight
Wings in the heart of a milky chalice!
Angel of evil! Angelic decoy!

The wanderer faltered on the road,
A mutter from the rushes flowed.
He errs through elms, a spectral maze,
There is no balm for his despair,
The darkness blurs his frantic gaze,
And storms are tangled in his hair.


The gravel slowly dries in morning rays
Too young to mingle blaze with their caress,
In gardens which their mistress loves on days
When she is pleased with cool and tranquilness.

Blue-flowered vines are wreathed around the door.
She strolls through asters, pinks, and mignonette.
As in the past, will they assert once more:
"In realms of bloom you are the coronet?"

Her ribbons veer the butterflies aside,
And in the wind a pair of palm trees quake.
Almost resentfully she scents the pride
Of things that only grow for flowering's sake.


JOURNEYS OF LONG AGO

I

Through the wood, across the valley,
On we trudged with serious word,
Flushed and childish overrated
Trespasses — our trifling tally —
Longed to have our doubts abated
At the shrine where prayers are heard.

Silent hope and higher power
Eased the burden of our going,
Oh, and then the sacred towers
Filled our hearts to overflowing!

And no scorn could makes us falter.
When the evening glimmered mild
In the tinted panes, we bowed
Gravely on the flags, and vowed
Not as yet before the altar
Of the Mother, but her Child.


II

The island-garden sleeps. No step, no sound,
And magic holds the palace dim and mute.
No priest, or prince, or marquis can be found,
No guard displays the banner in salute.

A breath of fever from the river fumes,
A fire falls, a fire mounts and flows,
On every colour greyish vapour glooms
And wilts the shrubs and flowers in formal rows.

The stranger is expectant and afraid,
He hastens up the path between the yews...
No glimmer of a child in blue brocade,
Or of the impress of his saffian shoes?


III

Across a plain of snow we sped,
And parting swiftly lost its sting,
The whirl of wheels that chugged ahead
    Hurried straight into the spring.

How thoughts revolved abreast of night
I know, and how we scarcely slept,
How mists were downed before the light,
    Gleam of day through windows crept,

Where rush and tiny palm and leaf
Of sheerest crystal were unfurled
Among the bracken, moss, and sheaf,
    Flora of a wonder-world!

What balms on brittle bark
Of fence and branches ooze?
Autumnal colours with sheen
Of lingering sunset fuse:
Red-gold, a stipple of dark,
Scarlet and curious green.

Who comes to the unknown soul,
Alone in its sorrowful maze?
A child in a flutter of blue —
Shy rustle of wind, the adieu
Of roses spending their toll
Of scent to the last warm rays.

By shimmering hedges and through
The crackle of withered trails
And sough of glossy bough,
Clinging together we go
Like siblings in fairy-tales,
And falter in dazzled awe.


THE CLASP

I planned it as an iron band,
As something cool and smooth and plain,
But not a mine in all the land
Had metal of the wanted grain.

So now it shall be otherwise:
A rare and lavish cluster tooled
Of gold as red as flame, and jewelled
With precious stones in flashing dyes.

ALGABAL

(1892)

ALBERT SAINT-PAUL

POET AND FRIEND WITH WHOM

I SHARED UNFORGOTTEN EXPERIENCES AND DELIGHT IN ART

PARIS

MDCCCXCII

INSCRIPTION

IN MEMORY OF LUDWIG II

WHEN YOUTH TRANSFIGURED MY DAYS WITH SO MUCH LIGHT
I FELT YOU CLOSE AND YEARNED FOR YOU IN SWIFT SURPRISE.
NOW ALGABAL WHO IS YOUR YOUNGER BROTHER, HAILS
BEYOND THE PALE OF DEATH, O MOCKED AND MARTYRED KING!

# THE REALM BELOW

O halls that boast of such fabulous treasure,
What lurks at your feet you never will know,
The curve of the coast gives the master less pleasure
Than dazzling domains in the waters below:

The mountains and springs of miraculous birth,
The houses and holdings his phantasies plot
Far under the tread of the creatures of earth,
And grottoes which luminous frenzy begot,

With walls where the whiteness of winter still clusters,
And others of ores in prismatic rays,
And showers of jewels suffused with the lustres
Of candles abloom with perpetual blaze.

The rivers that flared through the upper levels
In garnet, and ruby, and scarlet guise
Temper their triumph on downward travels
Ripple like roses in delicate dyes.

Deprived of their oars, on the wavy green
Of somnolent harbours, are bevies of skiffs
Which dream of venturesome journeys between
Ominous eddies and coral reefs.

He finds that the world he has formed and transcended
Is pleasing, at times, with its newness and might,
Where, save for his own, no command is attended
And he is the lord of the wind and the light.


The hall of yellow glitter and of sun!
On level domes among the stars it reigns,
And from the fiery crater flashes run:
Topazes interfused with amber grains.

The flat and unembellished golden tiles
— Entire towns' and kingdoms' looted store —
Are polished mirrors ranged in serried files,
And lion skins are broad upon the floor.

But one among the dazzled multitude
The glare and glory leave aloof and calm,
And thrice a thousand heavy urns exude
The breath of lemon, frankincense, and balm.

The room of pale resplendence lay beside,
Where white of light is fused with white of glow,
The roof is glass, the mats of weathered hide
Seem clouds from up above and snow below.

The cedar wainscot on the walls is wan.
Against it thirty peacocks stand in arcs,
Their breasts as flawless as the down of swans,
Their dragging tails enriched with icy sparks.

Each thing is graced with colours of its own,
With tarnished or metallic brilliancy,
With crystal, diamond, opalescent stone,
With alabaster and with ivory.

And pearls! The clear gifts of a sombre place,
They roll like fashionings which men beget,
But on the warmth and smoothness of a face
Will keep inviolate the cooling wet.

And there the globe of murra also lay,
Which he had played with in those early years...
The emperor's hand was stainless on the day
He held it to his eyes that brimmed with tears.

My garden requires no air and no sun,
The garden I built for my pondering,
Its birds are motionless flocks, and none
Ever has welcomed the advent of spring.

The trunks are of coal and of coal are the shoots,
The hedges and fields draw a scowling design,
A never harvested burden of fruits
Glitters like lava in groves of pine.

The greyish light of a cavern foils
The guess whether evening is close or dawn,
And resinous vapours of almond oils
Hover on beds, and furrows, and lawn.

But when my phantasy conquered my gloom
I asked, as I pensively made my rounds:
How can I evoke you in sacred bounds,
Black and large, and sombre bloom?


### DAYS

When ramparts tipped with copper seem to swim
In early rays, and all the gables glow,
While waves of cool through courts of basalt flow,
The emperor's doves alight and wait for him.

His robe is blue, of silken Seric twist,
A foil for sapphires and the Sardian gems
In hulls of silver, stitched along the hems,
But not a clasp or jewel on arm and wrist.

He smiled and his transparent fingers fed
The grains of millet from a golden bowl,
Then through the portico a Lydian stole
And to his master's ankle bowed his head.

Above the roof the startled birds careen.
"I want to die, for I alarmed my lord!"
And as he spoke a heavy dagger gored
His breast. A patch of crimson stained the green.

The emperor turned in scorn, but all the same,
Before the afternoon was done, he bade
Them carve upon the cup from which he had
His evening draught of wine, the servant's name.

Toward the east the walls are massed
Where, to honour mighty Zeus,
Majesty and marvel, vast
And exotic, strike a truce.

Clad in robes designed to lure,
Dancers open up the rite,
Boys, an offering made secure
In a country limp with light.
Heap the palm and olive leaves
For the priest, and scatter silver-
Dust, and sand, and fragrant sheaves,
Waxen lilies, and narcissus.

On the threshold pause and rest,
Where unveiled the image gazes
Only on a single guest
Who adores with constant praises.
He alone shall stammer words,
Ban his brother from the place
When the dual god accords
His eternal sign of grace.

Youthful voices — echo blooms,
Nards dissolve in scent and err
Through the heavy shaft of fumes
To the sweet caress of myrrh.

O mother of my mother, long revered,
How I am vexed by language that adjures,
You claim my spirit did not follow yours,
That actionless in idle air it veered.

Do you recall how many spears were hurled
When in the east I struggled for the crown?
My valour met with censure and renown
Before I even understood the world.

It is not weakness bids me shun your ways,
To me your doing spells futility.
Oh, let me go my fated course, but free
And undefiled by words of hate or praise.

Do not estrange my brother! For I guessed
Your secret aim, there was no need to ask.
You hold him shrewdly to his dulling task
And scheme to keep him servile and suppressed.

See, I am delicate as apple bloom,
More peaceful than a new-born lamb, but should
My soul be gashed, its stone and iron would
Ignite the tinder ominous with doom.

I pace the marble stair and half-way down
I come upon a corpse without a head,
My brother's precious blood is clotted-red...
I merely lift my purple trailing gown.


Cups on the ground,
Buckles unclasped,
Women and whores,
Slim boys pour,
Sink to the floor.
Naked are thigh,
Haunches, and breast,
Tattered flowers
Around their brows.

Perfumes unbound,
Aura of rest,
Wine-god has passed,
All shall die
At the banquet's close.

Roses caress you,
Fiery and full,
Heaped and wanted?
Milky and dull,

For your wonder?
Red as mallow,
Wilted yellow:
MANES hover,
Kiss and bless you.

Open the sluices,
Floodgate looses
Roses, flaunted,
Rain and river
Drowning under.

When envious sleep turns to leave me
Flung out on my silken sheet,
No teller of tales shall reprieve me,
No song that is lulling and sweet,
Of maidens from Attica's flower,
Who moons ago chanced to beguile,
Now draw me into your power,
Players of flutes from the Nile!

I lay in pavilions celestial
I ate of heavenly bread,
You sang of the flight from terrestrial
Abodes and the fame of the dead.

When sleep after long supplication,
Comes cooling my lids, Oh, beguile
And slay me in soft iteration,
Players of flutes from the Nile!


These words were said when living was a loss:
I want the mob to perish and to groan,
And let who laughs be nailed upon the cross!
My rage is turned against myself alone.


For I, the one, comprise the multitude.
As I am led by destiny, I lead,
And though my scourges strike them till they bleed,
They have their gladiators and their food.


When I forgot myself, when clad like them
I shared unnoticed in their empty round,
My hate for them, I fear, was not profound,
I had not gauged the harshness of my stem.


Then out I barred the rabble's hue and cry.
Without desires, mild and light I dreamed,
And almost like a sister's image seemed
The face a mirror showed my searching eye.


I must saddle ashen horses,
Race across the moors of dread,
Till the marshes end our courses
Or the lightning strikes me dead.

Many silent heroes whiten
In the fallow field, and flares
Of the firs are all that brighten
Corpse by corpse with sooty glares.

Red as brick the slender, shallow
Rivers run as straight as strings,
Sighs arise from them and hollow
Winds cavort in gusty rings.

Women's hair is loose and slashes
Through the pebbles, thickly sweeping,
Women's weeping cools the gashes,
Lavish weeping — honest weeping?


Agathon, close to my pillow bowed,
What your mouth concealed your lashes said.
What shall I do to brush away the cloud
— My brother and my friend — of tears unshed?

When veins abounding in radiance shrink
From dust and merciless wind, refrain
From rising against the gods who drink
Joy from the sight of heroic pain.

This your reward: Only you may guess
These proud limbs too dread ash and bones.
We never shall tremble in earthly distress,
We, who were born for the purple of thrones.


Somnolent peace, yet I cannot dispel
Rumble of riotous mobs, do I grow
Fearful of Ides the planets foretell?
Foul is the omen of serpents, but know:
Long before any has dared to rebel
Out of your reaches your ruler will go.


Music sifted
Down! A harp? Or horn that gave
Wings and lifted
Me, or thrust into a grave?

As if shaken,
And as though a god ordained,
Prayers waken
In me, Syrians, at your strains.

Brittle trebles — regenerate, quicken,
Brazen flourishes — laughingly squander,
Shrill arpeggios — sever and sicken,
Silver clashes — fire and wonder.

Shall I tender
Thanks, but oust you, Syrian seers,
Who engender
Lust to cling in earthly spheres?


## MEMORIES


Days of grandeur when in fancy worlds awaited my command,
Luckless day when I departed from the altars of my land.

There with gods I sat in counsel on their most exalted rules,
Down to earth their children journeyed as my paramours and tools.

Be again the boy who wanders through the woods to be alone,
Stops, afraid of thoughts that face him of a sudden as his own,

With your tender, daring pallor, mark of restless, ripening year.
Oh, that in the flesh, not only as a shadow you were here!


I have lost the days of bloom
When a tear was sweet. Has death
Chilled the butterfly to whom
Kisses clung in every breath?

54

Who on blade and clover dipped,
And through gaudy gardens flew,
And from every blossom sipped
Hurriedly the scent and hue?

Whom the night allowed a scope
Which the day did not procure,
Whom the night allayed with hope
That the tulip still may lure?

Will the tit's, the skylark's tune
Bring him back from where he fled?
Will he praise another June,
Does he sleep, or is he dead?


Wipe away the stinging traces
Of the years and fancied sin,
Child, elected by the Graces,
So the world may love and win.

Victors home from battle bowed
To your beauty, to their young
God the sons of mortals vowed
Homage with adoring tongue.

They give thanks to fate which suffers
Them to live with the Divine,
When on jasper tiles he offers
Gifts before the ivied shrine.

Men lament and women sigh
At your temple's gates in flocks,
And the scorned devoutly vie
For your hem to touch their locks.

Lave yourself and doubly fair
Rise before your fame lose lustres,
That once more you may compare
To the Hermae of the masters.

Against the square I saw her first, among
The white-clad sisters, stern and beautiful.
Around her neck and sloping shoulders clung
Like coronation robes the simple wool.

In the arena, when to mad acclaim
Of many mouths the victims strewed the ground,
When those about to die called Caesar's name,
Her eyes were cold, and tranquil, and profound.

And I recall the wooing wild and swift:
I snatched the priestess from the sacred fold,
And every country brought a bridal gift.
I gave her floods of fragrant oils and gold.

And doubting new delight in store for me,
I only found a source of greater pain.
Back to the shrine I ordered her, for she
— Like all the others — also bore a stain.

And now I shall evoke those hours: Under
The fig tree lay the children fast asleep
After their sudden mating, sweet with wonder ...
I feared their fathers soon would make them weep.

Ah, well for you I gave the drop of bane
I carry in my faithful ring, to use
If once, at fall of night, I should not choose
To be confronted with the stars again.

You are reprieved! My coming was benign,
For no awakening shall abate the rapture
Which only dreams so perfectly recapture
As from your features now I can divine.

I can still relive my first distress:
Tracking alien steps with guilty haste,
And I crushed my dearest dream for this!

When I conjure up the past and see
Early years of wildest agony,
How I beat on tombs: Oh, shelter me!

Now I find you almost swift and slight!
Gentle awe I grant you as your right,
Saddest solace, Son of Night.


Have victims gulled me, or an eagle's glide,
Or can the reader in the clouds have lied?

This virgin bud is never to enjoy
The bridal nectar which the winds convoy?

But with a flood of balm and spice assail
The tedious hours in a sultry jail?

And try to quicken life in sluggish veins
With sap of hemp, and wine in broken rains?

And must I forfeit youth, my love confessed
— Unheeded — to a pillar's marble breast!


AUGURY

Once I saw the swallows winging,
Swallows snow- and silver-white,
In the wind I saw them clinging,
Windy weather, hot and bright.

Saw the jays alight and glimmer,
Parakeet and colibri
Through the trees of wonder shimmer
In the wood of Thusferi.

Saw the ravens flap and slacken,
Daws of black and sombre grey
Over adders, near the bracken
Where the magic forest lay.

Now again I see the winging
Snow and silver swallows veer,
In the wind I see them clinging,
Windy weather, cold and clear.

THE BOOKS OF

ECLOGUES AND EULOGIES,

OF LEGENDS AND LAYS

AND OF THE HANGING GARDENS

(1894)

THE NAMES OF THREE POETS SHALL ADORN THESE PAGES:

PAUL GERARDY

WENZESLAUS LIEDER

KARL WOLFSKEHL

MUNICH

MDCCCXCIV

These three books should be prefaced by the statement that they are not intended as reflections of any particular epoch of history or development. They mirror a soul which has temporarily taken refuge in other eras and regions. Here — obviously — traditional concepts were just as helpful as the tangible environment of the moment: our still undesecrated valleys and woods, our rivers flowing in the aura of the Middle Ages, and then again the almost palpable air of the towns we venerate. In every age a spirit which shapes and integrates what is alien and past transfers it to the pale of the personal and the present. And what has here been presented of our three great spheres of civilization is only what some of us still maintain as a living heritage.

THE BOOK OF ECLOGUES AND EULOGIES

## ANNIVERSARY

O sister, take the jug of sallow clay
And come with me, for you did not forget
What still we cherish in devout renewal.
Now it is seven summers since they told us
— While at the well we talked and drew the water —
That on the same day our betrothed had died.
There at the spring which rises in the meadow
Beside two poplars and a firtree, let
Us fill our jugs of sallow clay with water.

## DAY OF RECOGNITION

Struck with amazement as though we were entering a region
Frost-bound when last we had seen it, yet now full of flowers,
We who felt old and sorrowful gazed at each other,
And our reflections were fused in the water below us.
Each for a moment held back while she probed the other,
Growing more certain in solemn and saturate silence.
Sister, from then on I gave you the name of Serena,
And we confessed the secret long buried within us:
That from the glimmering pastures, from Swan or Lyre
Over us, still we await a luminous wonder.

## DAY OF DESTINY

On evenings when the air was mild we chose
Our usual path, and bound in close accord
We talked about our kindred and our stem
To give each other confidence and hope.
Now for the first time you have saddened me,
A bitter grief, my sister, for it seems
That often westward toward the trellised grapes
You turn, serene and glad, and hardly hear
My words. Alas! What if the unknown lurks
There in the vines to snatch you from our midst!

66

## SHEPHERD'S DAY

The herds were trotting from their winter quarters.
Their young attendant, after many months,
Advanced across the plain a river brightens.
The meadows, glad to be awakened, hailed
With sappy green, and fields sang out to him.
But smiling to himself, he walked the paths
Of spring and was possessed with new divinings.
He used his staff to leap across the ford
And lingered on the farther bank where gold,
Which lazy waves had washed from sand and stones,
Delighted him, and fragile shells of many
Colours and contours presaged happiness.
The bleating of his lambs no longer held him.
He roved into the woods to cool ravines
Where plunging streams are steep between the boulders
On which the mosses drip, and bared and black
The roots of beeches branch. Beneath the silence
And gentle motion of the vaulted tree-tops,
He closed his eyes and slept. The sun was high
And scaly silver darted through the waters.
When he awoke he climbed the peak and reached
The solemn rite of onward flowing light.
He prayed and crowned himself with sacred leaves,
And up to warm and slowly shifting shadows
Of clouds already dark, he launched his song.


## THE FIELDGOD'S SORROW

Why should thè girls who came from under elm trees
With garlands in their hands and on their foreheads,
Oppress my thoughts and grieve me? At the edge
Of thinning woods, beside my quiet house,
I watched the meadows, green and splashed with colour,
Climb upward in a gentle slope, and hawthorn
Scatter the earth with overflow of bloom,
When flitting by the wayside they discerned me,

Began to whisper secrets and with laughter
And haste avoided me, although I called them,
Although my pipe implored with tender music.
And not until I drank and caught my image
Down in the shallow well: my matted locks
And furrowed brow, did I discover what
Their flying words had shrilled to one another,
What rang and echoed from the rocky wall.
Now I have lost what zest I had in poising
My fishing-rod above the pond, and coaxing
My willow-pipe — that proved so ineffective —
With agile touch. But through the misty greyness
Of dusk I shall beset the Lord of Harvests
With the lament that he denied me beauty
When he invested me with deathlessness.


DIALOGUE IN THE REEDS

"Oh, why do you rise through the ripples to eavesdrop again on my pleasure
The moment I waken at noon, when the loveliest songs well within me,
When wine-coloured bindweed invades the twittering gold-tinted grasses,
And halos of delicate glory encircle the network of bushes?"

"This hour is dear to me also for rowing through wax-petalled lotus
And rocking myself as in boats on the lily pads, upward and downward,
My body suffused with the radiant rays of empyrial regions.
But come, I will show you the charms which I found on the bank of these
        waters."

"We two are so different, and think what the gossip of flowers would be if
The gleam of my arms were confused with your shaggy and weathertanned
        shoulder!"

"Then find yourself other abodes to disport in, for these are the meadows
Which always — my earliest memories pledge it — belonged to my people."

"And we have been here since beginning of time we, the fair and immortal."

"This knife — here it is in my hand — which has served me to whittle
   the rind from
The sap-swollen branches and carve them to pipes, I shall plunge in my heart
Clear up to the handle and sink to my death with the coming of twilight."

"You shall not, for how it would vex me if blood in a sinister current
Should darken the mirror I cherish, the lake with its limpid enchantment."


THE LORD OF THE ISLAND

In southern seas — the fishers tell the story —
Far on an island rich in cinnamon,
And oil, and jewels that glitter in the gravel,
There was a bird who, standing in the rushes,
Could use his beak to pluck the topmost branches
Of even tallest trees, and when he lifted
His wings, the dye of Tyrian snails, to travel
In low and heavy passage, he resembled
A darkly drifting cloud. They say by day
He waited in the wood, but of an evening
When he had settled on the shore in flurries
Of seawind redolent of salt and weed,
He loosed the sweetness of his voice and dolphins,
The friends of song, swam nearer in an ocean
That brimmed with golden sparks and golden feathers,
And this had been his life since time began.
None but the shipwrecked ever saw him, for
When first the shining sails of men were favoured
By fortune, and a prow approached the cliffs,
He slowly climbed the hill and there his glances
Encompassed all the land he long had cherished,
And widely spreading his enormous pinions
He passed away with muted sounds of anguish.

## EXODUS OF THE FIRSTBORN

The lot is cast and we, who still are children, must
Already seek a new abode in foreign lands.
An ivy tendril from the feast still wreathes our hair.
Our mothers on the threshold gently sighed and kissed
Us long, and then with tightened lips our fathers went
With us until we reached the city-bounds, and when
They left us hung around our neck the tablets carved
Of spruce, but some of these we are to throw into
The grave when one of our beloved brothers dies.
We parted lightly. All of us restrained our tears,
Since what we do is done to serve our people's good.
And only once we turned our heads to look behind,
Then crossed without a twinge into the far-off blue.
We want to go! A noble goal is set for us.
We burn to go! The gods keep watch upon our course.


## SECRET SACRIFICE

Appeased and released
We said our farewells
To sun-lighted fields,
To Memnon, the blithe,
To Mirra, the blonde,
Who ask us to stay.
Their joys are not ours!
The temple resounds,
We follow the call
That leads us to serve
The Beautiful: gloried and boundless.

The grove is our screen
From the people we hold
In reticent awe.
With poppies and milk-
White stars we have plucked,
We garland the shrine.

70

We bathe by a shore
Where violets grow,
We kindle a flame
In gardens of grace,
And wait while we falter an anthem.

And when we are fair
With the freshness of youth,
The prophet will weld
Us fast to the bronze
Of pillars and lift
The veil from the god.
We tremble and gaze
In tortuous grief,
In luminous strength,
In fires of bliss,
And die in perpetual yearning.

## THE FAVOURITES OF THE PEOPLE

The Wrestler

His arm — Oh, admirable and amazing! —
Rests on his dexter hip. The sunlight plays
Across his stalwart body and his temples
Circled with laurel leaves. When he approaches
A slowly swelling clamour sweeps the rows
Along the street whose length is strewn with branches.
The women teach their children to repeat
His name with joyful tongue and lift them higher
To reach him with their palm fronds, but unsmiling
He sets his foot as squarely as a lion,
The glory of his birthplace after many
A year without renown. He does not notice
That thousands cheer, he does not even see
His parents proudly loom among the people.

The Lyre Player

How he advanced with a white fillet twisted
Around his locks, a sumptuous garment weighing
His slender shoulders, how he struck the lyre
Uncertainly at first with youthful shyness
Astonished even the austere and aged.
How faces kindled with the blush of yearning,
How many women flung him strings of jewels
And priceless clasps while he who still was new
To such ovation bowed, will be remembered
Wherever fruit grows on the holy tree.
The girls are full of endless eager talk,
And every boy in secret anguish worships
The hero of his sleepless starlit hours.


ERINNA

They say that when I sing the leaves are shaken,
That constellations quiver with enchantment,
And nimble waves delay to hear, that even
Men make their peace and solace one another.
Erinna neither knows nor feels it, mute
And lonely by the sea she stands and thinks:
Thus was Eurialus astride a stallion,
Like this when he was coming from the banquet.
How will he be when my new song is finished?
How is Eurialus when faced with passion?


AFTER THE FESTIVAL

You too, Menechtenus, shall take the flowers from
Your head. Now let us go before the flutes are lulled.
Though still they offer cups of joy to honour us,
I see compassion break through many a reeling gaze.
We two were not elected by the priests to those
Who are allowed to expiate within the shrine.

For we alone of all the twelve were not acclaimed
As beautiful, and none the less the well reveals
My shoulder and your brow are pure as ivory.
No longer can we join the shepherds in the field
And with the ploughmen walk the furrows' length no more,
We who have learned to ply the handicraft of gods!
Give me your wreath, and I shall fling it far away
With mine. Along the empty path let us escape
And lose the trail in thickets dark with destiny.


## THE END OF THE VICTOR

When he had defeated the dragons in poisonous marshes,
And giants who threatened the highways, when he, whom the people
Revered, had resisted the locks of the women he captured,
He battled on nebulous peaks with the wing-bearing serpent
Whose challenge and mockery struck his companions with terror.
They warned him in vain, and the fight was so long that his powers
Forsook him. The monster escaped, its perilous pinion
Inflicted a blow, and the wound would never heal over.
The light in his eyes flickered out, no venture could rouse him.
He clung to the narrow retreat of his home where he suffered
His anguish alone, and kept himself carefully hidden
From carrying mothers, who daydream of beautiful children,
From heroes-to-be whom the gods lend their favour and friendship.

EULOGIES ON SOME YOUNG MEN AND

WOMEN OF OUR TIME

## TO DAMON

Oh, may the luminous thought of that winter, my Damon,
     Never grow empty or dim,
Thought of our house near the northerly hill, where we tasted
     New and secluded delights!
Statues of marble ennobled it, naked and godlike,
     Which we admired and praised.
Then again we conversed, or you read me of battles
     And of desire and dream,
Read in a low and yet sonorous voice, and the fire
     Purred to the powerless wind.
Lamia who served us so noiselessly, Lamia who loved us
     Eagerly offered the cup.
Always communing with heavenly matters, a something
     Sheathed us like heavenly gleam.
And since we shunned every hostile intrusion, the quiet
     Flooded our senses with light.
But in the thaw and the tempest of March — Oh, I wonder
     Why we descended again
Down to the throngs in the square, to the portico's glory,
     Closer to creatures of earth!


## TO MENIPPA

Menippa, though your eyes — so well aware of how they glow —
Still lure me as in former days, you did not use the time
Which never will return, when you could guide me like a child,
When every word you spoke beset me like a fragrant breath,
And every flaw in you was but another charm. I hold
The gesture of that dancer dearer now than yours. The scar
Upon your chin no longer seems a miracle and I
Am not in serious danger at your side, although
While we were walking on the shore beneath a roof of branches,
You bade the slave who paced before us with a torch withdraw.

## TO MENIPPA

The lambs selected for the rites of gods, must be unblemished.
You know the rest: that the complacent and the idle scatter
Before the sharpness of your phrasing, that my wits are whetted
By none but yours, that once your presence daunted, that I likened
Your hair to queenly locks which glisten in a constellation.
And yet, in dust and drizzle of our days, I see you moving
No different from the girls you suffer near you, though you scorn them,
And to remain aloof from this would trouble and disturb you.
I grasp your inarticulate reproach, but I shall never
Accept you as an incarnation of the sacred seeress,
Nor as the voice of prophecy among the holy branches.


## TO CALLIMACHUS

We, your most faithful companions, gather on the landing.
Up at the rail of the readied ship, we see you lean,
Frozen with pain of the parting, torn from those who love you.
Long have you been one of ours, though of alien blood.
Are you preparing to barter sunlit skies where happy
Lore has developed, for misty, cold, and clouded coasts,
Home of a far-away people, and relearn the customs
— Simple and crude — which you no longer accept as yours?
Desolate hours await you, doleful in their passage.
Guest of the masters who taught us, friend at joyful feasts,
Who when he sang was commended by fastidious Phyllis,
Who gave a turn to his phrases equal to our own!
There at the court of barbarians, will you brook existence,
Bow to their sinister rulings, tyrant's ruthless nod?
You who have lived free from bondage! Sad concern assails us.
Rudder and anchor are moving, O Callimachus!
Churn of the waters has drowned the sound of farewell blessings,
Tears — although weeping be foolish — tears we half suppress.

## TO SIDONIA

I had persuaded myself that the poise and the pride of your bearing,
Joined to the beauty you knew how to heighten, outshone all the younger
Women, that not only indolent habit had prompted my friends to
Offer you homage. But I was aware of your eyes that are steely
Blue, of your lips that are contoured with shrewdness, and I was forwarned!
Once in the twilight we stood face to face (was it chance, or
Was it because you were wounded and sought him who never had sought you?)
Stood in the alcove concealed from the others by hangings from Persia.
Mocking and chiding I said there were persons who always are cautious,
Never forgetting their profit and goal in the flux of existence.
Then with amazement I noted your smile which so rarely is given.
"Judge," so you answered, "by something that happened a year ago, when I
Wanted to leave all my conquests, and triumphs, and riches to share the
Destinies of young Demotas who wooed me with mute adoration.
But he was more circumspect and discouraged my plan with his coolness.
Many a month did I need to revive from the smart of this blow!"
While you were speaking, our fingers drew closer, were woven together.
And from then on we no longer were strange to each other, Sidonia.

## TO PHAON

Before the harvest, when the pointed sunrays
    Softly blurred behind the mountain,
We walked together by the narrow streams and
    Slender trees which dot your region,
And vying with each other's words, recited
    Deathless cantos of our masters,
Inebriate with sound and lulled in rhythms,
    Stopped, withdrawn in dusk, and stood
Our arms entwined, who yesterday were strangers.
    Over us the feathery clouds retreated,
And ears of grain, the sheaves of a tomorrow,
    Moved in alternating ripples,
Still happy in the lavish seed they carried.

Sometimes we were stung by secret
Alarm that moments such as now we tasted
    Never would recur hereafter.
For many years they cast a gentle shadow
    On your ways and mine, O Phaon!


## TO LUZILLA

Now that in parting I give you my hands, O Luzilla,
You who are queen of the women in rustical Phlius,
Where I was banished by fate for a season of leisure,
Quelling my inner regret with a jest, I recall our
Arbour entwined with the clusters of purple wisteria,
Glister of fruits and the purl of the goblet. Below us
Sinewy drovers passed us with echoing tread.
Then with her sickle the reaper returned from the harvest,
Tanned by the sun, and we heard in the distance the lusty
Calls and replies of the boatsmen loading the vessels.
Friend, with your quiet awareness and strengthening solace,
Here in a network of useful endeavour, you dulled the
Edge of my want for the city I love, for the gracious
Sonorous cadence and wisdom of Attica's discourse.


## TO ISOCRATES

Speak! And at once we remember the years of our glory
    When even distant islands challenged us.
Bravely we battled and drafted the laws for the people,
    Our hand the scale which balanced destinies.
Hail, O Isocrates, hail to your youth, to your radiance,
    That only burns for action and explores
Ventures of others and crowns them with wild admiration
    Which even sets aflame a colder heart.
Would it be gracious to doubt or bear witness against you,
    So steadfast in your faith, and yet you wound
All those who love you, as guiltless and cruel as a child that
    Smilingly torments a fallen foe.

## TO KOTYTTO

Kotytto, flower sweet of scent but harsh in savour,
When richer grows your voice in melody, you scatter
Such joy, such warm and deep contentment, that the faceless
And compound multitude to whom you have devoted
All your attention, often stays its breath and kindles.
But in your converse, even with the tried who praise you,
Your way is stern and cold. You told me too in warning:
"I am not moved by gentle gestures and endearing words.
My spirit is replete with darkness. Flee from me!"
Yet in the morning wind, I cannot help but listen
Time and again before your door, and then I feel as if
I saw the swinging flags of grave and festal pageants,
And vessels, winged with golden sails, ride out of harbour.


## TO ANTINOUS

Your promise that in cooling green and healing blue
I should forget the town, was — when you gave it — faint,
And now has proven false. I see, but do not grasp,
These many woods spread out before me, all the fields,
And all the water with its talk that knows and asks.
My tears still fall, and on I wander to the lakes
Where new, delicious odours flatter (so you said),
And shores entice with shadow. Yet I much prefer
Your burning columns to the freshness of these trees,
For near them I have known a smile more lovely than
The melodies of birds, and words far sweeter than
The vaunted fragrance of these pines — Antinous!

## TO APOLLONIA

Trust in your fate, though it be grim, Apollonia, today.
Needed distress whitened your face, but it shows you will soon
Vanquish your pain, supple and strong. Then no longer shall flame
Leap, nor the storm topple your house, then no more shall we let
Hand rest in hand, cheek against cheek, lightly foot upon foot.
Goddess and world, wedded to Tros, like a brother to me,
Tros you restored once when he grieved over Pirra too much,
May I be far when you again straighten, flower, and shine:
Jewels your eyes, cherries your lips, yellow harvest your hair.

THE BOOK OF LEGENDS AND LAYS

## VIGIL OF ARMS

The tapers in the chapel flare and sway.
Before the altar, as the rite decrees,
The squire keeps his lonely watch. "When grey
Of coming dawn has brightened into day,
I shall be hailed with solemn pageantries

And knighted by a blow. Now that the lilt
And longing of the child have passed, I must
Devote to eager service spurs and hilt,
In holy war deliver thrust on thrust.

I must be fit and worthy to assume
The task, and dedicate this stainless blade
Before the throne of God, before the tomb
Which holds a hero, true and undismayed."

It was his sire hewn in stone, the curled
Design of flowers in slender arc about
His head, across his breast a flag unfurled,
His carven fingers folded and devout.

The visor darks his eyes. An angel poised
Above, his wing uplifted, holds the shield
Emblazoned with his coat of arms: a sword,
Its wavy edge within an empty field.


The squire fervently implores the grace
Of heaven, breaks the narrow bounds of taught
Recital, in his hands he bows his face,
All piety! But subtly on his thought
An earthly figure etched a mortal trace.

There in a garden, next to rosmarin,
She stood, far less a maiden than a child,
Her gown was long and stitched with stars, and in
Her locks the golden flecks were bright and wild.

He shudders, takes her for the tempter's snare,
And startled by a sight he wants to shun,
He runs his fingers through his mop of hair,
And staunchly signs away the Evil One.

The blood leaps to his temples, red and warm,
The candles harry him with shafts of blaze,
Then on the Virgin's knees, before his gaze,
The Saviour of the world holds out his arm.

"A servant in your army, I will do
Your work, no slighter aim shall ever stir
My spirit, all my life I vow to you.
Forgive a weakness which shall not recur!"

And from the altar, decked in white, a swarm
Of cherubim flew upward. To the wave
Of holy song a distant organ gave,
The squire's artlessness, the sire's calm
Merged to a spacious light and filled the nave.

THE DEED

A host of simple flowers threaded through the grass —
His mind still blank with youth, the squire roamed across

At break of day, close to his father's banquet-hall,
Then flicked into the well the pebbles from the wall.

Perhaps he saw himself in blood and glory laved!
When midday came, and still no emerald token waved

— The sign of hope — upon his neighbour's battlement,
To pledge him Melusina's love and her consent,

He trembled and then wept defiantly and long
Through mournful hours while the sun was full and strong.

But in the twilight, starved for death and wounds, he sped
On to the forest, pulsing with the beat of dread.

He did not heed the kindly words which bade him stay,
With tameless, boyish steps he darted on his way.

And when his hand, armed with the naked sword, had thrust
The monster spitting venomed flame, into the dust,

He strode along the path, which torches blazed for him,
His eyes, serene and clear, intent on heaven's rim.




FRAUENLOB

In the town of ancient ridges and gabled shrines,
Of spirals curled over rafters and doors,
Of stained-glass windows and towers which touch the stars,
Of hollow passages and blurred heraldic signs,
By the fountains at dusk and when morning dawned,
To the bubble of laughter and water's silvery sound —
A life full of stubborn dolour,
The whole of life a martyr's sombre story,
I was the prophet of your grandeur,
I was the singer of your glory.

Children marching in white parades,
Ribbons blowing, tapers, pennants,
Frocks aswirl in rainbow shades,
Sheaths for young and tuneful tenants,
Pale-cheeked girls who crave the Holy Bread,
Patrician daughters, titled, arrogant,
Who under sacred portals tread
In sumptuous fabrics of the Orient —
For you, my ladies, who lord it with unmoved heart,
Who grace the halls where festive boards are spread,
I ran the gamut of my art.

But who of you has ever deigned to offer
The cup, the wreath of oaken leaves to me,
And say she thought that I might well aspire
To don her weightless yoke obediently?
Were tears or gentle penance ever proffered
In answer to the wailing of my lyre?
I feel the foot of Death — and scarcely suffer!

Mournful bells! Behind a coffin virgins and brides pace slowly,
Swathed in dark attire. Only
Delicate hands, noble and tender,
Shall carry him to the chapel, vault, and crypt, and pave
A way of kingly splendour
For the dead herald of their loveliness.
Maidens and mothers weep in the stress
Of common widowhood, and pour the choicest wines,
Flowers, and precious stones,
With awe into the grave.


## AUBADE

"The dawn is still asleep in secret night,
And still your hall
(A sheltering wall)
Allows us limitless delight.
So why your stifled weeping,
Why your wounded glance?"
"The flight of hours is sweeping
My joy into mischance."

"Take comfort from my vow:
You always shall be chaste for me,
And I will gaze and greet
You as I would an angel, bow
Devoutly at your feet.
Beloved and holy all of you shall be,
Each part of you
The refuge I adored
With lids that downward drew
As one receives the Lord.

And whether morning or a distant quest
Drives me from you, against my breast
I keep the silken kerchief with your name.
It pledges strength and fame
As prayer before the din
Of joust and battle start.
Oh, may I never weep again save when
The watchman's bugle forces us apart."


IN THE UNHAPPY MANNER OF...

Loose from this letter softly the thread,
Welcome with grace what came in my stead,
Fancy it speaks for one who is dead.

When first I met you this was your request:
"There is a dragon man has never cowed."
I swiftly galopped to his cliffy lair
And stabbed him after battling breast to breast,
But that encounter singed my hair —
You laughed aloud!

"The Corsair's turban should be mine," you said
In jest, and blindly and beguiled
I rode to sea with clash and fight ahead,
And lost my arm, the left, for this conceit.
I laid the turban at your feet,
You gave it as a plaything to a child.

You saw how for your sake I was bereaved
Of joy, and blood, and thew,
Though I was threatened you were never grieved,
You barely thanked me when, through frost and fire,
Your glory grew,
And you were deaf to my desire.

Now from a wound nothing allays
I suffer, but to the last I shall phrase,
Beautiful lady, words in your praise.

# KNIGHTS-ERRANT

By evil glances they are harried,
Maligning throngs beset their way,
Some say an eagle came and carried
Them after birth, from worlds of fay.

They pass their years in quests, as though
From land to land they hoped to see
The country tilled with golden ploughs,
The home of their felicity.

They head for bouts of strength and leave
Their blood on coasts of ashen shale,
Their dexter hand they gladly give
To shield a woman, proud and pale.

In times of bitter need they save,
When angels come with darts of bane
To drive the guilty to the grave —
They suffer for another's gain.

When gusts of praise like incense leap,
And crowds exalt them with their psalms,
Hosannas and the palms which heap
The road, are false and passing balms.

But late, one evening, they draw near
The castle where the worn are blessed
With holy light, with tranquil cheer
That pledges them eternal rest.

To songs they turn their earthly marches,
In waves of festal sound they share
Transfiguration under arches
Imperishably new and fair.

# THE COMRADE IN ARMS

## I

It was where deer frequent the pool
That after dangers which beset
Our burning quests we stopped to cool
Our foreheads from the battle's sweat.

And now my brother is asleep
— Today the clash of swords was keen —
And I am proud that I may keep
The rest of such a heart serene.

He leaned against his shield, I took
His head upon my knees, his cheek
Had something of a tender look,
His bearded lip was stern and bleak.

In gloomy woods where evil coils
From many a bond he succoured me,
When nettles caught me in their toils
With flashing fist he hewed me free.

When I was lured by siren sounds,
Forgot his counsel to desist,
And mounted to forbidden bounds
He held me firmly by the wrist.

He never wavers or delays,
The wicked know his rage is swift,
The poor who kneel upon his ways
Receive his fortune as a gift.

He never will permit me other
Than straightest course before the Lord.
Of wax and iron is my brother,
And I am glad to be his ward.

II

Yet he was trapped by crafty foes, with few
And faithful men against a horde he vied,
He fell, but by the grace of heaven knew
The victory was his, before he died.

And to his burial even princes came,
The eulogies of friends, the muffled lilt
Of prayers and the drone of trumpets built
An arch to witness bright and early fame.

Now he is dead, where shall I turn? What hand
Will keep the hounds of ruthless life at bay?
Without his greatness I shall die. Oh, may
It not be too inglorious an end!


A KNIGHT GROWING FORGETFUL

Muted clangour! Do I hear
Horses being saddled? Spear
Whirring? From the terrace flow
Cries of fear?

Only doors that creak below.

Guests who laugh and jest? Dispatch
Of the men who come and go
Under eaves with leafy thatch?
Merry watch?

Tender strings? A singing sigh
Under fingers slim and slow?
Has a Golden Age slipped by,
Fair and shy?

Only doors that creak below.

## THE RECLUSE

The elders nodded by the window-sill,
The flower-season of the vines had just
Begun, when back from lands of miracle
My son returned and leaned upon my breast.

I let him tell the tale of his despair
In earthly travels, all his wounded pride,
I should so much have liked to have him share
The ease and sheltered calmness at my side.

But Destiny denied me her consent,
Rich was my ransom, yet her hand was sealed.
One dawn that promised early fame he went...
I watched his shield move through a distant field.


## THE IMAGE

I sang as the guild of our worthy sires had taught,
And passed by implacable pillars and tombs of stone,
But at vespers, behind the smoke of the kilns, I caught
The freshness of twilight wavering slowly down.

When solacing shadows invaded the colours spun
By day, when the chimes had died, and the meadows slept,
I knelt in my sheltering cell, released and alone,
Before the celestial image and pleaded and wept.

My eloquent eyes were lifted, my hands were twined,
The velvet psalter had never a prayer like this
That flowed from my spirit without beginning or end,
I opened my arm and dared the imploring kiss.

I waited and dreamed — abetted by miracle tales —
Of visible guerdon which always belied my belief,
In futile rebellion and hope I more wildly assailed
The guiltless image of glory, and greatness, and grief.

And if at last it leaned above my bed,
Or drew the symbols of grace and salvation, I doubt
My arm would have power to clasp, for the hour is sped,
The fiery love on my lips has burned itself out.


## STRAINS OF A WANDERING GLEEMAN

Words elude and words deceive,
Only song can seize the soul,
And if mine has missed its goal,
Though the fault be grave — forgive!


Like a village child who walks
In the meadow, let me sing,
I shall leave the halls of kings,
Fabled realms where giants stalk.


Mock me for my gentle smart!
Once, I know I shall confess
That I dreamed you, and caress
You since then within my heart.


From the buds the dewdrops run
Slow, and full, and clear
Where they glisten in the sun.


But the tears I cannot rein?
Yesterday I did not know
What today is my despair:
That my last delight would go
Should I never taste again
Rising sun and spring of year.

Shall I offer sheaves of bloom
So your innocence may waver?
Shall I cherish as my favour
Colours which you choose to wear?
On my lute before your room
Humbly play a pleading air?

Is not all this very plain?
Shall I wander on in pain?
Shall I say it? Shall I dare?


Is it much to plead
Once and silently,
After bitter need
Now to kneel to you?

Clasp your fingertips,
Only this of you,
Graze them with my lips
Awed and silently?

Do you call it much
If stern and silently
You endure my touch
And let me stay with you?


When I mourn, I think
This and only this:
That you are at my side
And listen as I sing.

Then I hear a tone,
Almost words you spoke,
Long they echo on,
And I feel less forlorn.

See, my child, I leave,
For not even my
Voice shall tell you why
Men must toil and grieve.

I am caged in gloom,
See, my child, I leave,
Fearing to bereave
Cheeks of early bloom.

I should make you wise,
I should wake your sighs,
That is why I grieve.
See, my child, I leave.


What a morning, what a day!
Breath of sun on brook and tree
Tunes your ear more swiftly to
Melting promise, melting plea
Which I shyly hid away.

No more silent and afraid
Should I be, if now we both
Walked the lanes that never fade.
I should tell you of my oath,
Of the praise which is your due.


Have you never felt before
What is throbbing at your core?
Wait a day and still a day.
They will show
If you go
To a smile or to a sigh.
Ah, you know you will not die
If again you must delay.
Wait a day and still a day.

They will show
If you go
To a smile or to a sigh.


A lord's child leaned from the sill
To the spring so green and so gold,
Followed the skylark's trill
With glances blithe and bold.

A fiddler! O fiddler, play!
And sing me your favourite strain!
The child listened long to his lay
And trembled with sadness and pain.

Why should he have sung such airs?
I tossed him the ring from my hand.
Knavish smith full of snares!
Bowed in his bondage I stand.

No spring will make me gay.
How pale is every bloom!
I will dream today,
Weep in the loneliest room.


DITTIES OF A DWARF

I

The smallest birds are singing,
The smallest flowers springing,
And their bells are ringing.

Where pale-blue heather grows,
The smallest yeanlings go,
Their fleece is silk and snow.

The smallest children shout,
Take hands and turn about.
May the dwarf peep out?

II

I leave my kingly post
To see your children wind
The dance. Among their kind
Will any be my host?

I, who am veiled and shy,
I have a crown and throne,
I am a fairy's son,
The king of trolls am I.


III

You will be rich and royal,
Many splendours, treasure troves shall be your spoil.

You will have spear and sword,
Favour of the fair shall be your long reward.

You will lack wage and name,
Only song shall yield you love and fame.


AWAKENING OF THE BRIDE

An anthem from the tower
When dawn is faint and frail,
Exalts the saints, and stories
The coming day of glories
With moving weight and power
Of horns in the chorale.

Am I still dreaming? No!
There at the gate — a voice!
For seven nights I waited.
A herald is below
From him whom I am fated
To love and make my choice.

Lily of the field,
Mary whom roses screen,
Let your joy imbue me
And again renew me
On the day of grace which crowns you queen.

Virgin wreathed in rays,
Maid of maidens mild,
Let your goodness alter
Those whose fingers falter
As they twine your shrine in moss and sprays.

Lady, guiding true,
What if undefiled
Fervently I render
Witness to your splendour,
Will you give what long I begged of you?

THE BOOK OF THE HANGING GARDENS

Now we shall fly into the land again
Which as a child you called your own.
You touch the ruby in your palfrey's rein,
Your cheek against his mane, and on a night
Of summer heat — all hint of peril gone —
You will alight.


When through the greyness a clear
Scarlet suddenly showed,
Fragrance of spices flowed,
Land of my people was near,
Tribal dwelling and site.
Tremors of pride and delight
Freshened my soul to the core
When the first stems with their solemn
Palm fronds in opulent column,
Bent down to greet me once more.


The roads your strength has carven out, reveal
    The coveted, the utmost pales.
But vaults that spill with booty: flags and steel,
    Bewilder you with ringing tales
Of smoking shafts with battered grooves,
    Of swords besmeared with crimson dye,
Of mantles crushed by rush of hooves,
    And frenzied arms flung upward to the sky.

And deeper voices quiver through:
    Forget, while we resound,
The majesty conferred on you.
    Rejoice and kiss the ground
Where rains of rose and gold
    Atone for languor, lust, and sin,
This ground: the only hold
    Where the sweet seed can grow to green.

The palaces reared of crystallic and nigricant stone,
The billowy tents where the bounties of heaven unfold
Are lit from above, and a wedge of the wavering flume
Enhances the flesh like marble with dim blue veins,
The bodies like berries that ripen to succulent gold,
And those as deep-red as blood and as pale-red as bloom.

Since I have determined to leave them behind me and fling
My soul to the glory of triumph, elated and pure,
Can I banish the grief which once more has imperilled my days,
By summoning wines with their heady aroma and sting?
The beat of my armoured battalions at dawn — will it lure
My limbs from the bed where I drowse under basil sprays?


When first the noble city owned defeat,
The walls no longer checked the cavalry,
The river swept the corpses out to sea,
The last of the defenders strewed the street,

And vengeful conquerors were dulled with plunder,
An ample light from dark horizons sped,
It dwelt consolingly upon the dead
And touched the sad and ruined town to wonder.

It clung with double splendours where the crowd
Scattered before the victor, as he rode
Into a temple, unappalled and proud,
And swung his dripping blade against the god.


A CHILD'S KINGDOM

You were already chosen when you sifted
Your father's soil in search of precious stones
To grace the crown through which you felt uplifted
In majesty, and to enhance your throne.

102

In level lands, remote from men, you founded
Your state among the leaves, a secret pale!
And in its dusk you heard a voice which sounded
Exotic pomp and deeds on distant trail.

Companions whom your very glance had fired,
Were given gold and castles as their due,
They trusted what you were, what you aspired,
And thought it would be sweet to die for you.

The nights your ecstasy grew full and fuller
Were when your subjects circled you and kneeled
To listen in the halls of boughs, and colour
And suns, to marvels only you revealed.

Above your head the banner, white and wide!
A tier of bronze wove azure tracery
Of fumes about your cheek that burned with pride,
Your forehead, stern and radiant as the sky.


Bridle your phantasies, golden
And crimson in stain.
Lower your lashes
Under the lilacs
And dream in the languors
Of midday again.

Birds grow silent in gardens
On buds and boughs.
With circlet and swirls,
Metallic blue whorls,
Their tails in curls,
They rock and drowse.

Distant drums of silver
And tin resound.
But no one sings,
No answering ring,
No lyre-string
Encumbers the mind.

Glint of the pointed pagoda
In shrubbery furled,
With extricate fusion
And lacy inclusion,
Dispels the illusion
Of being and world.


My macaws are white and crowned with
Saffron-yellow comb.
In the closure where they home
They are perched on slender rings,
Without call, without song,
Slumber long,
Never do they spread their wings.
In their dreams my white macaws
Journey where the date tree grows.


## PREPARATIONS

Your body with its young and virgin charms
Shall be immersed beneath the crescent's curve
In milk and wine, but with the swerve
From half to full, in fragrant oils and balms.
You shall have gems, a palace, maids that serve
And tend, and even priests shall come and lay
Their hands on you and bless you day by day,

To make you worthy of a regal throne,
To kneel in virtue, mute,
Awaiting the unknown,
So that — as rich and ripe as mellow fruit
Yet tender as a bud — the stern
Lord of the feast may see you and discern
That you are fit to be his own.

104

And you exult in trying hour on hour
Herbs of pure and magic power,
Guard your spirit close in lonely stages,
Raptures of expectance for its wages,
Till the curtain flow
From the paramount of ages
Whom, perhaps, your flesh will never know.


EVENING OF PEACE

The regions withered by the sun that poured
In stinging torrents, slowly are restored,

And clouds of black and lurid yellow fall
Upon the rigid pole, the naked wall.

The gardens stifle in a fragrant bath,
The shadows grow and seem to clutch the path.

The brittle voices drop asleep and blur,
The high are muted to a toneless whir.

The clamour of the end, the clash of hosts,
The glories of the banquet fade to ghosts.

And only seldom, dulled in mist, a sound
Of worlds in bondage rises from the ground.


Sheltered by the lavish foliage, where
Filmy flakes from starry flowers snow,
Gentle voices tell of their despair,
Tawny throats of fabled creatures flare
Jets the marble basins catch and throw
Down as little streams that fret and glide.
Through a screen of branches candles stare,
Milky shapes divide the moving tide.

In this Eden, halls and gayly-
Painted tiles take turns with fraily-
Flowered field and leafy valley.
Slender storks on forage stipple
Ponds the fishes streak with glamour,
Rows of birds in glistening dun
From the crooked ridges clamour,
And the golden rushes ripple...
But I dream of one alone!


A novice I was drawn into your sway,
I was not moved until I saw your face,
And wishlessly I lived the common day.
Elect me to the ranks that do your will,
These young and folded hands regard with grace,
Im merciful forbearance spare who still
Must falter on so new and strange a way.


Now that my lips are motionless and burn,
The path my feet have taken me is plain:
To other lords' magnificent domain.
Perhaps I still could bring myself to turn,
But through the spacious grating I divine
The eyes to which I knelt so long in vain.
They seem to question me or make a sign.


Tell me on what path today
She will come and wander by,
So that from my chest I may
Take the sheerest silks and choose
Sprigs of violet and rose,
That I lean my cheek to lie
Underfoot for her repose.

Now there is no deed I do not spurn!
To imagine talk between us two
And to let my senses conjure you,
To receive and serve, to have and yearn,
For nothing else, for this alone I burn
And weep because the visions which assail
In exultant darkness always pale
When the clear and cold of dawn return.


I am throttled by my hopes and fears,
Every word is lengthened into sighs.
So tempestuously my longings rise
That I slight the thought of sleep and rest,
That my couch is drenched with tears.
I reject the hint of happiness,
Beg my friends to leave me comfortless.


If I do not touch your body now
Then the fibre of my soul will tear
Like a bow-string over-strait.
Mourning is the colour dear to me
Who, since I am yours, know agony.
Slake and cool my hot and fevered brow,
Judge if I must suffer such despair,
I, who tremble at your gate?


Our delights are stern and spare.
What availed so brief a kiss?
Like a drop of rain was this
On a plain which, parched and bare,
Drinks but cannot quench its pain,
Cannot taste a second bliss,
And is cracked with heat again.

Beside the lovely flower-bed I lean,
Where haws with black and crimson thorn are hedged
Around tall cups with dappled spurs, and fledged
With velvet wings the bracken arches. Green
As water, flaky clusters curl their tips,
And in the middle bells! The grain of snow!
The liquid fragrance clinging to their lips
Is sweet as fruit from paradisian bough.


When behind the flowered gate our own
Breath at longed-for last, was all that stirred,
Did we feel that fancied ecstasy?
I remember how when softly one
Touched the other, we began to sway
Like the fragile reeds — without a word.
Tears rose in your eyes and had their way.
Very long like this you stayed with me.


When flung on heavy mats in holy rest,
Our tender hands around our temples curve,
And awe abates the burning of our limbs,
Then do not fear the formless shadows pressed
Against the wall in high and nether swerve,
The guards who can divide us at a nod,
The sand that traps the town in glaring rims
And is athirst to suck our tepid blood.


Against a silver willow on the shore
Your leaned, and with your fan you framed your hair,
The pointed slats in flashes seemed to flare,
As if in play you twirled the gems you wore.
And in a boat the leafen arches hide,
I wait. In vain I coaxed you down to me,
I see the willows bending lower, see
The scattered blossoms drifting with the tide.

Hush your tale
Of the leaves
Wind unweaves,
Quince that lies
Ripe and bled,
And the tread
Of the vandals,
Fall of year,
Of the brightning
Dragonflies
In the lightning,
Of the candles
That in frail
Glimmers veer.


Blithe in arbours dim with dusk we moved,
Lit pavilions, garden-bed, and lane,
She with smiles and I with whispers roved,
Now she leaves and will not come again.
Broken are the slender blooms and drab,
Drab and broken is the water's glass,
And I stumble in the withered grass,
Palmy fronds with pointed fingers stab.
Brittle foliage sibilant and massed,
Loosed by unseen hands to flight and fall,
Drives against our Eden's ghostly wall.
The night is close and overcast.


The shallow appetite for fame is reined,
Since now there is a treasure I must cherish
Which, after losing many things, I gained.
It makes the greed for other glories perish.

The hands which summoned subjects to their duty,
Forget to use the force in their employ,
Because to you, surrendered to your beauty,
I raise them in a reel of pagan joy.

The mouth which spoke prophetic words, resigns
Its office charged with sanctity
And bends to kiss a foot that far outshines
The carpet white as milk and ivory.


While in my dreams I rode to victories
And savoured sequences of words,
My country was beset with enemies,
They conquered half my kingdom with their swords.


And yet my craving for revenge is lost!
My last imperial act of all
Was when they caught the traitors from the coast
And led them to my scarlet judgment hall.


Then I could fix my eyes unflinchingly
Upon the prostrate who had dared withhold
Their tribute, and at every nod from me
A head from smooth and slender body rolled.


Now I am bowed and mourn my fair domain..
Only this shall ease my fate:
The bird that unconcerned for fields of ravaged grain
Sings in the myrtles, dark and wet,
Unremittingly his sweet regret.


I flung my circlet which no longer shone,
Aside. It clanged, and surfeited I turned to flee
The hall to which the treasure of the Orient flows,
The courts where fountains fall in silken strands,
The pillared walls of bronze and lazuli,
My very throne,
And travelled far to serve a pasha who commands
A realm like Shiraz, slumbering in mists of rose.

110

For many weeks I nourished his content
With songs of praise I chanted faithfully,
With wreaths of eulogies I corded.
In awe and reverence my head was bent
To him who silenced every mutiny
And over many foreign foemen lorded.

After his greatest conquest home he rode
One evening through the throngs which surged around.
I had prepared a dagger for his heart:
The candle's death shall mark his own! And yet
When up the stair in pride and majesty he strode
And I had mixed the festal draught, regret
Assailed me strangely, and I stole apart
With ashen cheeks without a sound.

The cymbals and the kettledrums combine
To jar the streets and palaces with thunder,
The soldiers take their pay in love and wine,
With looted splendours they array
The girls whose lips are smouldering and gay
In gardens where the yellow torches wander.

The slave moves on. A bush which grows before
The gate unfurls a blossom, bright and broad,
From which disgrace and glory spoke,
But he no longer trusts in fraud,
He only breaks a branch of sycamore
And leaves the region where his spirit broke.

The slave moves on, he knows his part is played,
On to the shore where mortals drink release
From torment, where their fervours drown in peace.
Now he can face the waters unafraid.

Where before the final lap
Gorgeous trains and riders stop,
Ramparts beckon from afar,
Travelers quench their thirst, the water-
Vendors offer him the jar
And address whom no one knows
For a former prince. No rancor
Clouds his soul, He thanks the giver
With a smile, but shyly goes
For his kingship broke, a slight
Contact even makes him quiver
And he almost fears the light.


He lay alone upon a ledge of stone.
How distant were his lands and all the proffer
Of mercy and command, as in a coffer
Buried in sand, the gold and gems he owned.
And deep into his hands he bowed his head.

But through the silence sighing whispers sped.

The wayside grasses, sad and trodden down,
The dialogue of cedar trees and alders,
The plashing drops that tumbled from the boulders
Divined the grief — so strange to men — of one
Who lost his kingly heritage.

And then he heard the river surge and pledge:


VOICES IN THE RIVER

Timorous creatures, adoring, deploring,
Here in our realm is the refuge your craved.
Here is rejoicing and here is restoring,
Softly in sound and caress you are laved.

112

Limbs turned to shell in a palace of surges,
Coralline lips in a resonant chain,
Tresses entangled in ledges and verges
Drift, and are caught in the current again.

Lanterns aglow like a violet ember,
Pillars afloat on a pivoting base,
Waters awakened to languorous timbre
Rock into rest, meditation, and grace.

But if reflection and melody cloy you
— Anodyne joys in perpetual swing —
Touch of a kiss shall deliver and buoy you
Hither and thither as ripple and ring.

# THE YEAR OF THE SOUL

(1897)

FOR ANNA MARIA OTTILIE

SHELTER AND SOLACE ON MANY

OF MY PATHS

MDCCCXCVII

## PREFACE TO THE SECOND EDITION

Even those who very nearly understood what the author had in mind thought that identifying persons and places would make for a better understanding of THE YEAR OF THE SOUL. But just as no one profits from looking for human and regional models in sculpture and painting, thus in poetry too we should avoid so idle a search. Art has transformed them so completely that they have become unimportant to the poet himself and his readers would be more confused than enlightened by a knowledge of the facts. Names should be mentioned only when they serve to indicate a gift or to bestow eternity. And it should be remembered that in this book the I and the You represent the same soul to an almost unprecedented extent.

AFTER THE HARVEST

JOURNEY THROUGH SNOW

TRIUMPH OF SUMMER

## AFTER THE HARVEST

Come to the park they say is dead, and you
Will see the glint of smiling shores beyond,
Pure clouds with rifts of unexpected blue
Diffuse a light on patterned path and pond.

Take the grey tinge of boxwood and the charm
Of burning-yellow birch. The wind is warm.
Late roses still have traces of their hue,
So kiss, and gather them, and wreathe them too.

Do not forget the asters — last of all —
And not the scarlet on the twists of vine,
And what is left of living green, combine
To shape a weightless image of the fall.


O urges from the years of youth which sweep
Me on in quest of her beneath these boughs,
Before you I must bend denying brows,
In lands of light my love is chained in sleep.

But if you sent her back, who in the flame
Of summer and the whir of Cupids would
Have shyly borne me company, I should
Acknowledge her this time with glad acclaim.

In wooden vats the ripened grapes ferment,
But I shall heap before her lavishly
What precious shoots and seeds are left to me
Of all the lovely yield the season lent.


Oh, hail and thanks to you who eased my stress,
Who lulled the constant clamour in my veins
With the expectance, dear, of your caress,
In weeks the glow of dying summer stains.

123

You came, and closer each to each we clung,
I shall devise a gentle word for you,
And praise you on our sunny paths as though
You were the very one for whom I long.


Up to the gate and back again we wander
Between the beeches with their gold and gloom,
And glancing through the bars, we pause to ponder
The almond tree beyond, in second bloom.

We search for benches where there is no shade
And alien voices never fret. In dreams
Your arm in mine and mine in yours is laid,
And we are bathed in long and mellow beams,

And feel beholden when the sunflakes glisten
Around us from the leaves alive with sound,
And only lift our heads to look and listen
When fruit, too rich with ripeness, taps the ground.


Around the pond where runnels bring
Their silent waters, let us stroll,
You calmly try to plumb my soul,
A wind ensnares us, soft as spring.

The leaves that yellow on the mould,
Diffuse an odour new and frail,
Echoing me, you subtly told
What pleased me in this picture-tale.

But do you know of wordless sighs
And bliss on a sublimer stage?
Down from the bridge, with shaded eyes
You watch the swans in slow cortège.

Beside the long and even hedge we lean.
Led by a Sister, rows of children pace,
Their voices rise in praise of heaven's grace
In earthly accents, steadfast and serene.

We, who are bathed in evening's latest rays,
Are frightened by your words, for you recall
That we were happy only when a wall
Like this was still enough to block our gaze.

Above the spring, niched in the wall, you bent
To cup the cool and dabble in the spray,
And yet it seems your fingers draw away
From the two lion heads with some constraint.

You wear a ring whose jewelled lustre dies.
I try to slip it off, but you invade
My very spirit with your misty eyes
In answer to the plea I could not hide.

Now do not lag in reaching for the boon
Of parting pomp before the turn of tide,
The clouds are grey, they swiftly mass and glide,
Perhaps the fog will be upon us soon.

A faint and fluted note from tattered tree
Tells you that goodness, wise and ultimate,
Will dip the land — before it learns the fate
Of freezing storms — in damask lambency.

The wasps with scales of golden-green are gone
From blooms that close their chalices. We row
Our boat around an archipelago
Of matted leaves in shades of bronze and fawn.

Today let us avoid the garden, for
As sometimes — unexplained and sudden — this
Elusive scent and lilting breath once more
Imbues us with a long forgotten bliss,

So that confronts us with reminding ghosts,
And grief that makes us tired and afraid.
Here from the window you can see how hosts
Of wind attacked the tree, how much is dead!

And from the gate whose iron lilies rust,
Birds light on lawns asleep in leafen stoles,
And others on the posts, in bitter frost,
Are sipping rain from empty flower-bowls.


I wrote it down: No more can I conceal
What, as a thought, no longer I can shun,
What I restrain, what you will never feel:
Our pilgrimage to joy is far from done!

And you, beside a tall and withered stalk,
Unfold my note. I stand apart and guess...
The sheet, which slipped from you, was white as chalk,
The loudest colour in the sallow grass.


Here in the spacious square of yellow stone
With fountains in the middle, though the day
Is gone, you still would like to talk and stay,
For brighter stars, you think, have never shone.

But keep from the basaltine bowl, it calls
For sepulture of faded bough and blade,
The wind is cooler where the moonlight falls
Than over there, where spruces throw their shade.

To spare you, I have let you guess askew
The reason why my sorrow is so deep.
I feel, when time has parted me from you,
You will not even haunt me in my sleep.

But when the snow has made the park a tomb,
Faint comfort, I believe, may still be told
By lovely residues: a note, a bloom,
In wintry silence, fathomless and cold.


## JOURNEY THROUGH SNOW

The stones, which jutted in my road, have all
Been spirited away and softly shrined
In banks of snow. To distant skies it swells,
The flakes are weaving at a ghostly pall,

And when they touch my lashes with the wind,
They seem to flicker as when weeping wells.
I look to stars, for no one guides my quest,
They leave me lonely in the spectral night.

I wish that I could slowly sink to rest,
Unconscious of myself in drifts of white.
But if the tempest whirled me to the edge,
The gusts of death decoyed into their keep,

Once more for door and shelter I should make.
Perhaps that hidden there beyond the ledge
Of mountains, lies a hope of youth, asleep.
A first and tender breath — and it's awake!


I feel as if a glance had slit the dark.
So shyly you elected me to go
With you, your voice and gesture moved me so,
That I forgot our path was steep and stark.

You praised the grandeur of the silent earth
In silver leaves and frosty rays, unsown
With infelicities and strident mirth.
We christened her the pale, the chaste, the lone,

And to her strength and majesty averred:
The sounds which floated through the stainless air,
The shapes which filled the skies, were lordlier
Than any night in May had yet conferred.


We took the usual path with joy and fear
Time and again in late and moonlit hours,
As though we wandered, wet with dripping flowers,
Into enchanted woods of yester-year.

You led me to the valley spells enchain
With languid perfumes and a naked light,
And showed me from afar where tombs incite
A dreary love to grow in frosts of pain.


I may not kneel and thank you who were lent
The spirit of the fields which nurtured us,
And when I try to ease your wistfulness,
You draw away in token of dissent.

And is it still your cruel plan to keep
Your sorrow — kin to mine — in secrecy,
And only walk abroad with it and me
Along the river glazed with shining sleep?


That evening, when the candles had been lit
For you, I said a benediction and
Gave you a diamond, the most exquisite
Of all my gifts, placed on a velvet band.

But you know nothing of the solemn rite
Of burnished candelabra, tier on tier,
Of vessels breathing clouds of stainless white
To warm the temple, sombre and austere,

Of niches brimming with their angel throngs
Reflected in the lustre's prismed glass,
Of ardent prayers told with faltering tongues,
Of darkness sighing with a faint: Alas!

And nothing of desires that awake
Upon the festive altar's lower rows.
Uncertain, cold, and dubious, you take
The jewel born of glitter, tears, and glows.


I taught you to discern the winning peace
Within these walls, the quiet rays which fall
From lamp and hearth, the croon in nook and niche,
You have the same and vague amaze for all.

I cannot fan your pallor into flame,
And in the room beside I kneel and break
My silent thoughts with doubt I cannot tame:
Will you awaken — ever? Oh awake!

But when I venture to approach the door,
You still are lost in dreams, your eye upon
The emptiness of space, just as before.
Your shadow blots the carpet's same festoon.

And there is nothing now to stem the plea
I never practiced and I know is vain:
O Mother — great and sad — concede to me
That solace spring within this soul again!

Your beauty while you mourn, my loyalty
Compel me to remain and cherish you.
That I may share your grief more perfectly
I try devoutly to be mournful too.

With tender words I never shall be met.
Up to the latest hour that holds us twined,
I must accept with stoical regret
The bitter destiny of winter's find.


The flower in its pot of sallow clay,
Against my window, sheltered from the frost,
Sags on its stalk as though it died away
And ill repays the loving care it cost.

To free my mind from memories of bloom
And lavish destinies it had before,
I take a whetted blade and cut the stem
Of the pale flower with the ailing core.

Why shall I keep what only serves to pain!
I long to have it vanish from my sight...
And now I lift my empty eyes again,
And empty hands into the empty night.


Your magic broke when veils of azure blew
From green of graves and certainty of grace.
Now let me — gone so soon — a little space,
As to the heart of sorrow, pray to you.

To rapid parting you must needs agree,
For riven is the water's frozen rind,
Perhaps a bud will be tomorrow's find!
I cannot take you into spring with me.

Where the sunrays swiftly slash
Palls of death on naked land,
Waters in the furrows stand,
In the sodden mires flash

And to rivers run united,
I have lighted pyres for you
And for memories of too
Brittle joys which now are blighted.

And I leave the blazing shrines
For my boat, and take an oar,
There a brother on the shore
Spreads his flag and gayly signs.

Thawing wind is swept in powered
Gusts across the fallow plain,
With the withered souls the lane
Shall again be overflowered.


## TRIUMPH OF SUMMER

The air, astir as though with coming things,
The sullen clouds which screen a fiery core,
The surging sound of homeward-pointed wings
Apprize me of adventure still in store

With you, who firmed my faith these many years,
Who were my sun where silent leaves attest
The alternating flux of hopes and fears.
For can delight — I ask — be manifest

To us, if such a night of stars and spells,
In gardens fresh with green, does not betray it,
If hosts of blooms with divers-coloured bells,
If burning winds do not convey it?

Ignore the poppies red as blood, the blue
Corollas, and the bright and brittle grain,
Remote from all reflection wander through
The wood and take each twisted path again.

The lettered birches shall not slow your pace,
Forget the fingers which have carven these,
Now learn that other names can fill with grace,
And turn your steps to younger, fresher trees.

Discard the sorrows and the wounds of old,
The gash of creepers, mouldering and spined,
The fronds of withered seasons! Light and bold,
Set foot on them and leave them far behind!

You want to found a realm of sun with me
Where we shall strive for joy and joy alone,
Where it will hallow grass, and bush, and tree
Before our vigours vanish with its own.

Oh, that so sweet a life sufficed, that we
Could linger here as grateful guests, for now
You find such words and songs that easily
Regret is banished to the highest bough.

You sing of humming fields, the gentle song
One hears before a door at dusk, you show
Us how to suffer like the plain and strong
Whose smile conceals the tear which lurks below.

The birds have fled from bitter sloes, the leap
Of wind and rain disbands the butterflies,
They glitter forth again in clearing skies,
And who has ever seen a flower weep?

A golden mullein nodding in the grass,
The silver tufts along the meadow's hem
Remember us and wonder if a less
Ungracious star has sent us back to them.

The branches touch our heads, may they eclipse
The fear which clings between us even now,
And let no idle query cool the lips
Which to a mated mouth have made their vow.

And let us guard against the dooms that brew
When flaming life of one the other laves,
And gaze together into summer blue
Which blithely beckons from the shining waves.


Have you his lovely image still in mind,
Who boldly snatched a rose from the ravine,
Forgot the passing day in such a find,
And thieved the nectar from a columbine?

Who when a flash of wings had driven him
Too far afield, turned back into the park,
Who mused and rested at the water's rim
And listened to the deep and secret dark?

The swan forsook the waterfall to sail
Around the island, built of moss and stone,
And laid a slender neck into the frail
And childish hand which smoothed his down.


When we are haunted by a past dismay,
And fear is rampant in our golden land,
"Feel no alarm at what recurs," you say
With confidence, "while we are hand in hand.

If only from my care you do not rove
Before the sharp effulgence dies away,
And placable and grave, the evening grove
Again affords you refuge in its grey."


It seemed as if another sky unfurled
When we had broken off the dream of old,
And smiling life permited us to hold
The only thing we wanted in this world.

And all at once the meaning of our days
Was: tensely to entreat the crowning hour
That knits us close together and devours
Phantasmal shapes and forces with its blaze.


Learn how to lavish even priceless gains!
Like plants consumed with long and searing drought,
So you, who live in regions of delight,
Shall cool your thirsty limbs in slender rains.

Know, while you take the loveliest that grows,
While sweet and sultry stars begin to burn,
While blaze and darkness ravish you in turn,
That you have had what fulness fate allows.

And nurse no foolish qualms because you woo
An image still a figment of your heart,
And always are impelled to keep apart
The kiss a dream accords you and the true.


When cool and early morning blows the wet
Down from the leaves of oak against our cheeks,
Beneath our feet the pointed gravel creaks
And pricks remembrance, ready to abate.

Your very voice sounds violent to you
When in the kindred pulse which presses near,
You recognize the quicker thud of fear ...
And passionless embrace dispels the dew.


These trees be praised, this earth of many hues!
They taught us how to touch a rapture doled
In passing, one that left its residues
Like bloom of ripened fruit within our hold.

The pennant flies! There is no stop nor stay!
The tears will brim from hours of farewell,
And doubting a return, you go away
Immersed in mournfulness you cannot quell.

But I shall listen through the dusk, if there
The last call of a bird will tell me of
The sleep which yields a wakening fresh and fair
In flowered field — the satin sleep of love.


## SUPERSCRIPTIONS AND DEDICATIONS

Friends, I cannot yet beget
Songs as I would have my songs,
Only shyly have I set
Rhymes like these in fleeting throngs,

To be proffered, to be told
Under silent roofs or green
Vines, to ease the winter's cold,
Make the fallow spring serene.

These are what I won from peace
After years of savage strife,
And from youth's abundant bliss
Salvage over into life.

135

I locked myself in dreams and shunned the crowd,
With frantic hands I groped for wider ways,
Alone and pure avowed to star and cloud
The first encounter with my young dismays.

Erect and free on rings of gold I wound
The flowers lavish life had given me.
For the ephebe whom timeless splendour crowned
Affliction ebbed to solemn melody.

To valleys of the gods, to bright Maeanders,
To lands where great and fervent codes obtain,
And to the south I let my spirit wander
To gain the halo born of martyr's pain.

And if I end the silent interim
And sing again, it only is that we
May glory in the hour day grows dim,
And my grave sister may confess to me:

"If living is my lot, I cannot do
Without the draught your chiming cup provides,
And in my darknesses the lights that flow
Like beacons from your wounds shall be my guides."


The word of seers is not for common sharing.
In curious kingdoms, earnest and alone,
When first his wishes roused him with their daring,
He summoned things with names that were his own.

And some were vast with clamorous commands,
Or hesitant like faltering desires,
And others leapt like brooks in April lands,
Or like Pactoli dyed in ruby fires.

Their melody and magic were his slaking.
They were — when in abandonment he flung
Himself into a dream, all else forsaking —
The temple's lyre-strings and holy tongue.

136

They were his choice when he had turned away
From mild, maternal tutelage and, burning
With ecstasy of nightingales and May,
Pored over fabled worlds of early yearning,

And when he prayed to him who let him waken,
In doubt and fear the pledge might be withdrawn,
And pleaded that the image which had taken
Shape in his spirit, grow into the sun.


When from gilded bars like a bird I flew,
Fortune followed me on eager feet,
From the wall the women threw
Roses on the street.

By the shores of wonder, halls with marble domes,
Tents of deities, where shudders brew,
Far from thronging guests I roamed,
And my songs were few.

Years went by, the funnels of my country cast
Smoke into the clouds, I only long
For a twilit dream, and rest,
And oblivion.


VERSES FOR THE GUESTS IN T . . .


I

A sinister fairy shall sing
Of shadows and death, while you
Are nursed at your mother's breast.
She brings you a christening gift:
Eyes that are veiled and strange,
Where muses discover a refuge.

Your glances will disparage
The games of callow comrades,
Austere and majestic thoughts
Shall guard and warn you away from
The work that debases.

When those who call you brother
Complain of their pain, confide your
Grief to the winds of dark.
The breast of the child shall bleed
Under his nail's armed thrust.

Do not forget: You must
Put to death your youth and freshness,
For only when their grave
Is wet with tears untold, it will beget
Under the matchless miracle of green,
The matchless beauty of roses.

II

You learned that only the house of want knows dejection,
But portals and pillars will show you a deeper dejection,

That only who dares the untried feels the bounds that are fated,
I teach that fulfilment brings with it the worst that is fated

For him who mourns through the day with an exquisite jewel,
Whose fingers listlessly play with the luminous jewel,

For him who is born to the folds of imperial purple,
And bows his pale and pensive face on the purple.


Though in the castle's dark and clanging hall
The many lyres hanging on the wall
Resound with fiercer joy and fuller fame,
Why is it that this first still holds the same
Delight and tremors for me, late and soon,
And that the chaste beginnings of its croon,
Awakened at a touch, still free the flow
Of tears today no less than long ago?

The traveller pauses midway on his road,
And after looking back on what he traversed,
Probes forward into clouds with timid doubt.
The hills and valleys he has crossed are worlds!
Behind him so much joy and stress! Can there
Be more to come? Shall he lie down to slumber
As if this were the journey's end, or venture
To brighter peaks, to jubilate more loudly,
Or moan more hopelessly in wilder chasms?
Was all this nothing but a morning's walk?


## RECOLLECTIONS OF EVENINGS OF INNER

## COMPANIONSHIP


### FLOWERS

In March we put the seeds into the earth,
While still we suffered in the angry vise
Of pain to which the yester-year gave birth,
And in the final bout of sun and ice.

We fetched them water from the glassy well
And tried to raise them, bound to slender stays,
We knew that in the light their buds would swell
And in the love and brightness of our gaze.

We kept them fresh with eager industry
And — leaned together — looked with questioning fear
Into the clouds, and waited patiently
To see a leaf unfold, a shoot appear.

We gathered them in gardens and above
Where vines were terraced on a neighbouring hill,
Enchanted by the golden night we roved
And held them in our hands as children will.

139

## RETURN

The harbour in the crimson west!
With precious cargo I return,
The white flag ripples from the mast,
How many a boat we left astern!

The ancient shores and roofs are new,
The ancient bells are new to me,
And winds persuade me gently through
The presage of a joy to be.

A rosy face, a word which broke
Through moving crests of jasper tide:
"So long you lived with foreign folk,
And yet our love has never died.

You sailed at dawn, but just as though
A single day you had been far
From them, the naiads welcome you,
The jetties and the evening star."


## ABDUCTION

Come with me, beloved child,
To the woods which few have sung,
By no other gift beguiled
Than my song upon your tongue.

If we bathe in silken blue
Where horizons film and gleam,
Then our limbs will shine and seem
Even clearer than the dew.

Frail and airy, to and fro,
Silver threads are spun to veils,
In the grass the linen pales
Delicate as stars and snow.

140

Under boughs, around the lake's
Edge we wander, gently singing,
Linked in happiness and flinging
White dianthus, clover-flakes.


RIPENING

A lavish sound, a throb of triumph swung
Across the grain in furrows late and lush,
The sparing words had not been spoken long
When poignant feeling wound us in its hush.

Where purple flames and perfect yellow merge,
Beside the trellis hung with fruit they slid,
They mounted to the vineyard's jewelled verge,
Where heavy clusters swell for crimson need.

I dared not cling to you, nor you to me
When slanted rays were loosed upon our brow,
Nor yet affirm in clumsy phrase what we
Received with mute delight, what bound us now,

And what in us, when day had quenched its fires,
Climbed to the clouds of lavender and rose,
What more than any dream and all desires
Shed slender glory through the evening glows.


WHITE SONG

For her I shall devise a dream of white:
A fancied castle, dipped in muted rays
And bordered with translucent blossom-sprays —
I see two children limned in early light.

Each carries flowers in a narrow sheaf
Glinted like aspens any breath can rouse,
And in it, higher than their tender brows,
A swinging flag: a silver cockle leaf.

They move, they wander slowly toward the lake
And sway on spacious marble steps, until
The lifted wings of nearing herons shake
The fragile burden in their arms, and chill

Petals of nards in spiral gusts exhale
Sweet vapours, where they merge, and float, and rise
To higher space. They grow more faint and pale
And are dissolved in pure and downy skies.


VIGILS

I

Your forehead clouded by the two tufts
Of your parted hair (they are blond and soft),
Your forehead shows me the sorrow of youth.

Your lips (they are silent) seem to tell
The story of souls condemned to hell.
A maddening mirror (your eyes), do not play with its spell.

When you smile (at last you have fallen asleep),
Your mouth is sad, you seem to weep,
And your head bends a little — your grief so deep!

II

I did not heed you and I went my road
In months of mist and greyness, when the goad
To ask, the urge to quest abate.

Who, in the months of mist and grey, will be
Beside the sombre gate because of me?
I think of you: Beside the sombre gate

Because of me you were, for me, though wall
And pillar creaked in silent fall
Of frost, and no one else was out so late.

142

III

What two middlenights, when he
Who himself was grief-impaled,
Met her anguish vengefully!

Ah, his eyes were never veiled,
He withheld his clemency!
Each could see the other's wound

Throb and well through thickly furred
Dark, but in aloneness found
Neither tear nor word.

IV

From deepest dream I rose and knew awaking,
To her as to a mirror I was bowed
And leaned my mouth above the lips that paled:

"The great compassionate shall be your slaking,
Only in thanks accept one who is vowed
To you!" But those I touched so burningly

Responded more than even dream allowed
That — though I shook with doubt — my senses failed.
O minutes slowed in bliss and ecstasy!

V

When such a tempest rages through the trees,
Is this not more than threat of yearning from
A violet glance, O blond and frolic bloom?

When cliffs are lashed by such a clash of seas,
Is this not more than that you skirt the shore
Alone, entreating heaven's ashen core,

That pale and shy as never yet, I find
You very like the girl, unheeded, blind,
Who calls along the road in deafening wind?

## PERMIT ME THIS GAME: YOUR SILHOUETTES

## NIMBLY CUT TO DECORATE MY HALLS OF

## MEMORY

Shall lips which anguish sealed between the thaw
Of April and autumnal rime, now cede
Their sorrow to the child and take their cue
From what? Oh, do not stop me, for I plead!

You stand upon the shore, the sail is caught
In savage winds. The ship may run aground!
So wait until you shape a gentle thought
To tell the stranger whom your wisdom found.


You who enhance a joy you never tasted,
Who staunch a grief which you can scarcely fathom,
And — though the signs be foul — foretell the fair,
In realms of kindness lavish and resourceful,
You have the right to boast: So many lives
Which, when the ship was shattered, drifted shoreward,
Abandoned by their gods and their companions,
Girl that I am, I helped them to renascence.


Hours of evening we spent with you passed so agreeably,
Lighting the lamp was forgotten — but not to your profit!
Was it delusion that drove you to utter the phrases
Chosen so crudely I may neither listen nor answer?
Should you be helpless to rein such impulsive expression,
Go from me, lest my amazement and sorrow compel you.
Keep the derision you feel for your failure in wooing,
Keep your contemptuous laugh from your care-ridden spirit.

So often, when the season shifts, I greet
You in the pause when night is still reluctant,
And spread before you sprays in faded colours,
Which you perhaps disdain, and then I leave.

144

This time the only comfort I can offer
Is that I shall return some harvest evening,
My hands transfigured by a lovely sadness,
And bring a token which may please you more.


W.L.

One of the few, the rare, who feel the fortunes
Of banished sovereigns, their exalted sorrow
And unrecorded death! Because you are —
If just for this — we bring our thanks. Your grandeur
Confirms us in the claim we make on grandeur.
With regal nod you take or cast aside,
You standard of our steps which sometimes falter,
And lodestar over every noble quest.


P.G.

In daily life, where one is like the other,
And hardly ever says what stirs within him,
Some meetings, none the less, gave rise to tremors,
And some farewells to tears we tried to stifle.
Those days on which you gave yourself and parted
The curtain of your wisdom were unrivalled,
Those evenings when — though nothing happened — glances
And words were proffered that remain forever.


M.L.

Like our transfigured horizons, brother in pride,
Like ripening harvest, your luminous yellow is spread.
Your lilac and wistful green are the tenuous foil
For hours unshapen, bent on laborious courses,
For sighs from dungeons: they bring no ease and are endless.
Your saturate blue is flung around wishless immortals,
And in your violet dark with an alloy of crimson,
Lurks our most deadly desire, brother in pain.

## H.H.

Finder of soaring songs and brilliant parleys
Adroitly turned, the lapse of time and parting
Permit me to engrave upon my tablet
Of memory, the former foe. Do likewise!
For on the rungs of ecstasy and motion
We both are netherbound: I shall not savour
Such glad acclaim of youth again, and never
Again will strophes strike your ear like thunder.


## K.W.

O happy we! Only the prophets may
Hold forth in such a voice, but on your course,
From laurelled cup it sounded day by day,
And yet I feel the ferment of remorse.

Though I respect your ways, I may not share
The smiles and pleasures — which are right for you!
I must return on seas of dull despair
Into my wonder-laden years of rue.


## E.R.

It often seems as if the fairest charm,
The highest exultation were obtained
In early days of youth, and that we warm
The barren span of life with what remained,

And then again that ecstasy untold
Escaped and haunts us — rarely though — by night,
And that on ruins of our young delight
We wander unremembering, proud, and cold.


## A.H.

You, gentle seer, who muse so helplessly
And sadly over dreams which never flowered,
Give us your hand, and we shall show you furrows
Where harvests of redemption can be sown.

146

With offerings of our blood and tears we gladly
Would tend them, miracles which still are hidden.
And you will clasp us, smiling and elated,
When they unfold before your startled eyes.


A.V.

You guess the contours of our bright dominions,
The many-coloured meadows topped with vineyards,
The westwind trailing through a row of poplars,
And soft as flutes of love, the streams of Tibur?
But here you lift your golden head: "Do you
Know dances of the mist on endless moors?
On grassy dunes the organ-boom of storms?
And all the tumult of tremendous seas?"


R.P.

Of what avail is wisdom on the verge of madness
That cows and overwhelms us with its glare and glitter,
But does not know when it becomes a weight and trespass?
How restlessly, O palest one among our brothers,
You err the mournful length and breadth of your possessions!
When will you weary of the conquest of new regions
And learn at last to plant and tend with care and pleasure
What grows, and blooms, and ripens in a threefold garden?


C.S.

We cherish you, and yet you are a riddle
Which tortures us. You smile: "Accept — as I —
That gulfs dividing us are fathomless,
And bow before their secret, even happy
You cannot plumb them." And imbued with sadness
We try to bridge them with our love, and follow
The life you lead, and do not feel afraid.
Your face is radiant with the look of victors.

A.S.

And was there really ever such a circle? Torches
Lit up the pallor of our faces, vapours mounted
From braziers for the godlike youth, and words you uttered
Uplifted us to loud vermilion worlds of frenzy,
So that for days we were bewildered, and our senses
Reeled as if poisoned by too lush a banquet,
So that our brows still burned with roses, and we suffered
For spying at the wealth behind the screen of heaven.


L.K.

And yet our home will always be the light
To which our winding paths at last will lead us.
Although you count yourself among the giants
And stubborn forces of the barren lowland,
Does not my clasp at every meeting tell you,
And that I often seek you out, how much
You rouse in me and are my own? You shun me
And so betray how I took root in you!


MOURNFUL DANCES

The harvest moon's unbridled flames have wasted
To shadow, but they burn within us yet,
And we, who were apart so briefly, tasted
Near the familiar stream a new regret.

You never challenged it before, and I
Cannot today provide you with a reason
Why storms and winter days are sadder, why
The air is gladder in the April season.

You run your fingers through your hair in anger
Because I find that your concern has paled.
I almost grieve, for now I weep no longer,
As once when far from Lilia, the child.

148

The walls are tapestried with velvet bloom
— A fashion grown from some ancestral mood —
Your arm in mine we come into the room
And tell each other death is good.

Upon the pane the frozen tendrils lace
And take us far from our accustomed earth,
Let us remain a while before the hearth,
The flames that fuse in tremulous embrace.

"Then you are sure the muses never will
Again accost the one they loved?" "And you —
Does the abundant light within you fail
And leave you too in darkness? Tell me true!"


The hours of August still wind you
In scents of the mild garden air,
Ivy and speedwell still bind you
A wreath for your wind-tangled hair.

Like gold is the wavering wheat, though
Perhaps less exultant and full,
Late-blooming roses still greet, though
The sheen of their colours grew dull.

Then let us conceal what defied us
And turn to felicity, for
The one thing which is not denied us
Is walking together once more.


Give me one more song
In chiming stanzas of a happier day,
You know it too: My peace is torn,
And now my hand delays.

Where shadowed spirits yearn
A rare and splendid vision rears,
But lost the memory that burned
In colours blithe and clear.

Where ailing spirits call
The sound assuages bitter stings,
The voice is sonorous and palled,
And yet it cannot sing.


The song the beggar dully sings
Is like my praise which beckons you in vain,
Is like a brook that bubbles far from springs
And which your lips, although they thirst, disdain.

The song the sightless girl repeats
Is like a dream I did not understand,
Is like my gaze that half retreats,
To which your glances scruple to respond.

The song the children chant aloud
Is soulless like the words which come from you,
Is like a bridge to those more cowed
Emotions which are all you still avow.


Three songs are what the village fool has learned,
And these he drones incessantly, the first
A breath from graves of elders who returned
Their souls to God before they breathed their last.

The other pure and consecrate, as though
It were the song of sisters while they span,
And serving girls who in an endless row
Have walked the evening lanes since time began.

The third is menacing: in sky-blue sheath
An ancient dagger, vengefulness and sin,
With sorrow handed down from kith to kin
And evil stars on many a roof beneath.

Region of mordant desires
Where you are wrecked on the strand!
Fly from your sunlighted shires,
Follow the ruthless command.

Put all your strength in your rowing,
Unimperilled by fear
Slowly your boat will be flowing
On with the wane of the year.

Ponder without trepidations
Glaciers where riddles arise,
And on the grave constellations
Fasten your questioning gaze.


The drowsy pasture woke and lured. She turned
Through clustering violets to the gate, her gown
As yearly picked to please a groom, and yearned
For him until the reapers' work was done.

Only a lark which carolled in the grove
Saw that her anguish and confusion grew,
And how on drifting days of summer's drove
She mused and wasted by the hedge of yew.

All that recalls her slender loveliness
Is — under strings of pearls — a silken lock
A faithful friend keeps in her treasure-chest,
And simple grass around a marble block.


Since now the grains within the glass are few,
Go after him: the wanderer drenched in dew,
Who swiftly vanished in the burning winds,
The child of stars, with flowers as his friends.

Who once, before the wheat was gathered, laid
His head into his mournful hands and, swayed
By no one knows what early curse, divined
That now the final day of youth had dawned.

151

Who callous to the coaxing of the sun,
Light as a butterfly above the foam,
While he was beautiful, without lament
That very day beyond our circles went.


Night of lurking dooms!
Palls of sombre velvet mute
Footfalls in the room
Where Love defends his suit.

Your wish has made him die.
Now toward the bier you gaze
Where pale and still he lies
Beset with candle rays.

The candles burn to ends,
You blindly leave the walls
Where Love was done to death,
And weeping fills the halls.


No longer do we blanch and stare
Like ancient lovers in despair.
Excess of dolour was our share,
We gently wince and softly bear.

How unafraid they were, how free,
Although they voiced their agony!
Our lot was long adversity,
And yet we suffer silently.

They used the axe, they used the blade,
But we refuse to fight and raid.
The peace we crave cannot be paid
With weal and woe which they displayed.

I know you come to me like one
Who, tuned to sighs, ignores the call
Of feast and play with merry throngs
When strings resound in pillared hall.

The window filters autumn scent,
Here few and gentle steps are heard,
The hopeless find a new content,
And timid pleas a clement word.

On coming, hands are lightly pressed,
On going from this silent clime
A kiss, and to adorn the guest
A simple gift: a tender rhyme.


This burden and this grief: to ban
What once I called my own,
In vain with reaching arms to span
What now — a wraith — is flown.

This torpor without cure or stay,
This idle no and none,
This groundless rising up at bay,
This course which must be run.

The weighing sorrows which oppress
An anguish that has grown
Resigned, the ache of emptiness,
This: with myself alone!


Foolish hope: until the utmost day
To rejoice in what must pass away.
Southward to the sea the birds have sped,
Blooms await the snow with drooping head.

Limp the stems your languid fingers wreathe,
They are all the season will bequeath.
Wish cannot evoke them on our ways,
Others will unfold in other Mays.

Courage! Drop my arm, and let us go
From the park before the sun is low
And the mountain mists begin to weave.
Come, before the winter bids us leave!


Only your subtle ear
Discerns what sings within,
What quivers shy and thin
And grows more faint and far.

Only your valiant phrase
Distils a balm from what
Was given as our lot,
And grants a peace that stays.

Only your fervent thought
Dissolves the pain so well
Which once at dusk befell
The light our morning brought.


No road too long, too steep for me,
My friend, if I can only be
With you, no gulf that threatens doom,
And penance calls from every tomb.

So wistfully we go our way
Through joyless fields of cinder-grey,
Across the withered thorn and gorse,
But free from anger and remorse.

My eyes are wet, I only look
For one whose hand will gladly pluck
The strings attuned and manifold,
One who will take our harp of gold.

154

The tempest tears across the endless fallows
And, filled with fair divinings, makes the rounds,
The earth is stifled for revenge, and hollows
Between the mountains echo broken sounds.

Those who are terribly distant seem to fret,
But from the tranquil firs a warning flows:
Did I not have your promise that regret
Should not disturb the dead in their repose!

I pass the wintry shrine we never harry
With idle pleas and tears, and all I pray
Of you, so soon to see them, is to carry
My greeting to the rays of youth and May.


By singing led that softly fled,
Along the shore how light your tread!
I see the hills where vapour twines,
The crumpled leaves, the thistle spines.

Your dreaming eyes already shift
To find a land of fresher gift,
Because your fancy flutters on
Into a rich and safer dawn.

And still I ask: When on the verge
The yellow cowslips gently surge
And green with reeds the waters swing —
Who'll come to help me start the spring?


In weightless vessels flee
From reeling worlds of light,
That lessened poignancy
Of tears requite your flight.

What cataracts of blond
Cerulean visions churn,
And glutted joys beyond
Mere rapture bud and burn!

Sweet shudders shall not arch
Your life for new distress,
So saturate this March
With silent wistfulness.


Lingering hours on the stream,
As if in wrath the waters scream,
And freshened by the rainy winds
The light now flickers and now blinds.

Astrand we loitered hand in hand,
She saw the grain which grew in sand.
She came, and stooped, and picked a spray,
And found a tune to fit the day.

Serene and bright her strain began
As of a goal which we had won.
Then sadness crept into the song
Of lost delight — how lorn! How long!


The hill where we are roaming lies in shadow,
While that beyond is all enmeshed in light,
The moon within its green and tender meadow
Is still a little cloud, adrift and white.

The roads into the infinite are paling,
The wanderers halt, delayed by whispered sighs,
Is it a hidden stream from mountains trailing?
Is it a bird that twitters hushabies?

Two moths which flew abroad before their hour,
Are playing at pursuit from leaf to leaf,
And path and field distil from bush and flower
The scent of evening for a muted grief.

Forests aflame on the mountain side,
Clustering tendrils in cinnabar pride!
Glistering grapes which your fingers enshrine
Soon will be barrelled and ripen to wine.

Long before sunrays had rounded the sheath
Homeward you came with sprig and wreath,
And you are happy with autumn's reward,
You, who inherit the summer's hoard.

He was not fated to savour the fruits
Who did not cherish the buds and the shoots.
If you ask, he will tell you: "They
Took my only joy away."


The sultry dusk, the pale and sober morrow
Are change eternal of her dismal faring,
A sternly charted course decrees the bearing
Of one so shy and all in tears and sorrow.

At stately gates she lingers and beseeches,
But there is none to vouch for her or second,
And not a single hand is raised and reaches
As flesh of her own flesh and beckons.

So now the tides of din and discord drive her,
Now turning with their evil prey she wavers,
And just as long ago, today she quavers
The spell that will approach and shrive her.


Though heavy vapours hang from bush and tree,
Your further journey shall not be delayed,
Speak to the pallid spectres unafraid,
And they will move, and touch you tenderly.

When wayside grooves and grasses turn to stone,
The hoarfrost bends the branches, try to hear
The anguish in the winter winds that veer
To withered solitudes and swell their moan.

Then you will lift your tired head and flout
The thought of slipping from the precipice,
Although the faintly lighted goal and this
One lonely star above you flicker out.


Since much is wan and torn, and sinks and crumbles,
The song is dead in floods of mist and dreaming
Until in gusts the brittle foliage tumbles —
The wound that once was wild, again is streaming.

But then from dripping clouds a sunbeam flashes,
And water straggles black across the ashen
Terrains, through frost a seldom thunder crashes.
And yet the song construes the grave procession

As clangour pouring from sepulchral glitter,
As torches high among the bended shoulders,
And asks if in the dross of what is bitter
The clear, eternal spark of joy still smoulders.


The storm aroused the heath
To sullen task. Through gloom
Of noon a hoot of doom,
Sung by the bird of death.

The arc of hills ignores
The hours' empty flow,
And branches fumble low
For blades on barren shores.

The shaft of darkness jails
The dismal land again,
A voice of night and pain
Is like a cry that fails.

Perhaps your vision is clouded
By branches which fall and ride.
Are waters driven and crowded
Against the tide?

You reach them and they rise higher
Submissive to alien trance,
Frantic haste of desire
Follows their dithering dance.

Take care and stop pursuing
A game that costs so dear!
Are your companions not wooing
The ways of yester-year?

You reached the hearth, but dwindled
To cinders was the glow,
The moon was all that kindled
The earth with deathly hue.

Your listless fingers crumble
The ashes. If you strain,
And grope in them, and fumble,
Will light return again?

See, how the moon consoles you
With soothing gait,
Leave the hearth — she tells you —
It has gotten late.

The lamp within the vault
Has live and timeless beams,
And how its ruby gleams
On shivering basalt!

The rounded window flings
A blaze that overflows,
Below the monstrance glows
With globes in golden rings,

And with a snowy lamb.
And do the timeless beams,
And do the jewelled gleams
Burn with an inner flame?

The hunt has passed, you slow
Your steps with idle bow.
Blood under firs, the air
Is taut with sound — from where?

This is no hound, no call
Of those who flee and fall.
You listen, crouched upon
The earth — shall you go on?

But hush! It comes more clear,
And you who rove and peer,
Divine a summons borne
On echoes of the horn.

The airs of evening blew
A less austere delight,
Take it and keep it too,
Or else another might!

But as if shackled and wan
The soul sings threnodies,
She feels a joy draw on,
She craves, yet cannot seize.

The airs of evening blew
Her signs of saving grace:
The saddest hour I face,
You know it now — you too!


Will you persist in looking for the deep
And early colours on a barren shore,
In ashen deserts wait for fruit and reap
The grain of summers that will come no more.

It is enough if filmed with cloud you find
The muted sheen of fulness you have known,
And through the sluggish air, the freeing wind
Blows us caresses from another zone.

And see, the hours of the past which beat
In us like burning wounds have paled and fled,
But all the things we took for flowers meet
Beside the well which now is dead.

THE TAPESTRY OF LIFE AND

THE SONGS OF DREAM AND DEATH

WITH A PRELUDE

(1900)

## MELCHIOR LECHTER

This edition, intended for a wider public, must do without the drawings of the first: the lavish marginal decorations and the pictures of an angel throned in the clouds, flowers pouring forth the waters of life, and the harp struck by the hand of ultimate passion. But I should like to set down on these pages the reverenced name which is so closely connected with them and shall adorn them forever.

PRELUDE

I

When pale with zeal I searched for hidden store,
For strophes weighed with grief and things that flow
In drowsy and uncertain round, I saw
A naked angel enter through the door.

He brought the spirit which was buried in . .
Itself a wealth of precious blooms, his hand
Was like the flowering almond, and a band
Of roses, roses clustered at his chin.

He did not wear a heavy crown and when
He spoke his voice was almost like my own:
"Dispatched to you by radiant Life I come,
An envoy!" So he said and smiled and then

He dropped his sheaves of lilies and mimosas,
But when I stooped to gather them, he too
Was kneeling. In delight I bathed my brow
And cheeks, and mouth in newly-opened roses.


II

"Give me the solemn breath that never failed,
Give me the fire again that makes us young,
On which the wings of childhood rose among
The fumes our earliest sacrifice exhaled.

I will not breathe save in your fragrant air,
Enclose me wholly in your shrine, accord
A single crumb from your abundant board,
I plead today from chasms of despair."

And he: "The reckless words which meet my ear
Spell flocks of wishes, tangled and at feud,
The ready granting of a multitude
Of boons is not my charge, what I confer

Is never wrested from me under stress."
But then against his knee I bent my arm
And all the tongues of wakened longing stormed:
"I will not let you go unless you bless!"


## III

My life was cut by inauspicious trails,
And many voices sounded harsh and shrill,
But now a blessed spirit holds the scales,
Now I am governed by the angel's will.

Though still too often on a dismal coast
The soul forgets and weeps, a quick command
Rings from the crier at the mooring-post:
"Up with the sails and on to fairer lands!"

When new disaster strikes and slants the keel,
When madness threatens from the left, the grave
Looms on the right, he swiftly grips the wheel,
The angry forces fawn upon his wave.

Imperiously he calms the warring tides,
The clouds give way to flawless blue once more.
Soon on a quiet sea the fleet will glide
To tranquil islands, to the promised shore.


## IV

Too long have I been thirsting for your bliss,
Henceforth no lord shall harness me like this.
Too lonely was his service and too grey
When you appeared upon my mournful way.

Let him return my freedom and reclaim
The fronds of palm, the solemn diadem,
A pledge of dawn with flowers still unguessed —
So I have you! My forehead on your breast.

Then he, the banner-bearer, crossed the glow
Of autumn and with lifted finger drew
Me back into his spell, his tones like those
That once in songs of fabled sirens closed

Around the soul, and with a long and sad
Look in his eyes — like that the Master had,
When standing at the Sea of Galilee
He asked the twelve: "Is all your love for me?"


V


No longer will you praise the gorgeous quests
On treacherous and sullen seas, and where
Abysses climb to crags abrupt and bare,
And eagles float around the jagged crests.

In these unbroken meadows learn to feel
The breath that tempers frosty April days,
And know the wind that parts the sultry haze.
Hear what their childish voices have to tell.

You find the secret of eternal runes
In hills with clearly contoured rise and fall,
Not only in the lure of street and wall.
How weak is now the Wonder of Lagoons,

Is great and ruined Rome, the world-wooed dream,
Compared to vines and tang of oaken grove,
To those that guard your people's treasure-trove:
Your waters, green with life, O surging Stream!


VI


Recall the terrors which, since you became
My own, were blotted from your memory,
For only I accord the cup of flame
Which shall enrapture you until you die.

You thanked me then as for the boon of boons,
That in my peace you were no longer faced
With savage heat of parching summer moons
Which drove you — homeless — out into the waste.

When you disdained my dizzy peak and cried:
"Allot an instant dedicate to choice,
And I deny the altar and the creed!"
The night was strident with your tortured voice.

The victim reared before the hearth, like sheaves
Of weightless straw the purple flared and ran
Along the columns to the architrave,
And all the temple burned, and shook, and shone.


VII

Now I am your friend, and guard, and guide,
So you may no longer share the feuds
Even of the wise. My peaks provide
Views of valleys and their multitudes.

Sturdy feet in endless come and go,
Cry of busy toilers: "Delve in things,
Profit from their use and you shall know
Joys on earth like those which heaven brings."

There, in swirls of incense, solemn throngs
Follow an ascetic on a white
Horse, and passion smoulders through their songs:
"Long the world shall have the cross for light!"

Only few have chosen silent ways,
Proudly distant from the active drove,
And the words their banners flaunt are these:
"Hellas, our eternal love!"

## VIII

"You never cite convention or disgrace."
"You, my disciples, of untainted blood
Are quick to recognize and choose the good,
Though covertly I still direct your pace.

I love you, when intent upon your course
In midday calm you call the rules of old
A dear tradition and reject the hold
Of self-reproach, compulsion, or remorse.

And you, who lived within the clan you chose,
In love you neither limit nor abate,
You hardly question or detest your fate,
But long the grudge you cherish for your foes.

And at the deeds which never should have won
Reward or blame, those deeds you vaunt before
Your peers, but which the populace abhor,
I only shrugged and smiled: "O son, my son!"


## IX

Ask not what word shall win the most applause,
Nor at the feast what song the wreath. Today
The yester-storm which swept the meagre grass
Is sacred westwind in the laurel spray.

Now it was warp of green in crystal lanes
Unflawed and brilliant in a burnished dawn,
Now fluid agate traced with darker veins,
And then like rubies darting frantic suns.

What as a drizzle, warm and gentle, drew
Along the withered walk which all forsake,
And only as a drop of fragrant dew
Fell from the flower to the hollow lake,

173

Grew into streams that tunnel through the lock
Of mountains, and in deepest midnights fling
The sudden jet that stabs the heart of rock,
And throbs and gushes as a crimson spring.


## X

If you are prisoned in those hopeless tracts
Where deeds of both the wan and vital pale
Unsung, then — as the body without fail
To all delight — my word exhorts to acts.

The lucid answer rises with my sun
When you demand: "What wind shall drive my ship?
Since every well is full, where shall I dip?
Where seize since all the fibres intertwine?"

And if you suffer from your fathers' fear
That you may lose direction in the drift
Of all-too many shapes that glint and shift,
If you are crushed by countless worlds in air,

Then come to where we work in unison,
Where through my sacred grove a paean rings:
"Though tens of thousands be the forms of things,
You shall give voice to one alone: my own."


## XI

You doubt you can evoke the glory of
The gods unless the flash you cannot bid
Lights up your brooding brow — a child that sobs
For laughing hours all-too swiftly sped.

On every word the rabble stamps its stain,
Sweet sounds are dulled when fools usurp the floor,
"O voice in storm and temple," you implore,
"When will you raise us with your strength again?"

The weary worker bowed his head and hand,
The stuff grew brittle, cumbersome, and cold,
Then through the chink a glint, a silver band
Broke suddenly, undreamed, into the hold.

How buoyant what but just was grave and dull,
Alight and purified what clung in dust,
A first and bridal lifting of the veil,
Now the Eternal says: "I call — you must!"


## XII

We who as princes choose and cast aside
And lift the world from ancient hinges, shall
We search forever, sick and sorely tried,
And think we miss the best that can befall?

We who are love's most faithful priests must quest
For it with hidden grief and hollow eyes
Wide with fanatic flame, and when at last
We seize what is our own, revere, and prize

And barely taste, again it flickers from
Our avid senses, colourless and wry,
And all our gods seem only shades and foam.
"I know your heart would break, that you would die

If I had not the spell that can abate:
Since all the forms you worshipped and forwent
Through you are valid and through you are great,
Do not lament too much what you have lent."


## XIII

The years like fairy-tales, when on a strand
Of filmy cloud and sunlight you were led,
My wards, to white and slender trails and had
Sheaved grapes, and wheat, and lilies in your hand,

175

Gave you a love that never died. And when
The branches beckoned with fantastic twists,
The dark and snaring thickets lured, and mists
Beguiled above the ooze of quaggy fen,

You felt reluctance as before the storm
Of masses interlocked in press and pace,
The false design of bodies that are base,
The overplus of limbs on monstrous form.

The love for light remained from early days,
For gentle fields and hills, and narrow pines,
Clean colours and uncomplicated lines,
And whispers from the spicy garden-sprays.


XIV

You left your house above and took the road
Which wound below, and chosen friends were near,
And there you tried to found your own abode
And looked about as in an alien sphere.

Your summits will no longer be your screen,
But in a robe unsullied as before
Upon your neighbour's arm you now will lean,
And yet you are a guest from distant shore

To all the many whom you wished to shun.
Their clasp could never hold you, and to fight
Their battles in their ranks were idly done.
For them your patterns are too recondite.

But sometimes pure and seldom fires shine
From them and show such closeness does not stain.
Then say: "I take your brother-hands in mine,
Allied in strong community of pain."

176

## XV

Back to the vanished years your spirit leant
And failed to grasp what starry fathoms ran
Between you and the worlds of other men.
How every head was bent in wonderment

When you contrived the temples for the Fleece,
More radiant than our pale, terrestrial beam,
And golden was the dye of every dream,
And all in the enchanted port was peace.

Then fruity summer led you onward by
Accustomed paths on stony hills, the slope
Smiled to the wanderer kindling him to hope,
And faces gave him greeting, hushed and shy.

These are the meadows: velvet threaded through
With flowers, the ready harvest, full and lithe,
The song of reapers beating out the scythe —
The earth from which you hail is calling you.


## XVI

Your goal shall be the shore, the market-place,
The supple sinews of the strong and slim,
The people's song and say, their shout and press,
And in the stream the glide of naked limb.

The struggle waged by man with man, and brute,
And soil will take new shape and colour: poise
In every gesture, and in dance, and gait,
The ring of singing girls, the games of boys.

But in a room with friends, by night you find
The rarest treasures, soon a silence reigns,
And then a glance is born, a trembling sound,
And revelation pulses through your veins.

177

The regnant word ascends, the magic seal,
A star in furrows of which no one knows,
The word of new delight and new ordeal,
A shaft that stabs the soul, and throbs, and glows.


## XVII

Now he may speak as from another star,
Who in the darkness set new fires burning,
Who found release from lifeless days of yearning,
Refrained from deeds until his hand was sure,

Restored the withered world with new delights,
And through his office pointed to his brothers
The field of true renown beyond all others,
And in new dances fostered secret rites.

No king will ever equal him in fame,
To whom the sybils with devout elation
And noble boys are bound in dedication,
The future lords whom nations shall acclaim.

The gods alone receive such incense wreathing
Aloft, as he from holy youth who chime
His praise and far beyond his rungs will climb,
Much of his breath infused into their breathing.


## XVIII

Some day they will examine your ravines
For echoes of your voice. "Is this the haunt,"
So one may say, "of vows, and tears, and moans?
How paltry!" And another dare to taunt:

"Are these the crests of hills so greatly praised,
Which gladdened with a glimpse of fabled lands?
Are these the waves which threatened where they grazed?
So shallow that our fingers touch the sand!"

And one may turn from you in sullen gloom:
"All he aroused was our surprise and awe,
How far away those passions and their bloom,
How could their fruits accord us any joy!"

But here the masters pattern and beguile:
Those who in Athens gave the gods their best,
The bitter lord of souls on foggy isle,
The son of Florence and Valclusa's guest.


## XIX

To whom but you is she to turn her gaze,
The soul afire you were first to show
The heights and happiness which fails to flow
From gaudy days like these. You deign to rouse,

And she approaches the eternal gate,
The longed-for rays in jubilant accord,
Floats down the hall to the immortals' board,
Salvation peals! A shaft of perfect light!

She finds herself in uninvaded zones,
She crosses chasms as an eagle soars,
Directs the galaxies of lesser stars,
And rushes forward to paternal suns.

Now you must curb her wanton haste, you lean
From sills of cloud and cover her who is
Shaken with tremors and replete with bliss,
True spirit, with the heavy wings of dream.


## XX

At every turn of tide she feels her thirst
For holy fare grow wilder than at first,
And as if, banished from the fragrant shore,
She sank in seas of sorrow more and more.

Forsaken by the guides which led her on,
The shining torch of Venus and the Swan,
For her the fiery god has only drouth,
She flutters like a singed and dazzled moth.

Then she recalls how many times she thought
The day an end, a flame that peters out,
A tomb engulfed in mists malign and low,
And yet the morning never failed to show

The valley swimming in a haze of blue,
Where mellow chimes, and secret strains, and through
The boughs of May her own reflection sang:
"Now look! And you will see you still are young."


## XXI

As long as drifts of sunset lit the hill
It was not hard to find the way, and still
I heard familiar calls along my trail,
Now it is grey and all the voices fail.

Now there is none who for a little scope
Of kindred going rouses me to hope,
Whose even slightest solace I desire.
No wanderer walks in darkness so entire.

And when the cricket's chirp, the final tone,
Falls silent, even memories are gone.
The woods are cold, the vapours close around
The path and drain the dregs of light and sound.

From dark terrains, where sleep has conquered, wheel
The chill and mist of graves, and yet I feel
Your breath that fans the spark to mounting fires,
Your great and watchful love that never tires.

180

## XXII

"And must I always thirst and wait? The sun
Not yet at noon, the worst is still ahead!"
"Your want and torment would be far from done
If 'Come and take' this very day I said.

You thrive in struggles meet for you and know
That from my mouth upon your bleeding weals
A balm of tenderness will always flow,
But you will never find the spell that heals."

"And those who reverently touch my knee,
Who lay upon my breast a youthful cheek,
Those who were guided by a sign from me?"
"Disciples love but are afraid and weak."

"So to the end I must contend alone
And never rest in faithful arms? Reply!"
"You stir me to compassion, for no one
Indeed remains with you — save you and I."


## XXIII

We are the selfsame children who in awe
Of your imperial 'tread, but undismayed,
Are ready when the battle-trumpets blow
From open reaches where your flag is spread.

We journey at our stern commander's side,
He probes among his men to choose and bar,
No loving friend, nor kisses of a bride,
Nor tears can make us faithless to our star.

And in his glances joyfully we read
What in prophetic dreams he knows will come,
If honours or oblivion be decreed
By his uplifted or his downward thumb.

181

He gives in fief what bliss we are allowed,
What fame and force. He beckons, and we vie
To serve his greater glory, strong and proud
To go into the darkness and to die.


## XXIV

We who through many years composed and spoke
Our odes in praise of magic life, we must
Be just as glad and ready to evoke
The dim divinings of the dark and dust...

The pillowed head still mutely acquiesced
And dwelt on former honour, gain, and bout,
The flowers of our childhood stirred without,
And rocked and heralded consummate rest.

And then the last and lovely image strayed
And slowly vanished into singing wind,
All had withdrawn and gone was every friend,
But he who never faltered, watched and stayed.

Delaying anguish in its sullen spate
With numbing wine shed from his aspergill,
And easing tortured glances of farewell,
The angel at the bed stood tall and straight.

# THE TAPESTRY OF LIFE

## THE TAPESTRY

Here men are oddly meshed with beasts and plants
Which silken fringes frame to harmonies,
Cerulean crescents in arrested dance
Are scored and trimmed with silver galaxies.

The arabesque is crossed with barren lines,
The single parts are tangled and at strife,
And the enigma of the snared remains
Until, one night, the fabric leaps to life.

The patterned boughs begin to stir and veer,
The creatures locked in arc and square come out
Before the knotted tassels, limned and clear,
And bring the answer that dispels your doubt.

It is not at your beck and call on each
Accustomed day, and not what guilds could share,
And never for the many nor through speech
It comes incarnate rarely to the rare.


## PRIMEVAL LANDSCAPE

From brooding pines an eagle upward swept
Into the blue, and toward the clearing stepped
Two wolves. They lapped the shallow pool and swung
To stark attention, marshalling their young.

And then across the glossy needles whipped
A flock of hinds, and drank, and shyly slipped
Back to the dusk of woods, but one remained
Alone among the reeds to wait his end.

Here the lush grass had never felt the blade,
But hands had been at work, for stems were laid
And further on a plough had ridged the sod,
Where in the fertile odour of the clod

And happy in the white and stinging sun
With fields and gains their novel toil had won,
Arch-father delved, arch-mother milked,
Shaping the fate of all this human ilk.


## THE FRIEND OF THE FIELDS

You see him walk the furrows through the gleaming
Of dawn, the shiny sickle in his grip,
And reach into the wheat to weigh its teeming.
He tests a yellow kernel with his lip.

Then on between the vines you watch him steady
The wayward shoot with bast on sturdy prop,
He feels the grapes, too green and still unready,
And prunes a spray grown overlong with sap.

To find if it will stand against the welter
Of wind, he shakes a sapling, probes the cloud,
He binds his favourite to a shaft for shelter
And smiles on one which firstling fruits have bowed.

He draws the water with a gourd and pours,
He often stoops to pull the quickening grasses,
Beneath his foot the region spills with flowers
And ripens to a harvest where he passes.


## THUNDERSTORM

On every path the vagrant flickers pale and wane,
A sudden thunder flails the full and upright grain.
The midnight storm attacks the wall of massy boughs
And crashes through the lairs where boars and vultures house.

The ruthless king has spurred from cloudy castle-hold
And hunts with great cortege, his charger geared with gold,
The faithless queen who joins the wind's unbridled race,
Delivered up to any wanton saviour's grace.

186

Often he thinks he has her in his dour fists,
But she, with whispered laughter, lithely from him twists
Until he seizes her and holds her in his grasp
Crosswise between his horse's neck and girdle's clasp.

She grinds her glistening teeth and sobs in caged despair,
In tameless rage she shakes her mane of loosened hair,
Around her naked limbs the slanting torrents fall,
Composed her icy bosom faces coming thrall.


## THE STRANGER

She came alone from far away,
They shunned her house in cold dismay.
She told the palm, and baked, and stewed,
By moonlight walked without a snood.

Bedecked with gauds she often lay
Against her sill on holy day,
And sweet and bitter was her smile
To spouse and brother bane and guile.

The morrow-year when through the dusk
Danewort she dug and buttercups,
Some said the swamp had sucked her down,
But others swore, before the town

She disappeared midway, and had
As only pledge bequeathed the lad
As pale as linen, black as night
Whom she had born in Feveril light.


## LAMBS

When days are done with memory-laden shadows
In half-forgotten beauty's faded frame,
Waves of white lambs draw slowly through the meadows
From the broad clearing to the darkened stream.

Lambs of the mournful moon, the lusty sun,
You hardly guess or covet unknown treasures,
Lambs that are shallow and a little vain,
Proud of the golden bells which grace your wethers.

Old in our eyes, you think that youth will keep!
Lambs of a happiness which now seems hollow,
Lambs that sedately tread or lightly leap
With feelings which we now can scarcely follow.

You probe, but from a ledge you never shied!
Lambs of the carefully encircled meres,
Lambs of a faithfulness too old, but tried,
Lambs of beyonds that hold no fears.


QUEEN OF HEARTS

Out of the church the frightened sexton ran
By nooks and corners of the crooked lane,
And pious parish ladies heard his cries
That upward now the Image turned her eyes,

And that her lips were parted — almost spoke!
Repenting their most recent sins, they flock
And fling themselves to earth before the shrine,
Even the righteous shudder at the sign.

At fall of night they billow through the door
In grave alarm, but she in white attire
Who was the first to come and answers to
The name of Queen of Hearts, the fair, the true,

She, only she had grasped the miracle,
Her fervent pleas had broken through the veil.
She paces with her head a trifle bent
In azure trance and marvelous lament.

188

## THE MASK

In lighted halls the silken puppets flutter.
One used her paint to hide her passions and,
While maudlin couples weave and whirl around her,
Discovers that Ash Wednesday is at hand.

She steals to the deserted park, the narrow
Embankment, gives the masque a parting glance,
And bends above the ice with freezing marrow.
A crash, the silent cold — and still they dance!

None of the handsome lords and ladies noted
Her down below, in weeds and pebbles wound,
But when they roved the paths in spring, a muted
And gurgling sound came often from the pond.

They must have heard that curious murmur rising,
The light of heart in eras far from grave,
But found it hardly more than just surprising,
And merely took if for a whim of wave.


## IMPRECATION

Is there a path behind the willow logs
Where the grasses crouch when the tempest passes?
Does not this river wind to the poisonous bogs
Green with will-o'-the wisps in erratic flashes?

Serpents uncoil, and the flicker and flame of a tongue
Dart from a gullet which threatens and brands with corruption.
Rider, vow your life to avenge a wrong,
Hate him and hate until you achieve his destruction.

Only the dead will cure you of wild desire,
Calm the anger in your smouldering cry,
Cool the cheek which he has fanned to fire.
Curse him till the waters wash him by.

189

Lips that are too white to sneer and fingers
All-too slack to deal another blow,
In his breast a shining dagger lingers,
Down beneath the bridges let him go.


## THE DOER

I sit at the window I slighted so long. Now unfold
Your wings, as so often before, and scatter my way
With blessings, O twilight, I always have yearned for, now hold
Me close while I yield to the solace and peace of today.

Tomorrow, when slant falls the light, it will all come true
What haunts me in hours that shackle and stretch on the rack,
Then rising like shadows behind me are those who pursue
And mobs ever ready to stone will be hot on my track.

Who never has measured his brother for gauging a blow,
How simple his life must be! And who never knew
The hemlock that deadens, how thinly his thinking must flow!
If only you guessed how I mock at the best among you!

For even my friends will say on the morrow: "Here ends
A life in which promise and glory ennobled the way."
How gently I swing in the somnolent dream of the land,
How drowned I am in peace of parting day!


## BROTHERS IN SORROW

You wander through greyness, are time growing dim,
Companioned by none but a beckoning gleam,
United and speechless, for all has been said,
You bear with an anguish you cannot evade.

Who gives himself wholly — how slight is his prize!
Young foreheads desire a sky beyond skies.
You wander through greyness, are time growing dim,
Companioned by none but a beckoning gleam.

190

And sometimes when touches more fervent reward
And move you, when words are in tender accord,
When eloquent silence has woven its spells,
It seems as if hope, though reluctantly, wells.

With tremulous fingers held close to your breast
Though just for an hour, you try to arrest
The passage of evening, but those who have gone
With you on this journey — they dream of the dawn!


## THE DISCIPLE

You speak of raptures I shall never treasure,
I pulse with love that binds me to my lord,
I thirst for glory while you covet pleasure,
I live for glories of my lord.

More than in any work of your pursuing
I am adroit in labours of my lord,
My lord is gracious, valid is my doing,
I only serve my gracious lord.

I know that many died who dared the journey
Into the land of darkness, but my lord
Is wise, with him I go to any tourney,
I trust the wisdom of my lord.

And if he gave me no reward, my guerdon
Is in a glance accorded by my lord,
There may be richer, but my lord is sovereign,
I shall not leave my sovereign lord.


## THE ELECT

They loudly acclaim your fairer rebirth,
A halo transforms the child of the dusk.
What seldom is won was early your fate,
The masters upheld your praises in song.

What courts and exalts you modestly took,
Your forehead was bent, but proudly you felt
What things will submit if treated with awe,
And thus you preferred to journey through life.

With glances that probed, with love as your drive,
Your untainted hands reached forward to seize.
You trusted and mused with malice toward none:
The statelier urge of the kinglier beast.

What crowns you today, will weigh him with thorns
Who squandered himself, who let the leaf wilt.
But while you revere you cannot be false,
You keep both yourself, O youth, and the wreath.


THE OUTCAST

Your passions roused too soon, you toyed and tampered
With everything: with beauty, love, and fame,
And majesty, and when in life you found them
They seemed insipid and their tints had dulled.

You pried too tensely on the road, the market,
Lest there be shades of moods you might have missed.
Your soul, which slipped into the soul of others
So greedily, was left unsown and waste.

You gathered seldom colours, shards, and sounds
And cast them to the blind, bewildered throng
That brimmed with praise, until you felt elated,
But wept in secret. Sorrow saps your strength!

Before the pure your gaze is shamed and shifting,
As though they saw through you. Unworthy of
Yourself you came adorned and yet unhallowed,
Without a wreath to the great feast of life.

## PILGRIMS TO ROME

Rejoice you never lost your kinship for
This gracious land, your fathers' paradise,
Which broke their misty, northern dreams, and more
Than of their native soil they sang its praise.

There scents, and sorcery of marble limbs
And painted frieze evoke a lordly goal,
There you will lose the flower of your stem,
So fair a mistress chains your drunken soul

Forever, though for evil: once she hurled
Your sires into bonds who loathed the lean
Trust in the throne, the Wonder of the World
And the imperial poet Conradin.

Your longing follows the enchanted glide
Of silver galleons through eternity,
And swept with bliss you lash the rope beside
A kingly palace on the bluest sea.


## MONASTERY

Flee from the noisy throng with few companions
And build your order domes of peace among
The quiet hills — your dream when you were young —
Before your strength is sapped by icy venoms.

The gentle chimes of even hours lull,
Your labours in the virgin earth are praises,
The day of toil revolves in seven phases
For you and those I gave you, chaste in soul.

They clasp but do not crave. They are united
As friends who never fret and never fear,
The evening drains a word, a kiss, a tear,
And this the faith to which the pairs are plighted:

To keep delight and grief alike restrained,
To lift their glances up to azure beauty,
Divine renouncing, consecrated duty
As once a monk of Fiesole ordained.


## SYMBOLS

This is your destiny: brief spans of lithe
And brilliant bloom, and then a brawling welter
That shuns the day — the vipers breed and writhe!
And tender shoots depend on secret shelter.

So find the cool enchantment which is sealed
In early masters, learn to shield your breast
With virgin spells your own Madonnas yield,
With him who forced your beauty to its crest,

Holbein, the paramount! When thunder sallies,
Look to the gloried from the Main and Rhine,
And though the sterile worm destroy your valleys,
A grove will flank the uninfested shrine.

Accept the age-old rules which govern pain:
Time and again the light that was, will teem.
With swelling sails the spirits always strain
Back to the land of legend and of dream.


## JEAN PAUL

When we who scorn our country, always itching
To roam, are charmed by lovelier lands, you prod
Us back again, tormenting and bewitching,
Alive with passion that betrays the god.

In you alone we fuse, no sage has fired
Our grey domains like you, from sea to moor
You sing the radiant south which you desired.
You like our people, vast and yet unsure

194

Hide steel and tinder in a murky vapour
Imbued with blaze that glistens wild and mild.
In woods of magic you uphold the taper
And in our fields you are both lord and child.

You stir the languid mind with starry leaven
And spread the couch where frenzy ebbs away,
A golden harp of choirs tuned in heaven,
Flute from "the hills of bloom, the slopes of May."


## STATUES: THE TWO FIRST

The landscape taught you how to build your house:
No higher than the nearby tree allowed.
Here virgins offer you a lock of hair,
And youths unite in fervent covenant.

In azure clarity you see them all
Prepared for your profound and buoyant fête,
They glory in the flesh and its desires
And move, serene and proud, through early bloom.

Your towers vanish in a mound of vapour,
The winged spirit fled the heavy furrow,
The body must be crushed and strive to heaven,
The stubborn stone to tracery of roses.

When your ascetic, much too pointed fingers
Are clasped, your eyes intent on far horizons,
Divine that everyone will kneel in rapture
Before the miracle, and weep and tremble.


## STATUES: THE THIRD

How fair I thought you, Lady, sheathed in veils,
And how enchanting that, through every grief
Of day, you still awakened the belief
That far from halls and heights an Eden hails.

How often when the sluggish blood grew wan,
A single flash from you could rouse the worn,
The ailing, the disheartened, the forlorn,
What is the force that beckons on and on?

"O child, you never knew: What made you press
Ahead like this was only want and rue,
They dyed the distant hills more blue for you,
And stress I often healed with new distress.

Since you have grown impatient, come and cleave
The veils — they will not serve you any more.
Now see what many years you cherished for
The dew of diamonds shimmering through the weave!"


STATUES: THE FOURTH

When firm and grave she comes to us today
With ruthless eyes, we do not shirk her call,
For now we niche her in the marble hall
And bend before her noble will and pray.

We, who were comrades, used to loathe her rule,
Do you remember? You, the Morning Spark,
You, Branch from Alien Stem, you, Kiss of Dark?
Whenever with her glances fixed and cool

She found the cove where in and out we wound,
We gathered up as many glittering gauds
As arms, indulged with pleasure, could surround
And turned our rudder from the haunted swards.

In brimming boats we sailed the sunny bay
With boys and women, flag and song and shout,
Until with all we had we put about
To where the next enchanted island lay.

## STATUES: THE FIFTH

For only I lead even you, the wise,
From charted courses. When I lift my eyes
Your structures pale and crumble, you pursue
Me everywhere as foolish children do,

Forget your work, your rights, and your desire,
Strange to yourselves and wholly in my hire,
Without demur accept the wounds I deal,
A holy madness forces you to kneel.

When I contrive the cruelest laws: that none
Shall know the sweetness of my lips who won
My body's most profound embrace, you thrust
All doubt from you and only bear and trust.

I change your narrow firmament to proud
Horizons rimmed with clouds of flame and blood,
Where calls from chasms sound like feeble cries,
And curse of death like singing of schalmeys.


## STATUES: THE SIXTH

When in my hands I weigh the clay-coloured jars,
Through the remains of the weatherworn crust I see
Bodies of heroes who seem to dance in wars,
Gestures of bathers, careless and free.

On the angels, aglitter with torturous glaze,
I discover a throbbing vein and a curving bone,
Hot with the fevers which maddened their makers, I raise
Impious lips to the sculpture and sully the stone.

Anguish and yearning are wakened by sonorous names:
Sumptuous princes in ruby and gold, their heads
Look at me gravely out of their mouldering frames
Set against silvery darkness and shadowy reds.

And I ponder how beings who long are dust
Yielded themselves to the snare of these locks and this gaze,
How were the kisses that flamed from this mouth to which lust
Senselessly circles upward like smoke without blaze?


## THE VEIL: THE SEVENTH

I flung it out, and those who at their board
Chose native fruit, were dazed and paused — a mist
Of distant glow, and swiftly in the east
With ramparts, tent, and dome a city soared.

Once it was swirled like this: and houses caught
In hopeless rows, were nacre in the husk
Of rain, the world was dimmed to silver dusk,
The peak of day and yet a moon of thought.

It folds and falls: Like shepherds on a new —
Made earth are these, and girls advance like those
Who brought the goddess gifts in long agos —
A shadow under myrtles are these two.

It spreads, and through the gate you know so well,
They go by tens like children of the sun
Who found a joy that lasts, though lightly won . . .
Your longing changes as I cast my veil.

THE SONGS OF DREAM AND DEATH

## AZURE HOUR

### TO REINHOLD AND SABINE LEPSIUS

This hour in its azure
Has set behind the arbour now,
It brought delight and pleasure,
Amends for days of duller hue.

Suffused with calm elation,
With flocks of roving clouds it flies
Consumed in conflagration
And yields its fulness as it dies.

Oh, that time stopped, we ponder,
To this one hour dedicate,
Though even now the wonder
Of darkness vaults a richer fête,

As measures, deep and ringing,
That saturate with joy and pain,
In newer Edens clinging,
Still touch and conjure as they wane.


## HOUSE ON THE DUNES

### TO ALBERT AND KITTY VERWEY

Could there be another roof that wholly
Cloaked in peace, and free, and proud, and ample
Often called the sad and numb
Guest from far away and charmed him?

There you like to probe in what his spirit
Meets your own, in what it always differs,
Musing when at dusk the soft
Shadows lengthen over Holland.

200

Through the reeds caressing phrases flutter
To the beat of surf, but stronger voices
Always lurk, and when their sound
Soars in freshening ocean-wind

Sorrows cannot chain him. Ships, a whistle!
Lust and strife of towns! Was not the sungod's
Son astray in clouds and crushed
In a frenzied hunt for rapture!


## A BOY WHO SANG TO ME OF AUTUMN AND EVENING

### TO CYRIL MEIR SCOTT


I

Those who have lived in dreams see when they wake
A glimmer of the glory they abandoned
For earth and agony, and weep in silence
Filling the hours with their memories

Of purple shores where children, golden-winged,
Advance on weightless feet and wave a welcome
To tired souls that just escaped their prison
And — still bewildered — turn their vacant eyes

To lands of wonder drenched in dazzling light.
You try to shun the truth, O fellow captives!
For you the shadow of a smile still lingers,
Although you both are forced to walk the rut

And languish in the musty air again.
One flying glance which sparks behind the grating,
Revives the hope in your oppressive desert.
What pale and sudden beam has kissed your hair?

## II

Now you have broken with the god you longed for
In former days, he looms with vengeful temples:
"You called the pricless laws I gave a yoke
And left my house too arrogant to bow.

Is not your present service more debasing?
Does it not weigh the hands you wring in pleading
More than the links of rhythm which you broke?
Do you not cry for grace, and wake, and weep?"

As once we knelt in want and supplication
Before the Saviour's bleeding feet, we prostrate
Ourselves in homage to a different god
And are uplifted by the trance and tremor

We felt before, but tinged with other passions,
More exigent and less resigned, when muted
The rays fall through the dusk of prayer and tint
The panes of our cathedral gold and wine.


## III

I waited through the summer, now I shudder
To see the scarlet banners blow, confronting
The merry reapers with the thought of graveyards,
Of fruit ungarnered which the storm will scatter.

Now I have lost my careless faith and hasten
To use what time is left and pluck a little
Of what remained, to garland leaves and flowers,
Half-withered wonders in my mournful hand.

With reverence and awe this timid hand
Holds out to you these gifts I took at random,
So small a sign of all my dreams of splendour,
Yet lit with unaccustomed tears, the merest

202

Suggestion of the jewel I wished to capture
For you from fortune, just as what I utter
In low and broken tones is but a fraction
Of the whole tale of flaming love and hatred.


## SADNESS IN JULY

### TO ERNEST DOWSON

Summery flowers lavish their scent but you,
Morning-glories in bitter breath of grain,
Have led me to the weathered paling far from
The gorgeous gardens and their sesame.

Out of the past you summon dreams: the child
At rest on virgin earth in furrows of rye
In harvest glows beside the naked reapers,
The gleaming sickles and the empty jug.

Drowsily rocked the wasps in the song of noon
And in the shadow of ears, a tenuous screen,
His forehead, flushed with heat, was spattered
With poppy petals, sprawling drops of blood.

Nothing I ever owned can be filched by time.
Thirsting as then, I lie in the thirst-stricken field.
My listless lips can barely breathe: How tired
I am of bloom, of wanton bloom! How tired!


## CAMPAGNA

### TO LUDWIG VON HOFMANN

Ensconced above, we saw the evening meadows,
The wreckage of a world in burning shadows.
We walk the stern and empty plain aghast
At stirrings from the present and the past.

For was our mourning less before the gloried
Façade of columns, fabled wealth, the storied
Stupendous tombs? And what are kings unbowed
To us since then, and nations great and proud?

We feel in parting that this noble furrow
Forbids the sorrowful to sow and burrow.
There in the clouds the Ageless Gate is limned!
A veil with cinnabar and violet rimmed

Floats over morbid green of fields and hedges.
Frascati pales against the mountain edges.
Once more this hill shall lock you in its spell
And yield the bloom of death, the asphodel.


SOUTHERN BAY

TO LUDWIG VON HOFMANN

Along green cliffs seraphic gardens pour
Their flowers which blend into the rippled blue,
And early wisps of glowing wind undo
The metal hardness clenched around his core.

The mountains touch the lilac sky with tongues
Of flame, the sapphire cave is dim and tranced,
Beyond, to shining space the ships advance...
And kissed with ecstasy which made him young

He quickened to the play of swinging loins
And sighed, and said, and sang a single name.
A potent breath within the magic frame,
Like wine and honey, sea and temple groins,

Transported him to tranquil realms of dream
Where lulled by cypress trees in song he lost
The urge to ruthless work and lands of frost,
Slowly unloosed on gulfs of crimson gleam.

## WINTER SOLSTICE

### TO CLEMENS FRANCKENSTEIN

Does the sun or moon effuse this flare
On Byzantium's lifeless roads? A glare
Flashes eerie flames which fall
Over trees and through the hall,

Paints a world of pleasures that elate
You, the orphaned wanderer at the gate.
And you yield yourselves, and weep, and cling
Lip to lip in hush and wondering.

What a bloom the barren seasons hold!
Even at a bier, or small and cold
Here on earth, you never shall forget,
Nor shall this grow dim for you or set.

Fearlessly you face the gulfs of night
With your eyes where action is alight.
In farewell they vision and foretell:
Such a ray can never pale!


## BROTHERS

### TO LEOPOLD ANDRIAN

In wayward youth when we could not discern
And praised and blamed with undivided powers,
Our love was for the land which many spurn:
This ailing Austria of yours, of ours.

Like you we showed the simpler, gladder souls
That death in beauty is the crown of all,
Until we felt we had more vivid goals
And listened to a more insistent call.

205

We saw the varied stores of earth emerge,
And wishes caught us in a freshening flood,
As friends we tried to wrest you to our urge
With what you too still had of growth and bud.

For brothers, far too fervent faith we gave
To you, to savour as a sound, a sight
Your grace, enhanced by yearning toward the grave,
Your downfall sheathed in iridescent light.


THE FIELDS

TO CARL AUGUST KLEIN

Salient curve of the silver sky
Arches the endless expanse of your somnolent fields.
Can you unriddle the fate which their furrows conceal,
All that we two for years passed by?

Under the willows dripping with new
Catkins, the children are listening entranced to the sound
Of a flute, buoyant and careless they caper and bound
Into a dusk of vermilion and blue.

Shining baubles weary the crone, and her gaze
Turns to the gentler resplendence of Thuja trees,
Only the care she bestows upon graves gives her ease,
Dimly she croons of a region of rays.

And those who slipped from the snares of delight,
But who, like us, on terrestrial wishes are fed —
Brooding friend, do you seek them in symbols and dread
Our adventure into night?


206

## JOURNEY'S END

### TO RICHARD PERLS

We paced the temple slabs while you deplored
The rot of ailing worlds, and I avowed
Contention and its promise of reward
And leaned against a pillar, young and proud.

You were amazed that, though I roved so long,
I still believed in what remains the same,
And in the dusk of Flanders, overhung
With mist, devotion fused with fleshly flame.

Then to the Awful Mothers and the vast
Titanic forces you went on alone,
I hated every dim and futile quest...
But now, aghast to learn that you are gone,

In dreams I wander where you loved to cling:
To the pagoda's green and ghostly gloom
Of not attempting, seeking anything —
So you, a victor, haunt me from your tomb.


## GARDENS IN SPRING

Shimmers of green-golden leaf
Break through a thicket of gloom,
Shadow of innocent broom
Over a passionless grief.

Flowering almonds in gardens below,
There I saw eyes full of dream and fire —
Back to those paths of bloom I shall go,
Smoothness and fragrance for hands of desire.

Butterflies drowsily cling,
Bushes clipped into cones,
Birds from more radiant zones
Rhythms more lavishly ring.

Feathery fountains sparkle their spray
More iridescent than fall of a stream,
Will they delight me, light me today,
Shall I adore you, sweet eyes of dream?


MORNING TREMOR

Can such a grief be moulded,
And breath and brightness such as this?
A morning be unfolded
That brings us new and sudden bliss?

The paths the soul had pondered
Took shape and wound through wood and field,
Uncertain perfumes wandered
And then cascaded swift and wild.

Blurred as by tears, the glimmer
Of tree and house which welcome us,
A candid, festal shimmer,
The cherry bough that hangs across,

A current and a glitter
Torment and ravish, weigh and free,
A medley sweet and bitter,
A singing without melody.


THE PULSING

This pulsing tells us what was banished,
What rose instead of former fill,
Instead of Joy that waved and vanished,
Now time and path are blank and chill.

In bonds of sleep we err and circle,
How every word is loud and shrill
Which like her last about us quivers!
How every stone is weighed with ill

Because our self was what we imaged
So long! How stifling wall and sill,
The home of things which once she cherished!
And though we fought to steel our will

— For steadfast purpose scorns and questions
The trifling goals our greeds distil —
We never could subdue this pulsing
Which only grief can slowly still.


LAUGHING HEARTS

Hearts full of laughter, you for whom joy emerges
As a girl that floats from the clouds and scatters
Gifts, the only beguilements you woo with your wishes
Food for your hope which grows greater from fête to fête.

You who have woven the loveliest beams of sunlight
Into a cheek as fragile in texture as roses,
Bear the hours of gloom as a transient penance,
Plead with grace and banish sombre reflection.

Hearts full of gambols which I seek out and admire,
Swiftly effacing myself so your bliss may be boundless,
You, the unburdened, who move me and silence desire,
Whom I adore to your own, almost smiling amazement,

You who entwine me in turns of gregarious dances,
Never aware that my mask is what renders me like you,
Hearts full of frolic, you that in friendship embrace me,
Oh, how remote from you all is my heart and its pulsing!

209

## TIDES

First she was deluged, ached with floods of light.
She slurred the gifts which homage brought, and in
The stubborn pride of youth that will not speak
She often missed her share of happiness.

She grew, she fared abroad, and then she wooed
What soon escaped. With burning want her glance
Beset the living who denied their love,
The dead whom she had not yet learned to love.

And once, when grief was all she had, it seemed
A hollow, worthless thing. She looked, and probed,
And shivered like a child who cannot see
But whom the coolness tells that dusk has come.

And now her early pain returns and rends.
She is the same, yet every fibre knows
That much has gone, but change can never change
What rouses her and what she still pursues.


## DAY SONG

### I

This, my day, was your dawn:
Full of promise, and out
Of the valleys of childhood
Rang jubilant shouts.

You were circled with glory,
And wreathed, and sublime,
Then you dipped glossy locks
Into lilac and thyme.

They praise you and hasten
With clamorous needs,
As emeralds to silver,
As ripples to reeds.

210

They follow with joy
Whom your smile summoned on —
O my day, so unflawed,
Yet so swifly withdrawn!


II

Still dazzled by rapture, my
    gaze toward him yearned,
To one who had conjured with
    love he was turned.

My praises on pinions
    across to him swung,
Till westerly heaven
    around him was flung.

And whom shall I woo though with
    ardor more dim,
For he is the world and who
    else is like him!

So sadly I wandered and
    listened and leant
To chasms intent on
    their sombre command.


III

By the stream whose sighing haunts us,
Where the poplar tree high sways,
Dwells a bird whose question taunts us,
Who through leaves and windy sky strays.

And the bird tunes a sing-sound:
Meadow-sweet and alder bloom fled,
Each is close within a ring bound...
And the peaks before you loom red.

He leaves memory as dreamhold
Who to happier ones his way takes,
From his fingers trickles dreamgold
Which he scatters when the day breaks.

Lift your head which in pain bends,
From below perhaps a dream flies,
And then wait until my strain ends,
And then stay until the gleam dies.


## NIGHT SONG

I

Gone the mild
And the dim,
Come and leave
Is my fate,

Storm and fall
That destroy,
Gloss and May
That delight.

What I did
What I bore
What I thought
What I am,

Like a flame
Turned to smoke,
Like a song
In the wind.

II

I was stirred by the flight
Of the sumptuous dark,
Of the sheaves drowned in light,
Of the sighs to the stars,

By the women who guide
While they serve us, how fair
As they circle and glide
In the surge of their hair!

By the youths who accord
Me their burning applause,
I commended their word
And my lips touched their brows.

Through you only and late
Have I learned, noble friends,
What is destined to fade
And what shines without end.


III

Be wine in the bud,
Be fruit that decoys,
Content with your mood,
But shun what annoys,

What rots and despairs,
The hurried and loud.
Revealed to the rare
And veiled from the crowd

Be avid for awe,
It brims, never churns,
Make beauty your law,
It warms, never burns,

Till somnolent planes
Transfigure your ray,
In golden refrains
Your life ebbs away.

## DREAM AND DEATH

Glow and fame, so our world turns to day,
Like the great we subdue cliff and bay,
And the mind, still unchained, bold and young,
Strides the plain,` rides the sea far outflung.

Shimmer dawns on the road, visions range,
Bliss and grief seethe in wild interchange.
He who bade, broods and weeps, bowing down:
"You, my joy, you my star, you my crown!"

Now the dream, pride of prides, sunward flings,
And its force quells the god who gave wings.
Then a voice thrusts us low, makes us fall,
We so poor faced with death, we so small.

All this whirls tears and pounds, flames and flies,
Until late in the night-vaulted skies
It is linked in a calm jewelled wreath:
Glow and fame, bliss and grief, dream and death.

# THE SEVENTH RING

## (1907)

POEMS OF OUR TIMES

## A POEM OF MY TIME

You people of my time, you thought you knew,
You judged and called me to account — and blundered!
When in your savage greed for life you clamoured
And swarmed with clumsy feet and brutal fingers,
I seemed a prince inebriate with perfumes
Who — swayed in languor — scanned his even measures
In fragile charm or cool and poised aloofness,
And wan with glories that are not of earth.

You never guessed my youth was filled with hardship,
That anguish dogged me when I stormed the height.
You never guessed my dreams of blood and danger.
"He too shall be my friend!" And so the rebel
Attacked the foe's domain with torch and dagger,
Longing for deeds, but not for deeds alone!
Though shrewd, you did not see the smile, the shudder,
Were blind to what was sleeping thinly veiled.

Then to the magic hill the piper beckoned
With amorous and coaxing tones, he showed you
So strange a treasure you began to scorn
A world you had so recently extolled.
Now that some few attempt Arcadian murmurs
And vapid flourishes, he grips the trumpet,
His spurs torment the flesh that sagged and rotted,
He clashes on again and heads the charge.

When dotards leer and drool that this is manhood,
You sigh: "Such majesty and so debased!
The song of sunlit clouds deformed to screams!"
You see a change, but I have done as always,
And he who blows fanfares today and hurls
A jet of fluid fire knows: Tomorrow
The sum of grandeur, force, and grace may spring
From the untroubled fluting of a boy.

216

# DANTE AND THE POEM OF HIS TIMES

When stricken with her loveliness I reeled
Close to the portal, when consumed with fires
I pondered through the bitter night and roused
The care and pity of my friend, when only
Her favour and my song to her spelled life,
I stirred the scorn of those who never question
Why we, on earth so transiently, should love,
And sigh, and plan as though we lived forever.

Then I became a man who burned with shame
That evil leaders sacked the realm, the city
And where the cause was just I flung my fortunes
And words into the scales and fought corrupters.
My pay was theft and exile, and I wander
A beggar, year by year, to alien doorways,
By order of the mad who soon will turn
To nameless dust while I shall be immortal.

And when my dim and often stranded course,
My sorrow for our self-begotten anguish,
My anger for the lax, and base, and wicked
Was hammered out in metal, many noted
The ruthless message, once their fears had ebbed.
And though not one deep in his heart was wounded
By fang and flame, from Adige to Tiber
They hailed the man who had no peace, no haven.

But when I fled the world and heard the choirs
Of angels, saw the precincts of the blessed,
And sang, then they declared my lyre sounded
Childish or senile. O you fools, I took
An ember from my hearth, I blew and hell
Rose up before you, but I needed torrents
Of blaze to light the highest love to glory
And to exalt the sun and all the stars.

# GOETHE ANNIVERSARY

Through misty fields at summer's end we made
Our way and reached his city in the first
Faint dawn. The massive walls, the flimsy platforms
Were still unstained by throngs and day and seemed
Transmuted to a pure, unearthly grandeur.
We stood before his silent house, we lifted
Our reverent gaze and left. Today, when many
Will shout their praise, our greeting shall be mute.


A little while and hallowed rooms will seethe
With those who do not trust until they handle.
The glaring colours flicker in the alleys,
The merrymakers sport. They like to drape
Themselves in draping heroes, and attempt
To use him as an emblem for their factions.
They listen only to the loudest voice
And do not see the height the spirit longs for.


What do you know of all the dreams and songs
That rouse your awe! The child already suffered.
He roamed the ramparts, stared into the well.
Unrest and pain in youth and pain in manhood,
His sadness veiled in smiles. If now he came
To life, more beautiful than ever, who would
There be to pay him homage? None would take him
For what he was: a king who passed you by.


You claim him as your own, and thank, and cheer,
You who, indeed, are filled with all his urges,
Only on lower levels, like a beast's.
Today the nation's mongrels do the barking.
But you will never guess how many secrets
He who has long been dust, still guards from you,
And that in him, the radiant, even now
Much that you think will always last, has paled.

218

# NIETZSCHE

Low yellow clouds and frosty storms are drifting
Across the hill, half harbingers of autumn,
Half early spring's. Was this the wall which circled
The Thunderer who was unmatched among
Surrounding thousands made of dust and smoke?
He launched his last, his duller flashes here
Upon a lifeless town and shallow foothills
And left a long night for the longest night.

Do not disturb the jog below. Can stabs
Destroy a squid, or shears uproot the weed!
The rule of fervent silence shall continue
Until the brutes who soil him with their praise
And fatten further on the reek of rotting
Which helped to strangle him, at last are stifled.
But you shall live in glory through the ages
With crowned and bleeding brow like other leaders.

You, the most luckless, fought to set us free.
What destiny oppressed you that you never
Could feast your eyes upon the promised land,
Created gods, but only to dethrone them?
Dissatisfied with rest or what was done
You wrecked the treasure dearest to your spirit
So you might yearn for it with new desire
And cry aloud in aching loneliness.

He came too late who might have pleaded with you:
There is no way across the icy summits
And haunts of ghostly birds! Now you must learn
To stay within the circle drawn by love.
And when his voice, austere and full of torment,
Rings like a paean into azure night
Across the surf, we mourn: It should have sung,
This herald-spirit, it should not have spoken.

# BOECKLIN

Let trumpets mark the entrances and exits
Of the romantic fraud, the paunchy trader!
Safe from degrading praise you leave the silent
And scattered groups of those who share your visions.
And journey toward the sun lured by the calmness
Of steadfast Tuscan pines, and by the Flower
Of Cities, and beyond beside Liguria's
Candescent mountains, the maternal sea.

When vain and ugly haste began, when limbs
Were understressed or overstressed, when some
Took filth for gold and others stormed the heavens,
You fled the everyday of brazen revels:
"They ceased to prize the only thing that lifts
From scum and offal. I shall take this jewel,
Unflawed and many-hued to alien regions
Until they see again and want it back."

Your world is realer than that servile world!
You shaped a realm of warm, unhampered bodies
With clear delights, with hot and sweet desires.
From silver air and slender boughs, from meadows
In bloom, from waves of magic green and midnight
Of caves, you conjured up the age-old tremors
And, in the frame of laurel-leaf and olive
A promised land in mists of timeless legend.

You staked the bounds of grief, the surge was gentled,
You forced lament to pour from golden lyres,
And over wilderness, and plague, and ruin
Vaulted the deepest blue of patient hope.
Because of you we stand with lifted foreheads
Instead of weeping through a barren darkness,
And only you — O warder, thanks! — protected
The sacred fire through an age of ice.

PORTA NIGRA
INGENIO ALF .... SCOLARI

Why did I have to waken in your era,
Who knew the stateliness of Treves when she
Still shared the fame of Rome, her sister city,
When eyes lit up and widened as they followed
The trains of clanging legions, in the stadium
The Franks with yellow hair who fought with lions,
The tubas at the palace and the god
Augustus, purple in his golden chariot.

Here the Mosella flowed by gracious villas.
The sounds of revel when the grapes were gathered!
The girls who bore the jars — what curves of teeming!
I scarcely know this rubble. Mist is gnawing
At what remains of ramparts once imperial.
The sacred images defiled! In cases!
Beside the flimsy structures of barbarians
Only my cherished gate is still intact.

In sombre crape of years, but full of pride
It flings derision from a hundred windows
Down at your shabby shelters — wreck the stones
That mock impermanence — down at your people,
Your princes, priests, and servants, all of them
Inflated masks with empty eyes, your women
Whom even slaves would find too cheap a bargain.
What is the worth of everything your honour

Now you have lost what is most priceless: blood!
Though shades, we breathe more deeply. You, the living,
Are only ghosts, laughs Manlius, the boy.
He would refuse to rule you with a scepter,
Who earned his wages by so base a calling
You shrink from naming it: "I waited, salved
With Persian scents, beside the gate, by night,
And sold myself to hirelings of the Caesars."

221

# FRANKISH LANDS

This was the dismal crossroads which I faced:
There, from the chasm, tongues of wicked fire,
Here regions which I shunned, where loathing festered
In me for everything they praised and practiced.
I mocked their gods, they taunted mine. O boastful,
Impoverished folk, where are your poets? None
Is here, for one lives out his days in exile,
The other's frantic head is touched with frost.

Then magic called me from the west — so rang
The sire's tribute to his ever lavish
Young land, whose glory thrilled, whose travail moved him
To tears though he was distant, to the Mother
Of aliens, of the fugitive, and hated.
The sound of rivers gave the heir a welcome
When in the early light the witching valleys
Of Meuse and Marne were spread in sweet abundance.

And in the town of merry grace, in gardens
Of wistful charm, at night near gleaming spires,
Enchanted arches, youth was all about me
Exhilerated with the things I cherish.
There bard and hero kept alive the secret:
Villiers who thought himself the peer of kings,
Verlaine in fall and shrift devout and childlike,
And — bleeding for his concept — Mallarmé.

Though dream and distance give us strength and nurture,
The air we breathe comes only from the living.
And so to friends still working there, and others
I saw entombed, I give my thanks. How often,
And even after I had gained a foothold,
When in my dreary land I strove, still doubtful
Of victory, this was the verse that braced me:
"RETURNENT FRANC EN FRANCE DULCE TERRE."

# LEO XIII

Today, when brazen idlers flaunt the purple
With loutish hubbub and the mien of brokers,
Our spirit, agitated by the presence
Of majesty and avid to revere
Turns to the grave, paternal brow that wears
The triple crown, to him, the true anointed,
The hundrey-year-old shadow of a life
Well-lived, who gazes from his sacred stronghold.


When he has ministered to all, his vineyard
Gladdens his leisure hours, white and tranquil
His fingers curve around the heavy clusters.
His fare is bread and wine, and weightless mallows,
And in his sleepless nights he is not racked
By stale ambition, for he fashions verses
To praise the world's delight, Our Blessed Lady,
And her omnipotent and radiant Child:


"Come, Holy Boy, and keep the brittle world
From crashing to destruction, Sole Redeemer!
A gentler age shall bloom beneath your sign
And rise untouched from all these desecrations.
May joys of long desired peace return,
May love bind each to each and make them brothers."
So says the poet, and the prophet knows
New love alone begets a new salvation.


When vested in the symbols of his office
And born beneath the baldachin, a pattern
Of lordly splendour and divine dominion,
Half-veiled in incense and in gleaming tapers,
He spreads his blessing over the entire
Terrestrial globe, we kneel and bow: believers
Melted into the thousand-headed unit
That, moved, by mystery, grows beautiful.

# THE GRAVES IN SPEYER

Our fingers twitch when in the ravaged choir
We see the graves which have been desecrated.
Our tears of anger must redeem these precincts,
And with our blood the blood of long ago
Must now be called and conjured lest it vanish,
Lest those to come confront a plundered temple,
And lifeless stones, and furrows drained of substance.
The spell is cast, the train of lords appears.


The sanctum's builders, stern, imperial foreheads.
Supreme in penance, firm in failure: Henry
The Third, the strongest ruler, follows Conrad.
In Roman toils, with his insurgent son,
The Fourth, a toy of Fate: imprisoned — free!
But haughtily he silences who taunts him
With ash and sackcloth: "Other places brought
You infamy far greater than Canossa!"


Rudolf, the founder, rises with his kindred.
He sees the glorious rulers of his line
To the last knight, the noble Maximilian.
He sees the shameful wounds which still are bleeding
From broils of monks, revolt, the scourge of strangers.
He sees the thousand-year-old scepter broken,
And now the bolts of lightning on the relics
Of those for whom we sound our constant grief.


Then, summoned by his Staufen ancestress
From regions of the south, a splendid guest,
A people's god: the greatest of the Fredericks
Approaches arm in arm with golden Enzio.
His gaze unites the plans of Ottos, Carls,
With his own boundless dreams of the Levant,
Wisdom of Cabbalists and Rome's decorum,
Banquets of Akragas and Selinus.

PENTE PIGADIA

TO CLEMENS KILLED 23 APRIL 1897

When Turkish bullets struck him in the fight
Beside the olives of Epirus, only
We were in tears at this too early wilting
Of flower-laden spring. Fate had protected
Her favourite from the sharpest pain, from battering
On bounds and emptiness before the end.
A sweet dejection hung about his parting
From earth still unexplored, from hidden fortunes.

He lay and knew that there was no returning.
His fever painted the Aegean islands,
The peaks of Attica with greater magic
Than what he really would have seen. In surges
Of Pindar's song of songs he heard the praise
Of heroes mounting in accord with verse
Which he devised. And then they shot the wounded
Who could not walk. They shot him through the heart.

A gracious light was shed around his birth.
He could have had applause and fame but effort,
Except toward fervent deeds, seemed vain to him.
In gratitude for endless joys which Hellas
Confers, he helped her late and languid children
In war, and now our sons whose vapid pleasures
Have blunted them to suit their future office,
Are still admonished by his wounds, his laurels.

We prize him, jubilant that those who perish
To guard the word, the image, who are brimming
With god, are still begot by icy earth.
And when their names are called, a current pulses
Within our veins like noble wine and gives
The pledge of other days when we shall waken
As if renewed and, loosed from bondage, feel
The lure of dark beyonds, of daring quests.

# THE SISTERS

## SOPHIE OF ALENÇON       ELISABETH OF AUSTRIA

Whoever saw their queenliness which flouted
The very pose of cheap equality
And guarded ancient grandeur, grace, and judgment,
Was moved by majesty and felt the breath
Of matchless pain and power that detested
The base. They calmly went their noble courses
And wore the glory of their hair more proudly
Than others wear the flash of tainted crowns.

The younger, having mourned a barren bridal
With one whose radiance madness had not lessened,
Made the three sacred fleurs-de-lis her emblem
And lived serene in love and smiles for others.
A ball for charity brought her fulfillment
Of fate. They tried to save her in the tumult
Of screams, in acrid smoke, but she decreed:
"The guests come first!" and fell in gusts of fire.

The other quickened tears, at first with kindness
And youth, and then with kindness and despair.
The clamour of the people left her mute.
Untouched by day's concerns, she bore the riddle
Of hidden likeness and the far-blown shimmers
Of worlds just lit with dawn, until her torment
Drove her to sea, to land, and back to sea
Again, and to the blade which took her life.

But was not this alarming, avid fury
The gentle ordinance of stars? Both suffered
From bitter fear of growing old and withered,
And both were swiftly freed before their winter,
While life still wreathed around them all its fulness
And lent them charm. Or did this give them beauty,
That by a secret spell they were prevented
From breaking with a time-worn prophecy?

226

# CARL AUGUST

Do you recall, my friend, in that first year
Of storm, how by the trellis where the clusters
Hung bluish-black, you flung yourself defiant
And naked to the grinding hail? How often
We dared the dark and rose from dreary pallets
— Unstained — to greet the dawn? And how, whenever
We felt a tender glance, our blood ran swifter
Until a sacred word called us to work?

Child of your native soil, with generous urge
And yielding depths you were the only one
Essential to a circle graced by many.
You had the blind allegiance men have lost,
That serves and does not ask for goals and profits,
That leaves in silence when it doubts its value,
Disdains rewards and thanks, and disappears
Into obscurity without renown.

Then duty — or you thought it duty — caught
Your youth and forced it into galling harness.
When everyone was harvesting the choicest
Fruits in his garden, you were chained to toil.
Boundless in sacrifice you stumbled deeper
And deeper into martyrdom. When others
Slipped from their inner chains, you faced your downfall
And yet revered the ancient, lawful bond.

From rack and ruin you shall tell your critics:
"What matter if one more in thousands flaunts
His paltry talents! If he stores his cargoes
In solid lofts, or speaks in pompous phrases,
While that which feeds us all: the pith, decays!
What of my little life that tides and cracks
Against the cliffs, if dauntless in the storm
Our people's faithfulness is kept unbroken!"

# THE DEAD CITY

The new-made port has drained the country's riches,
The crescent of its rough and glittering walls
Is reared around the spacious gulf, processions
Of streets where with the same display of greed
The rabble trades by day and feasts by night.
Only contempt and pity climb the crag
Up to the mother-town. It lies impoverished
With blackened stones, forgotten by the years.

The lonely fortress lives, and dreams, and sees
How strong its tower looms in deathless suns,
How silence guards its shrine, and those who dwell
In alleys overgrown with grass, have bodies
That flower through the torn and faded cloth.
It does not grieve, it knows the day will come
When up the mountain from the splendid castles
A train of suppliants will drag its way:

"A barren pain is blighting us, we sicken
In surfeit and unless you help, we die!
Give us the stainless waters of your summit,
The clean, thin air! We are content to lodge
In stables, yards, the arch of any gate.
Here, take these gems, such as you never dreamed of,
More precious than a hundred cargoes! Circlets
And clasps of greater value than a kingdom!"

But stern the answer: "We cannot be bought!
The goods you cherish most are dust and shards.
Those seven who once came, at whom our children
Once smiled, they shall be saved, but all the others
Are doomed. Your crime is in your very numbers.
Leave with your trinkets which will only madden
Our youth to loathing. See, their naked feet
Thrust them across the ledge into the sea!"

# A POEM OF MY TIMES

I am your conscience, I the voice pervading
Your malcontent that curses and condemns:
"The base alone still rule, the great have perished,
Belief is washed away and love has withered.
How can we flee the foulness of the earth?"
Let torches show you where the era's ruin
Consumes us, where you shape it with the passions
Of your own senses, with your ravelled heart.


You turned away from grandeur and from beauty
Because it was your purpose to deny them,
And wrecked their images — the new, the ancient.
Beyond the body and the soil you lifted
Your house of smoke, and dust, and fog. The spires,
The walls, and arches rose and grew gigantic,
But clouds which floated higher could have presaged
The final downfall long before it came.


You fled to caves: "There is no day," you clamoured,
"And only he who kills the flesh will see
The rune unriddled, he shall be immortal."
Like seekers after gold who pale and fevered
Were bowed on crucibles with ore and fluxes
While sunlit paths unrolled beneath their windows,
So you concocted souls from filth and poison
And spilled the residue of healthy saps.


I saw the Pharaohs gazing through millennia,
Their eyes of stone conversant with our visions,
And heavy with our tears. They knew as we
That deserts shift with gardens, frost with blaze,
Night comes for sun, atonement for delight.
And though despair and dark engulf us, one thing
That always was (none knows it) is eternal,
And youth and flowers laugh and songs resound.

# PAGEANT

## THE COMBAT

Out of my cavern I rage,
Sated with sun and with blood,
Lurk in the flowering field,
Watch for the lovely-locked god,
Who with his jubilant step,
Who with a song on his lips,
Mocks at my life in a tomb.

Now he shall reel from the wrath
Born in the lap of the dark,
Reel from the clutch of my fist,
Throttling the rose of his flesh.
See how he walks! Like a child!
Down with the cudgel, a mere
Grip shall destroy whom I hate.

Look to yourself, for a light
Strikes from his eyes like a bolt.
Deep in the dimness of caves,
Fight in smouldering glows,
I was the victor of hosts!
Coward, lower your lids,
Show me the strength of your arm!

Ah, he wields light for his sword.
Whom he touches, he fells,
Sets the heel of his foot
Hard on my labouring breast,
Smiles and sings as he stands.
Sated with sun and with blood,
Robbed of my glory I die.

# THE LEADERS

## THE FIRST

Upon a garish float I saw a crowd
Half naked in their gold and finery,
Who sat, and sprawled, and talked, and laughed aloud.

And in the road stood One, naked from head
To foot, until they reached and passed him by,
And then, afraid to lose them, on he sped

With shouts, and circled to outstrip the train,
And all along the course the people veered
Toward him, and linked their hands to form a chain,

And sang, and leaped around the float, and pressed
Forward, then doubled on their tracks, and neared
Again in wild delight and tameless zest.

## THE SECOND

The courts are humming: Here a builder goes
Around the beams with calipers and rule,
Another crowns the roof with blooms and bows.

Some drive their horses forward with a shout,
And others load their wares. They look about
And yet their eyes are lusterless and dead.

There on the green a feast is on, they sing,
And many women raise their voices too,
But song and laughter have a hollow ring.

And One goes by and tosses back his hair.
He stops to pray into the evening air,
And youth is still a wreath around his head.

231

# THE PRINCE AND THE LOVER

## THE PRINCE

> Because you are —
> If just for this we bring our thanks.

They who in spirit build transcendent worlds,
Who stride through lands and forge them into realms,
They can indeed elect, but not create you,
The bearer of the crown's intrinsic splendour,
Who grew in mansions vast with veneration,
Through which you paced in golden pomp, with mercy
And pride, from early childhood seeing, thinking
Not as the rest, nor touching what they touch.
The strongest and the wisest kneel to you,
And you enchant and rule them with your smile.
They feel the grace which only you can give,
For which your sire moulded you, your slender
Anointed hands from which salvation pours
On whom they rest, the radiance of your glances
That change the people's burden to delight.


## THE LOVER

> "These eyes are filled with faith and dreams, with longing
> To find the image thought begot.
> A Sunday sadness dwells within these eyes."

Who could regret the sacrifice, the fruit
And beasts, because they brought no help to man
And fumed upon the altar in the rite?
The window frames a glad and eager crowd
Dispersing with a muffled sound, and westward
The purple greys. I give the southwind dreams
For the serene and happy who avow me.
But those who pass below, exclaim: "Now come
The days of work when you will drive your brothers
To battle. You will have to build your cities
And store a heritage for lusty scions,
For every mortal learns the greed for harvests."

I grieve, but I am grateful for what is.
I spent my breath upon the whirling feast
To garment you with sweetness and to bless.
I streamed my body's blood into the dusk
For you, beloved, O all of you beloved!


## MANUEL AND MENES

> I saw that one of greater worth than I
> Had risen through a change in destiny...
> > Manuel II, 2


## MENES

After the night when you appeared to us
A flash of lightning lit my path: the stretch
Which lies behind and that which winds beyond.
The grace that makes the boldest hope come true,
The blessing of the olive branch, the scepter
Which I was fighting for, were yours by birth.
I told my comrades to await your day
And lay aside their weapons. My defiance
And doubt, my planning and impassioned fervour,
Dangerous quests in seasons without rest,
My leadership which promised early harvests,
All this was nothing when you gave your oath.
And when renouncing almost numbed my spirit,
I looked at you and I was whole and strong.
A wisdom overwhelmed me, sweet and sad:
Each age that passes on but does not die
Links with the next, and so my deed with yours.
I quickly left the friends who pressed my arm
To warn me. You are now in power! Command!

## MANUEL

You have surpassed me through this final triumph
Which you have won, and now you share my work.
You found a guide, but I have found a warder.
We knew each other by the sign. Come closer!
The thief of crowns obeys his greedy hand,
The true heir his vocation. I, the lord,
And you, the aide, are equally ordained!


## ALGABAL AND THE LYDIAN

The even scales of the tremendous balance


## ALGABAL

The loot of legions does not move me, nor
The freights of fortune riding through my gates.
At every breath we draw, the dreaded foe
Comes nearer step by step, he blots the gleam,
He murks the cup. No spell can stop his course.

But there are times when, at the garden's edge,
I want to kill the day, so slow to sink
Into the sea, or lying on my couch,
I wait and count, and painfully attempt
To hasten empty hours to their end.


## THE LYDIAN

You, my companions, boast of supple bodies,
And practice them in morning games without me,
Or from your low estate proclaim the midnights
When vibrant with your lust, you shook and shuddered
Until you thought that only gods could match you.

234

The only truth I know is frenzied greed for
The unattainable the moon has tossed me.
No sorrow cows and clings like this desire!
Day has no charm for me. O final rapture:
When my cool blood will quench the conflagration.


## KING AND HARPER


### HARPER

You drew your cloak across your face and then
I saw it was a tear which you were hiding
And, lord, a gesture of distaste for me.
Today you have not spoken to your servant,
And yet you cannot frown on him you ordered
To stay beside you, ready with his music.
Have thankless mobs, perhaps, rebelled again?
Or the proud priests defied you? I have guessed it:
The jealous god has grudged you victory!


### KING

You spied on my disgrace, so you shall listen
To what you ought not: More than foes you speak of,
The foes I shall defeat, he who professes
To love me, will destroy me: you yourself!
Now you must bear a lot which none can alter,
You whom I hate and yet cannot dispense with.
You do not know you poison me, your fingers
Toy with my sword and shield, still red and slimed
With terrible saps — so you may catch the echo.
You cast the arms I chose to deal destruction
Into the water, stirring it to circles.
Your careless hand despoils my field, my orchard,
The labours of an endless, scalding summer,
To cool your sated palate with the fruit.

My nights of fevered torment only serve you
To scatter them in whispers and in tunes.
You split the holy musings which consume me
To coloured bubbles, to an airy nothing.
And your nefarious pastime melts my great
And kingly sorrow to an idle song.


## SUMMER SOLSTICE

Torpor weighs on us in the hall of candles,
　　In the smoke of the braziers.
Rigid ivory our moveless bodies,
　　Laved in smoulder and shadow
Of the long-drawn banquet, in adornment
　　Which the curves of the arches,
Floor, and panel lavish, fluting conjures,
　　And aroma of wine.
Then a nightwind bursts through all the windows,
　　And our torches are darkened,
Shudders tingle through our hair with sweetness,
　　We abandon the goblets,
Drag across the flags and over highways
　　Garlands withered and loosened,
Break through city gates into the hamlets
　　With our echoing dances,
See the field astir in orange sunrise
　　With the crowd of the reapers,
Shepherds, planters — naked rush to counter
　　Their luxuriant vigour,
Fix our eyes, remote and glazed with visions,
　　On the eyes of the earthbound
Creatures, shy and unaware, who slowly
　　Turn to flame in our fires.
Candid limbs are clinging close and twisted
　　Round the sinewy brown ones,
Firm as vines about the mother branches.
　　They are swirled, they are tangled
With the dewy clods, the trampled grasses,
　　And the dust of the seeding.

236

Cries of lust and terror ring through thickets,
    Of the hunters and hunted.
Shaken fingers for the locks still fumble.
    Some athirst past endurance,
Hot with chase and flight and splashed with juices
    From the fruit over-ripened,
Drink from callous lips the blood and spittle,
    In the fume of the grain sheaves,
Others lean and kiss the kindred flowers
    On the breast of the chosen.


## WITCHES' DANCE

We laugh at your elations
You mismade generations.
Your blue and bleary sight
Sees only lying day,
But ours, filmed with night,
Can spy the secret stay.

You only know the pelt!
We find a thousand terms
For clash of clouds and flurries,
For hosts in bay and belt,
For thousand sombre germs
Which darkness shrouds and buries.

We dance with twisted shoulder,
We feel at ease and fair
With swollen gut and limb.
We savour stench and moulder.
In whirling waves of blare
We hear a measured hymn.

We feed the slot with must,
The colour of the foam:
They float from earthen verges,
They fly from starry surges,
From east and west they home,
The forms of flesh and dust.

237

We shake our sieve until
The portions which you own
Of all the treasures spill.
But left within the chalice
Is something made of stone
And like a creature's phallus.

No force will make you see,
You wander blind and blank.
We feast on mired bank,
In carrion pits of slaughter.
The glint of poisoned water
Shows us all truths that be.


TEMPLARS

Once in a Golden Age we merged with all,
For aeons now the crowd has shunned our call.
We are the Rose: the young and fervent heart,
The Cross: to suffer proudly is our art.

On unknown courses, silent and austere,
We turn the sombre spool, we turn the spear.
Through coward years our flaming weapon rings,
We scourge the people and we challenge kings.

We do not join the customs and the bout
Of those who look askance at us and doubt
And fear because their hatred never felled
What with our savage love we caught and held.

Whatever loot our swords and slings have gained
Pours negligently from our spendthrift hand,
And though our rage devises harsh decrees,
Before a child we fall upon our knees.

We veil the flashing glance, the loosened lock
Which once betrayed the lord in beggar's smock,
Shyly from forward swarms who on our shade
— When we are gone — confer their accolade.

We nursed at alien breast and so our sons
Shall never be the children of our loins,
They never will be weak, dilute, or old,
For unborn fires quicken in their mould.

And only one of ours can complete
The needed change or do the iron feat
To which they summon us when chaos reigns,
Only to stone and curse us for our pains.

And when in wrath the Mighty Mother scorns
To lean and couple at the lower bourns,
Some world-night when her pulses scarcely stir,
Then only one who always strove with her,

Ignored her wishes and denied her will,
Can crush her hand and grip her hair until
Submissively she plies her work afresh:
Turns flesh to god, embodies god in flesh.


## THE GUARDIANS OF THE FORECOURT

At first I had you reared in poor terrains,
Buried in sorrow, searching full of fevers,
That yearning might be flooded through your veins
And make of children prophets and believers.

But then I lent you for a little time
A sunny land where grapes and roses cluster,
To show you heaven and the most sublime
In rows of earthly mornings lapped in lustre.

And so you grew in pride and solitude
That — waiting — never stoops to grosser pleasure,
I fanned your inner flame until you viewed
The stainless image and eternal measure.

And so you cast the fullest light upon
The brow you crowned with bay and vine, the glory
Of rain-wet rye along a road, the dawn
Of magic, bright across the ancient valley.

You bring atonement to the gaping ground
Which avarice and malice gashed and looted,
You make it green again, you make it sound.
On virgin heath the naked dance is footed.

You dauntless swimmers peer through every shell,
You find the rarest fruit in every furrow,
Your wakeful spirits seize the shining spell
Unfailingly and store it for tomorrow.

You bear the mark! And whether you are set
In dingy walls or silks and silver portals,
You shall remember — though the rest forget —
That once you were descended from immortals.


THE ANTICHRIST

"He strides from the mountains, he stands near the pines,
We saw it: He changes the water to wines,
His voice can evoke the departed!"

If only you heard how I laugh in the dark!
My hour has come, now the quarry is snared,
Now fish fill the nets with their swarming.

The mob is afoot, both the foolish and wise,
They crash through the cornfields and tear up the trees,
Make way for the train of the Risen!

The sky has no marvels I cannot confer,
A hairsbreadth amiss, but you do not discern
The hoax, for your senses are blunted.

240

The facile I bring for the laboured and rare,
Make something like gold out of clay, or a sham
Like juice full of fragrance and spices.

And what the great prophet eschewed I have taught:
The art without clearing or sowing or toil
To live on the stores of the furrow.

The lord over vermin extends his domains,
No treasure escapes him his joys never wane.
And down with the rest, with the rebels!

You cheer, you are charmed by demoniac ruse,
Exhaust the old honeys, and only when doom
Approaches you feel you are beggared

And hang out your tongues, but the bucket is dry.
You flounder like cows when the barn is afire —
And grimly the trumpet is sounded!


HERO'S CHILDHOOD

Scornful of his sister's play
And his friend's he leaps abysses,
Climbs through stony wildernesses,
Out for nests of birds of prey.

With his limbs and shoulders bare
Firm he stands, his head erect
To the wind, and sets a snare
For the creature he has tracked.

Over barren space his clear
Artless song resounds, the ringing
Of his Pan-pipes marks the swinging
Rhythm of his tawny hair.

In his dreams he fights and kills
Monsters, straddles kingly steeds,
And at home — though rarely — spills
With the tale of daring deeds.

From his bath in icy tides,
From his sleep in sunny heather,
He is burned as brown as hides,
But his eyes are cloudless azure.

Men who mock at him and jeer,
Men who shrug their shoulders now,
Once before his tents shall bow
Low in reverence and fear,

Reel and tremble at his grandeur
When he rides through his domain.
Rich in weapons, pawns and plunder —
Kneel unbidden. They will stain

Beards and brows with ash and soot,
Crouch before his gaze that brands,
Sue for grace his ruthless hands,
Lick the dust which crusts his foot.


## THE OATH

"Come and close around me, you shall be
        Linked and bound to my decree:
You, escaped from prisons, ashen grey,
        You who foundered on your way,
You whose dagger for himself was ground,
        You I caught before you drowned,
Precious harvest scattered through the land,
        Savage forces fate restrained."

"We were bonded by the strongest seal
    When our arms were pierced with steel,
Quickened by the same candescent flood
    When one drank the other's blood.
Since we follow you our fortune flowers."
    "From your oath I draw my powers."
"Through your breath we kindle and unfold."
    "Through your marrow I am bold."


"Only you can point the goal in store,
    It is etched into your ore.
We whose fists are hard and trained to fight
    Carry out your every rite.
You who guides us in our stress, command,
    Though we may not understand.
Plough across our flesh and none will try
    To rebel or reason why."


"Even now I see through shrouded skies
    The fulfilment and the prize.
To their trenches our opponents pour,
    For my sons are crying 'War!'
Earth will help the hands it made and knows,
    Heaven harms detested foes.
Walls are nothing, hosts cannot prevail,
    For my sons are crying 'Hail!'"


THE COMING


Now is the day!
Waken what lay
Sheltered, heaving and quaking.
Decades of dark
Earth remained stark
Drank unseen without slaking:

Pitiless threat,
Agonized sweat,
Madness helplessly crying,
Anguish and thirst
Branded and cursed,
Futile pleas of the dying.


Furrow is split,
Cover is slit,
Sunward the seedlings burrow,
Fled from the gloom
Deep in the womb,
You are the lords of tomorrow.


Armies of light
Ride from the night,
Clash and the air is aquiver.
Chant of revenge,
Plunder and singe,
Saviours, destroy and deliver!


So you divide
Land from the tide,
Wastes are quickened with showers.
Heroes afire,
Heroes' desire
Shape the spring and its flowers.

244

# TIDES

When touched by the breath of my anguish
You float in the swirl of my dreams,
I fumble, and famish, and languish.
When day slowly darkens, it seems
As if a harsh lover were pressing
The supple young tree in embrace,
Or fingers grown cooler, caressing
A downy and luminous face.

But when the deep shadows draw nearer,
And thought has you gently in sway,
The glitter and sound become clearer,
And visions descend on our way:
The night shakes her locks, and a flurry
Of stars are released into flight,
We follow and cling in the scurry
Of flakes and their haloes of light.

From figment and fancy I bounded
So high that the earth left me free,
But yours was a sorrow you sounded
For others, for you, and for me.
And now you have learned to desire
This soul in its pallor and drouth,
My mouth with its fervour and fire
Is quenched in the bloom of your mouth.


Today our words shall dwell
        on only starry phases,
I hunger to exult
        but wan and dazed I stand:
The son of wisdom threads
        the Veda's cryptic mazes
And frees the blind from night
        by laying on his hand.

Unconscious of his poise
    a child of Eden raises
A gem more rich and strange
    than any emperor's land.


Star that shall govern this year!
Now in the season of budding and storm
Tell me of temperate summers to come,
Garland with flowers the yellowing ears,
So that the days full of tumult and fears
Calm to the smiling of light, that a still
Wisdom preserve me from perilous ill
Haunting my wanderings, clogged and obscure.
Make my shadowy wishes sure,
Solve the enigmas that trouble and chill.

Prodigal nights when your forehead lay
Bowed on my knees, when the faltering tones
Breaking from dull subterranean zones
Fused into song. You followed the play
Proffered by forces at feud and at bay:
Grace I was granted at destiny's hand,
Sorrow I suffered in far-away land —
Followed while dawn-clouds deepened and glistened,
Just as beautiful Dunyazad listened
Long to her sister's tales without end.


## LOOKING BACK

My thoughts which dwell on you and only you, have changed
    The room, and town, and silvered lane. I go
Completely filled with you and from myself estranged,
    In magic nights across the purple snow.

The pledge of hot horizons over harvest lands,
    The pledge of summer — was it all borne out?
So does the wanderer, home from years of roaming stand,
    Grip his own arm, and tremble with a doubt.

246

For one who waits, his slumber spins a witching net,
    And gentle love supplants his ecstasy.
To be apart from you is sweet despair and yet
    The harbinger of pleasures still to be.

You yielded wondering, and willingly sank down,
    And moaned beneath the overflow of bliss,
You rose: Around your limbs a stainless glory shone,
    You were bewildered by the breathless kiss.

And then an hour came — they rested in embrace,
    Their lips still burning from a wilder hold,
And to the room, through which the stars serenely gazed,
    A dawn had come, suffused with rose and gold.


## SONG AND RESPONSE

### SONG

I tremble, for today, beneath our joy I find
    Much that was strange in you and still remains,
As though you took for spray and gusts of passing wind
    What brims my heart and circles in my veins.

Can you not hold the fires that offer you their blaze?
    Release me from the clamour of my fears.
Was it, perhaps, my glance, caught in your lifeless gaze?
    Was it my breath that shook your voice with tears?


### RESPONSE

A dying and submissive murmur tells
    You of a soul which here lies drowned
And, muffled by the weeds, a soughing wells
    Up from the depths with listless sound.

247

Perhaps a firefly with whirring glow,
    Or else a flower, smooth and slight,
Will lure you who — uncertain where to go —
    Half wants to stay this anxious night.

Perhaps these sparks that flicker up and die,
    And melodies with mournful toll
Will touch and hinder you from passing by
    The prison of a sunken soul.


The ways on which we meet are full of pain,
As though they led into the fields of death,
The air is grey, but spends a fertile breath
Of new unfolding through the slender rain.
In meagre files the faded hedges stand
And guard a gully where the light is bleached,
As if uncounted rigid fingers reached
And groped to cling each to the other's hand.
The birds are few, their plaintive call is low
And lost among the leafless oaks, but one
Alive and secret thing is closely spun
Around the sombre boughs: green mistletoe.
That days ago through wet and chilling haze
A brief, seductive shaft of brightness fell
Upon this ground, the pallid grasses tell,
The first young blades and, under withered sprays,
The dark anemones in mourning clusters.
Furred with their silver down they bend and still
Hide in the clouded purple of their bells
A golden diadem and inner lustres,
And are like souls that in the dawning lull
Of half-awakened wishes and the sting
Of lurking doom in winds of early spring
Are still afraid to open fair and full.

You say that cliff and wall are gay with early green,
　　But what I see is only dross and doom.
The tranquil meadows sound the knell of death for me,
　　You launch your song on cataracts of bloom.

Those who would not remain, although they wept to part,
　　Surround me while you stand with smiling gaze.
Let us return, for scalding noon may bid my heart
　　To word a sorrow fanned to sudden blaze.

I can no longer bleed in silence: You deceived
　　Yourself for your survival, for my fall,
I am still thankful for the moments I believed
　　That you were beautiful and I enthralled.

Farewell! You shall not see my eyes when, dazed and drawn,
　　They close, my lashes wet with pain and rue,
And when beyond the plane where life is wholly gone
　　The sun pours glossy gold through leaden blue.


Sombre Soul — you questioned me — are you in mourning?
　　Is this your thanks for all our great delight?
Weightless Soul — I said to you — swiftly to mourning
　　Delight has changed and stricken me with blight.

Pallid Soul — you questioned me — and has our fire
　　Gone out for you? How matchlessly it burned!
Heedless Soul — I said to you — I brim with fire,
　　My sorrow's sum is only want that burns.

Cruel Soul — you questioned me — can more be proffered
　　Than youth accords? All that I have I give,
And can a heart beat with a nobler offer
　　Than this: Take of my blood so you may live.

Frothy Soul — I said to you — what is your loving
　　Compared to what I gave? The merest shred!
Secret Soul — you said to me — you spur my loving
　　Though now through you my airy dream is dead.

249

# THE MIRROR

I stumble on at every journey's end
Along a shore where nothing blooms, and take
My thoughts, and dreams, and wishes there to bend
And gaze at their reflection in the lake,
So they may know themselves at last. But they
Discerned an image always dim and wan.
"Those are not we," they said in musing tone
And then they wept and slowly went away.

But all at once through bitterness and dread,
Through shadow, and decay, and old despairs
I felt how Joy encompassed me with splendour.
Inebriate within his arms I swayed,
I snatched the star which glittered on his head,
I leaned against his feet and was allayed.
At last and utterly in savage flares
I flamed, and utter was my self-surrender.

Come blithely to the lake, my dream, my thought!
How low above the mirror you are bowed.
You still have doubts? Is not your likeness caught?
Perhaps the dancing clouds of autumn move
The glass, or withered tendrils draw a groove?
How anxious one against the next you crowd!
You do not weep, but as at every close
You sigh: "Those are not we — we are not those."



You pile your shallow panniers with largesse
You took from me and revel in your prize.
You do not know the names which I devise
For you in scores, the kisses that caress

You secretly, too young a squire who
Confuses victories with jousts and from
So brief a feast so blithely goes. To some
I say "enough" but "thirst for more" to you.

250

And this our sole concern: that for conferred
Felicity we store the fruit and grain
So that not we but others have the gain
Lest lovely light and charted trails grow blurred.


GIVING THANKS

The summer field is parched with evil fire,
And walking in a field of trodden clover
I saw my head in waters thick with mire
Which wrath of distant thunders shot with red.
When nights are frantic, days are full of dread,
The cherished gardens seem a stifling stall,
A poison like untimely snow films over
The trees, the lark ascends with hopeless call.

Then through the land you wander, light of foot,
And it unfolds in colours you have strewn,
You bid us strip the boughs of shining fruit,
You rout the twillight where the shadows grow.
Did I not weave for you, your tranquil glow
This crown of thanks, then who would know that far
More brightly than the sun you lit my noon,
And night more gloriously than any star!


CLOSE

Although the colours of the earth no longer
Are rich when sun has set, but dimmed with dust,
And each into a different region must
Go with his sorrow and confess: I hunger!

And though the inner urge to you is growing
More faint, I feel that I must turn your way,
That I am yours, that you possess my day,
And boughs of spring still weave around our going.

Another odour comes from silver-stripen
And brittle blades than flaxen grass, but all
My memories of stream, and slope, and wall
Evoke one only wish: Be glad and ripen!

And when a whisper lures that after burning
The fallow aftermath, on alien site
I may be free to find a new delight,
I feel as though a kindred blood were yearning.

The road was long, so now let me recapture
Our common faring and these bonds that fold
Us close in secret and compelling hold,
And all my former anguish and your rapture.


The field of loosened earth is sick and craving
When after barren cold it feels the thrust
Of plough and prong, the touch of milder air,
And heaves in storms that shake the drowsy year.
Now this shall be my draught, my fertile laving:
The trembling freshness of your naked breast,
The fragrance of your softly tangled hair,
The moisture of your mouth, your breath, your tear.


There were no shards and no destruction,
There was no chasm and no pall,
There was no yearning, no seduction,
A single hour gave us all.

A host of blossoms welled and rippled
In crimson light of sorcery,
And spring's primeval clamour stippled
The bird's untrammelled melody.

Ecstatic thrust that broke the traces
A frenzy nothing can destroy,
The gift of new and fragrant spaces,
A reel of senses fused in joy.

252

The joust that never notes the wounding flick
Until veiled eyes hide in a lap and weep,
That probes until it touches to the quick,
    Now in the dream grew deep.

The savage kiss that suffers while it brands,
That craves a draught withheld, and dies in wild
Relentless terror of the vacant end,
    Now in the dream grew mild.

Parting at night that leaves a bitter sting
When silently I look at you and treat
You like a stranger, though I writhe within,
    Now in the dream grew sweet.


What are these walls, in darkness strangely massed,
The paths which hedge us close with twisting verge?
I feel how shapes or ghosts around us surge,
Sprung from the spark of an impetuous past.

They torture me, a stifling ring is drawn!

You conjured them within a sultry shrine
Through all those summer days of glaring heat,
And let them linger in a vague retreat
With aftermath of showered myrrh and wine.

They hover through the wind of early dawn.

Perhaps they floated over bed and bough
And did not quite dissolve until I came,
So that their breath might kindle me to flame,
While he they followed finds them nothing now

But shades that haunt because their soul is gone.

The year had not yet rounded since the day
We read our hearts, when pointed grains of frost
Fell to the earth from yellow clouds. Then must
What seeds we sow be watered with dismay?

For tender feuds, for ardours swift and bold,
For all the joy which swept us to the skies,
For all the need we mourned, for all our sighs
A single circuit of the earth was doled.

The grapes that only just were clear, and full,
And heavy on the vines, are plucked and spent:
The clusters trodden to the vapid hull
And brews the months of darkness will ferment.

Must this delight like all the sheaves grow sallow,
Like blade and bush deprived of grace by grace,
And fly irrevocably with the swallow,
Dissolve in summer haze without a trace?


Now let me call across the meadows tided
With snow — your image very far and faint —
How first my pastime, then my balm, you guided
My year without your knowledge or intent.

You came when jewelled blooms were full and glowing,
And when they mowed the field we met once more,
I always took the path which through the blowing
And reddening harvest drew me to your door.

So tender was your word that I commended
Myself to you when leaves grew brown and dry,
And when you left, a broken call ascended
From the deserted valley like a sigh.

And so the shimmer of two eyes has granted
The last reward of every come and go,
Your gentle song was what the seasons chanted,
And all befell because you tuned it so.

254

## FLAMES

"Why do you drive us up and up to range
In tempests more and more remote and strange?

When we have barely calmed to glistening rest
Another mouth fans us to wilder crest,

Which ridges polished bars with slanted swirls,
Transfixes scorching drops to fickle pearls,

Until we seethe and overflow, and pour
Our strength on steel and earth and are no more."

"The distant breath which often touched you, bears
The same and secret stuffs which feed your flares,"

The Lord of Torches says, "and when you quite
Destroy yourselves, you burn with fullest light."


## WAVES

At first you lap against the bluish pebbles
Where in the hollow wood the pathway trebles.

As brooks you ripple through the sunlit land
And spatter tears across the grassy strand.

Into a boundless tide the current hurries
You on with thunderstorms and pelting flurries.

On myrtle cliffs you wildly rise at bay,
On barren sand dissolve in foaming spray.

Your waters harbour bodies nacre-tinted,
You carry cargoes, splendid and unstinted

Until the gusts drive you to empty pales.
You crash on rock and reef with moans and wails.

255

Now you are scourged through hidden depths, forgetting
That there is any dawn or any setting,

That there is urge or aim, and wind or lee...
A shoreless river winding through the sea.


ENCOMIUM

You are my lord! When on my path you rise
In many changing shapes and yet familiar
And beautiful, I bend my neck before you.
Now you have neither garments, wings, nor weapons,
All that adorns you is the clustered wreath
Around your hair. You touch: a fragrant draught
Of rapture floods the mind which feels your breath,
And every fibre quivers from your blow.
Who called you "the assuager" in the past
Had never fancied that your slender finger,
Your rosy heel could deal such devastation.
I fling my body back in patient pain,
Yes, even when you come with your battalions
Of beasts that brand their mark with pointed talons
And mangle with their fangs, extorting wordless
Laments and sighs of anguish. As you breathe
The scent of mellow fruit and sappy green,
So they the fetid odour of the jungle.
The wet and dust they reek does not repel us.
Nothing that weaves around you can be foul!
You cleanse the taint, you heal the gash, the sweetness
Which fans from you effaces every tear.
In threat or thrall, if only we are steadfast,
Each day shall end in triumph as our service
To you: the homage dauntlessly renewed,
A smile surrendered to the starlit blue.

# MAXIMIN

## ADVENT I

To some you are a child,
To some a friend, to me
The god whom I divined
And tremble to adore.

You came at last when sick
With waiting, weary of
My prayers I began
To lose myself in night.

I knew you by the beam
Which flowed into my dark,
The step to which the seed
Replied with sudden bloom.

## ADVENT II

As a sad people once
Cried for a saviour, flung
Their windows wide, and made
His bed and set his board,

But maddened by delay
Began to blame and jeer,
So I renounced. Three times
I was deceived: the child

Who could not find his dream,
The youth who yearned and failed,
And now, with life half done,
The man who scoffs at hope.

## ADVENT III

Now spring is here again,
You bless the air, the path,
And us on whom you gaze...
So take my faltered thanks.

The Maker breathed a soul
Through everything in space,
Before our clumsy mind
Asked him to speak and act.

Where such eyes are alight,
The withered branches bud,
The stark earth tunes her beat
To so unstained a heart.


## RESPONSES: THE MIRACLE

Do you still invade forbidden
Spheres with tangled hair and pray
That you may approach the Hidden?
See him in his earthly day,
Dust through which a flame is ridden!

More than for the rest, his splendid
Light is flung about your brow,
That the one whom he commended
Deck your shrine with bloom and bow
To the dream you bore and tended.

With his hand he curved the streaming
Clouds of sunset into halls
Vaulted with a gentle gleaming,
Now the miracle befalls:
Dream is blended into dreaming.

## RESPONSES: INTRODUCTION

Though you have crossed the wasted valley, far
From summits once your course,
You have been chosen as you are
To see the promised pales,
You tasted of the source,
Now tread the open trails.
The yellow wheat is framed in purple fields,
The altar, wreathed with roses, yields
A buoyant flame, and under boughs a sheen
Quivers and warms the air, and day
By day the angel's anthems sound.
His mouth shall burn you clean,
You are on holy ground,
Kneel down and pray!


## RESPONSES: THE MISTAKING

Through day and darkness, at the mountain where
The Lord had risen, the disciple mourned:
"So you have left your faithful to their sorrow,
Forgetting earth in your transfiguration?
I shall not hear your voice again, nor ever
Again embrace your feet and touch your garment?
I begged a sign, but you did not reply."
And then a stranger came: "My brother, speak!
Such torment is ablaze upon your cheek
That it will sear me if I do not quench it."
"Leave me to a despair you cannot solace,
I seek my Lord who has forsaken me."
The stranger vanished. The disciple fell
Upon his knees and cried aloud, for by
A glory clinging in that place he knew
That crushed and blind with pain he had not noted
It was the Lord himself who came and went.

## SORROW I

"Oh, wait for this message to reach you:
The day without you is profane,
I hunger for you and beseech you,
To die in your stead were a gain!

If one is decreed by the Powers
To cross the dark verge, it is I!
The night flings me down in the flowers,
Respond to my agonized cry!"

"Let me float away into heaven,
Arise from the ground and be whole,
Remain on the earth to extol
And witness the grace that was given."


## SORROW II

The forest shivers.
In vain it clothed itself in leaves of spring,
The field your foot made consecrate is numb
And cold without the sun you bring.
The fragile blades on hilly pastures quiver,
For now you never come.

What use are buds which you do not awake,
The many sprays your fingers do not wind,
And what the wealth of blooms you do not bind,
Whom shall the fruit, you have not tasted, slake?

The sound of saplings cracking,
Stem after stem — what now will fall?
The early green is growing worn,
The grass, so lately sprung, already shorn,
No bird sings, only frosty winds are clacking
And then the axes call.

## SORROW III

Dull is the air, deserted are the days,
What adequate observance can I render?
When shall I flame your light through all our days?
I who am only glad when I surrender
To graves the pomp and ruin of my days,
Devote myself to mournfulness and render
Songless and lifeless all the dragging days.
Accept the dirge which dust and darkness render,
Accept the offering of my empty days.

## ON THE LIFE AND DEATH OF MAXIMIN

### THE FIRST

Your eyes were dim with distant dreams, you failed
To guard and tend the holy fief and knew
That everywhere the glow of life had paled.
Now lift your head, for joy has come to you!

New miracles of spring have put to flight
The year you suffered slow and icy gloom,
With hands like April buds, with locks of light,
A god appeared and stepped into your room.

Unite in happiness, no more alloyed
With cravings for an age of vanished bliss,
You too have heard the summons of a god,
It was a god who granted you his kiss.

You also were elect, so do not mourn
For all the days which unfulfilment sheathed.
Praise to your city where a god was born,
Praise to your time in which a god has breathed!

## THE SECOND: PILGRIMAGE

Why does the stranger, moved with awe, draw near
The walls and tracks, unending and forlorn,
Through busy come and go of court and stair?
Here one who shaped our destiny was born!

Where houses frame the square, and grasses wedge
Their way between the paving stones, where trite
And stunted flowers skirt the shaven hedge,
Your glances first were lifted to the light.

How dusty is the air, the noisy road,
The roll of wheels, the ceaseless tread and trot!
As Mary, Anna's daughter, bore her load,
Here you, your mother — and they saw it not.

But once in spring a grey and silver dew
Fell from the sky and flashed on every stem,
The stunted flowers nodded silver blue,
And all the children thought they smiled at them.

This house, so like the rest, is journey's end.
We bare our heads within an empty hall
Which sent you earthward. Did three kings not bend
Down to a star which led them to a stall?


## THE THIRD

You watch over us
            in your unattainable glory,
For now you are one
            with the word which we heard from above.
In all that we do
            we attempt to fulfill your desire,
The smile of a king
            is more dear to his subjects than gold.

And when in the evening
         our memory dwells on your story,
Our arms try to reach you,
         we tremble with longing and love,
Our lips grow impassioned
         and yearn toward your mortal attire,
As if you were with us,
         O Light, and still caught in our mould.


## THE FOURTH

Choirs of heaven were tuned to enthral you
Seeking to slip from the snare of our praise,
So that O Changed One, it might not appall you,
And you reproved us and fled from our maze.

You, to the peace of the seventh elected,
Were so remote from our day, yet we knew
— Taught by a sign — that you had not rejected
Earth and the love we awakened in you.

When for the journey to stars you enlisted,
You were impaled by a beam from below,
And while the light of your glances was misted,
Muted with sadness your voice seemed to flow:

"Spring, you enchant me this year beyond measure,
Budding of boughs! Could I see it again!
See once again and with you whom I treasure,
Loveliest blooms of a sunny terrain."


## THE FIFTH: UPLIFT

You call on us who weep in dark and anguish:
         Fling all the portals wide!
Let sallow tapers gutter down and languish,
         Set mourning rites aside!

What strength and light you gave to cast reflection
 Upon your brief sojourn,
Let each effuse to work your resurrection,
 Your luminous return,

Embodied in our marrow, our desires
 And their incessant plea,
In all the beauty which still feeds our fires
 And fills our memory,

Throughout the days which left us cold and jaded,
 You were the burning thorn,
You gave us roses which have never faded,
 You went when spring was born.

We must accept your radiant incarnation
 Which spurs us to intone
Your praise in song, to seek the liberation
 From shades that drift and moan,

For you and for ourselves, to curb the sorrow
 That rides us to our doom,
And scatter blooms, today, tomorrow
 Until we hide your tomb.


THE SIXTH

You harbinger of joy have guided
Me from a sullen winter to
An island where enchantment tided,
Where fragrant trees and flowers grew.

You shared the secret of your spacious
And hidden realm with only one,
You loved your warder, and the gracious
Gift of your youth was his alone.

And in the grove the sacral spender
Revived the ardent haste of him
Who offered firstling fruits — a splendour
Once clear to me, now far and dim.

With fiery verve the Helper speeded
His bolt upon the arid rod,
And all the flames which had seceded,
United to be one with God.

From heights I saw where I had quested
In vain, I was reborn and knew
The distant land which you invested
With meaning when the clouds withdrew.

Our temple-halls were pure and gloried,
You raised your lids, and all the stained
Fled to their sties, ashamed and sordid,
And none were left but the ordained.

The earth resounds your name in paeans,
Our hearts and minds grow whole and wise,
And from the timeless dark of aeons
I now compel your star to rise.


PRAYER I

Call of holy trumpets drove
Through the air on which I drifted,
And my mouth and hands were lifted
In a prayer for your love.

Purer victim never came
To your shrine with greater gladness,
Less ensnared in haste and madness
I shall never seek your flame.

You have quickened me to burn,
I abide by your decision,
Free me from my body's prison,
See I sorrow, see I yearn!

Loose at last and lull to rest,
Hear my wooing, hear my sighing,
Let me die for you where dying
Makes me yours and serves you best.

Do not doubt me or appraise,
I am yours, so take and keep me
Fuse me with yourself and sweep me
Through your white and inmost blaze!

## PRAYER II

If our office is to cower
To your tempest and to lie
Crushed in dust before your power,
You, the ruthless Lord-on-High,

Why the summers when we darted
Free and naked, fervently
Called you neighbour who imparted
Light-begotten ecstacy?

Why the sombre frenzy under
Which our pride and vigours grew,
When we seethed with all your thunder,
Fancied we were close to you?

Snatch us from our lowly station!
Suddenly to stars we sail,
Kindred to your incarnation
In a cloud, a wave, a gale?

## PRAYER III

How grateful am I, sun, for all I see
When first I cross the threshold and attune
To warmth and light with which you garment me.
How glad the morning and how clear the noon!

A gentle wind is in my hair, my blood
Is sweet with garden fragrance, and I lay
A loving hand on many a crimson bud
And cool my cheek against a snowy spray.

O afternoon, with threat, and dream, and flame,
With plans the demigods and magi laid,
You gave me worlds to play a kingly game
While all around my boat the waters played.

And then the dusk for which I always yearn,
When I am kindled by the holy rite
That conjures what I loved until return
Of tranquil sleep submerges my delight.


## INCARNATION

Now that you are strong and high,
What you prophecied was done:
You have changed our pact, and I
Am the child of my own son.

At my board you have your share
In a bridal secrecy,
Drink from wells that freshen me,
Walk the path on which I fare.

In my blood you are reborn,
Not a wraith or afterglow,
Clinging in your love I know
Sacred union dawn by dawn.

Yours the gloss, and grain, and hue
Of my spirit, and the blaze
Of my every fibre rays
Distant fires caught from you.

With your ichor I have stilled
My desire crouched to take,
With a breath that never slacks,
With your essence I am filled.

So that tears and ecstasy,
Clouded foam and light combine
To a fused and living sign:
Dream begot by you and me.


VISIT

Sun is aslant on your small
Garden and gently edges
Into your house among hedges,
Down through a gap in the wall.

Flutter of birds on the lawn,
Tips of bushes are blowing,
People coming and going
Now that the heat is gone.

Pick up the bucket and shed
Water on gravel and clover,
Spray it on ramblers and over
Gilliblooms, golden and red.

Cut back the ivy, too wild
There on the slope, by the settle,
Scatter a carpet of petals.
All shall be fragrant and mild

When at the falling of night
He as a pilgrim passes
Once more, perhaps, through places
Touched by terrestrial light,

Parts the branches, asway
Over the path, with holy
Breath, descends to your lowly
Ground and elects to stay.


TRANSPORT

Air from another planet floats around me,
And darkness steals the faces from my sight
Which only just, with friendly eyes, had found me.

The trees and paths I loved are turning greyer
So that I hardly know them, and the light
Which comes from you, beloved shade, purveyor

Of pain, is fused with deeper incandescence
And fills with fervour when the savage phase
Of strife and struggle drifts into quiescence.

I melt in sound, I flow and circle, serving
The mighty breath without a wish, in praise
Beyond all utterance, and thanks unswerving.

I shiver in a tempest of elation,
Of rapture like a woman's when she screams
Crouched in the dust in throes of supplication.

And then I see how gauzy vapour masses
And thins in flawless space imbued with beams
Which only strike the farthest mountain passes.

As smooth and white as whey the ground is shifted.
Across enormous chasms, high and higher,
I feel how over last of clouds uplifted

To seas of crystal radiance I am swung:
Only a flicker of the holy fire,
Only an echo of the holy tongue.


## DARKNESS OF DREAM


### ENTRANCE

Vista of pageants, this is adieu,
Forest of ivory shafts, unfold!
Foliage and fruit of carnelian and gold
Cling to the branches high in the blue.

Midway in hollow of marble, water
Wells and spills in a blossomy rain
Over the rim, as if grain after grain
Slowly fell on a luminous platter.

Coolness and wonder curve to a ring,
Dawn in the treetops! Creatures who dwell
Here are surrounded by silence and spell.
Wings of dream, whisper! Harp of dream, sing!


### ORIGINS

Hail to a laughing array:
Regents of sumptuous treasure,
Guardians of gifts without measure,
Ruling with godlike sway,
Circlets you carry and psalters.
Never again will it seem
That all the stars once were captured
By one spirit enraptured
As in a childhood dream.

270

Hail, O meadow, blessed with sun
Where, while sacred grapes were pressed,
Came — when wilds and beasts were gone —
Pan and Hebe, blossom-dressed.
Rugged hunter, shaggy hound
Fled from limbs of marble shimmer,
Halls by Rome's proportions bound.
We were still allowed a glimmer!
And beneath the piercing tines
Breath of legions upward rolled,
Of their boys and concubines.

Here their clay, their brass, their gold!
See the host which mounts the ridge,
Cohorts tread in rhythms regal,
For the Caesar-scion's eagle
Open every gate and bridge.

The Church then reared her head above these stones, and she
Grew stern and scourged the flesh she found too bare and free.
But she was heir to pomp, aflash in death-like sleeping,
And gave the standard set for height and depths in keeping
To minds that in Hosannahs wheeled above the clouds
And on the slabs of tombs in self-abasement bowed.

But near the stream in a palace of reed
On by the tide of our lust we were swirled,
Singing an anthem which no one could read,
We were the masters and lords of the world.
Sweet and inciting as Attica's chorus
Over the mountains and islands flung:
CO BESOSO PASOJE PTOROS
CO ES ON HAMA PASOJE BOAÑ.

LANDSCAPE I

Across the year's untrammeled glory flows
The listless spirit which had lost its way
At noon within a forest, where dismay
Drips from autumnal saffron, rust, and rose.

And leaf by leaf is loosed, a lighter patch
On sombre smoothness of a languid pool
Where even now a boy whose eyes are cool,
The ruthless spouse of darkness, keeps his watch.

And through the vague and soundless solitudes,
From bough to bough the evening flings its glaze
And turns the sultry yellow into blaze.
Then brooding mist envelops brooding woods.

The climbing nightshade weaves in fragile sprays
Around a wall of naked crimson thorn,
The forward thrusting hands are tired and torn...
If only sleep would come into the maze!

But timid flickers break through tangled gloom,
And from the dusk another brightness sifts,
Across the jutting crag a meadow drifts
Far off ... In masses of violas loom

The rows of slender lances, tree on tree,
A silver glamour fills the vaulted blue,
A fragrant wind diffuses warmth and dew,
And blossoms fall upon an open sea.


LANDSCAPE II

Love, does October live for you again,
Our joy in roaming through the sombre maze
Of firs with shafts of green metallic stain,
Through cinnabar of foliage turned to blaze?

272

As silent guests we visited this tree
And that. I went alone and so did you,
In loving feud each listened secretly
To boughs which sang a dream not yet come true.

At first a laughing stream that swiftly wound
Through sunken crevice was our guide, but soon
It flowed more slowly with a sadder sound
Until we hardly heard its twilit croon.

And by our wandering we were so beguiled
That we forgot the hour, forgot the trail,
But then — out picking berries late — a child
Pointed the path through underbrush and shale.

On crumbling ridges hung with leaves we passed
And step by step we felt and forced our way,
And there behind the thinning sprays at last
The distant roofs, the open valley lay.

We flung our arms around a mossy bole
And left the tree which marked the forest's end,
Then on through meadows to a gracious goal,
And tides of gold transfigured air and land.


LANDSCAPE III

This is the half-way house, and moonbeams seep
In through the pane. From distant firns they flake,
Pale with the dawning day. I am awake
And bend above you who are still asleep.

Through meadows fanning out, and up the peak,
On granite range, my happiness was you:
The magic in your eyes of gentian blue,
The downy texture of your shimmering cheek.

On winding trails which runnels once had hewn,
We toiled, and on our mountain sticks we bore,
And your untainted breath refreshed me more
Than cooling fountains on a sultry noon.

When morning calls you in a soughing tone
You will return to fields of fruit and rye,
The walls are shadowed with a mute goodbye.
From here to sterner heights I go alone.

In narrow clefts of ice that never moves,
And past the snow which piles the bed of rocks,
I reach the menacing, gigantic blocks
Where frozen water stands in sullen grooves.

The cembras dwindle, and the wind is lord!
The climb through rubble grows more rough and waste,
Where every track is ruthlessly effaced
Harps of the chasm sound their chord.


NIGHT

Gone are the trivia of noon.

Infinite woods overgrow
All that we are and we know.
Voices of magic surround
Us who in darkness are bound,

Us who are vowed to a swoon.

Trees are the rungs leading straight
Up to a luminous gate,
Lure into trackless illusion,
Drive into dazzling confusion.

Does the earth shake for the clasped?

274

Your breath in me! Is it this
Air from the precincts of bliss,
That has entangled our bodies,
Woven together by shadows?

Welded in perilous clasp?

Listen! A whisper awakes!
Sacred the water which breaks
Out of a flower-spun gully.
Unprompted cadences sally,

Cut through the thicket, and stream

Summons to living delights,
Call us, whom darkest of rites
Took as gratuitous prey,
Us, who are ready to sway
Into an ocean of dream.


## THE ENCHANTED GARDEN

Kingly the solitude, garden, in which you lie,
Seldom you open your gates to the passerby,
Refuge of silences, curtained in thickets and sprays,
Gravel so rarely disturbed on your sun-flooded ways,
Garrulous fountains which trellissed blossoms enlace,
Vases of granite uplifted in burdenless grace.
Songbirds enliven the leaves with their twittering crowd,
Glassed in the somnolent lake is impalpable cloud.
And the reflections of palaces fringing the side
Flicker like fiery wisps in the cool of the tide.

One, the abode of the princess: Her chamber gleams
Sea-green and silver. She lives in her sorrowful dreams,
Weighed with her chaplet of pearls and her frozen brocade,
She has no friend whom she trusts who could offer her aid.

Tears in her eyes as she chooses a gem from her sheaf,
Radiance suffuses her features in spite of her grief.
Flower whose fragrance is wasted, yet never grows less,
Sensitive heart full of love which it cannot express.
Time and again when the sun has set in the trees,
Evils of day have been softened to reveries,
Low on her lute she devises a dirge, and the bold
Planets are stricken with wonder and soften their gold.

Garnet and gilded, across the lake is the hall
Housing the prince and the sorrow he buries from all.
Heavy the crown on his forehead, translucent and white,
Irksome to him is his retinue's ease and delight.
Young and yet old, he stretches his arms to the blue,
Sighs on the terrace and mingles his tears with the dew.
Since he has broken his innermost law which disdains
Any approach on the wonted and intimate planes,
None whom the chill of his majesty does not astound,
Who does not lower his lashes and bow to the ground
Faced with a visage so laden with beauty and drouth.
Bitter and sweet is the smile which has contoured his mouth.

Wide are the doors of the palaces once in the year,
Barriers fall, the magnificent deign to appear.
Only the reverent, only the chosen may come,
Those who divine the whisper of bloom to bloom,
Know of the gratitude told with a faltering tongue,
Charm and aloofness of all that is fervent and young.
He shall be far who has plotted in raucous ravine,
Lived in the swamp and the pasture of venomous green,
Henchman of ice-blooded spectres and sinister spies,
Who, like the beast, is unmoved by the wind from the skies.

Then from the portals the festal procession ascends,
And on the terrace the prince meets the princess and bends
Low to her nod. They advance and their hands interlace,
Their steps alone do not shatter the spell of the place.
Rapture immerses the circle which kneels at the sight,
Long was the time it was shorn of its dearest delight:

276

Kissing the tips of an opaline finger, the hems
Touching the sandals encrusted with luminous gems.
Many the prayers which mutely and tearfully mount,
But the procession has solemnly turned at the fount.
Once more the sovereigns graciously look upon these
Gathered in homage, and then through an arch in the trees,
Trailing their satiny robes they are gone, and the slow
Evening transfigures the garden to amaranth glow.


## ROSES

In waves of white and fire-coloured blossoms
On bushes scattered over hill and hollow,
You were entangled, sang, and clung, and buried
Yourself in fragrance. You were deluged in
A cataract of roses, and they drifted
A changeful joy upon your mouth at noon,
And while you slept, the sprays and garlands sheathed you:
            Surges of roses!

Why did you loiter until dusk? You stumbled
Through walls of brambles where you lost your self.
Blindly you kissed the thorns and felt their sting,
And now you crouch, your forehead bowed and bleeding
And, stirred by night, a plethora of blooms
Is swirling down. Then let their crimson petals
Fall over your disgrace! Now learn the graveness
            And grief of roses!


## VOICES OF THE CLOUD CHILDREN

We of a filmier heaven
Secretly haunt your domains,
You of a lustier leaven,
Tied to your meadows and lanes.

277

We who are weightless and swift
Know it were best to refrain,
Yet we are driven to drift
Toward you again and again.

You who with ruthless and bold
Fingers dishevel our wreath,
Claim we are mocking and cold,
Clamour with faltering breath.

You who are sturdy as steel
Crush our defense, and we must
Calmly accept what you deal,
Though we are downed by your thrust.

Oh, let us love you and throng
Closer with undulant grace,
Though we can never belong
Wholly, nor match your embrace.

We a more delicate breed
Lean to you: Bridle your passion!
Your year and this year forbid
Fuller and sweeter possession.


RITES

To the grove where shadows thread,
Where our fathers' spirits passed,
Where the trail was overgrassed
And the pilgrims, seized with dread,

Walked in bonds to symbolize
Thraldom, where they slashed their own
Flesh to worship at a throne
Hidden from all human eyes,

Where in white and floating frock
Stood the priest, his cudgel stained
With the scarlet drops which drained
Slowly from the rough-hewn rock,

Now our hosts are headed there!
Naked save for golden, wide
Breastplates, two by two they stride,
Wreaths of leaves around their hair.

No more strangled victims! Now
Jets of purple wine are thrown,
Hiss against the burning bough,
Gush and trickle from the stone.

And instead of wild acclaim
For the gash, we dance and throng
To the beat of solemn song,
Through the purifying flame.

In the echoing and high
Vaults of ashes, odours sift
And between the foliage drift
Cobalt shreds of cloudless sky.


CONCEPTION

When you showed me leagues of wonder,
Gave my eyes the strength to see,
I was conjured by your thunder,

Helpless in the storm that ferried
Down to black immensity,
Then to craggy summits carried

One reborn to other glory.
And it seemed to me as though
— Clear and solved — your secret story

For an instant permeated
Me, your grace had set aglow
And your greatness devastated.

As if cliff and ground were quaking
And submerged, as if the thought
Of that hour were awaking

When you dazzled, when you held me,
And I yielded wholly, caught
In a rapture that compelled me.

Every heart-beat shall be idle
Save when you arouse my blood,
Fashion me to fit your bridle!

Lock in clouds that cling and glisten,
Take me for your vessel! Flood
All of me! I lie and listen.


LITANY

Deep is my sorrow,
        darkness surrounds me,
Lord, I am coming
        home to your halls.

Long was the voyage,
        weary and numbing,
Barren the altar,
        ripe my despair.

Parched for your vintage,
        thirsting I falter,
Much have I striven,
        stark is my arm.

Rest to my stumbling
          feet shall be given,
Nothing regales me,
          portion your bread!

Breath to incarnate
          phantasy fails me,
Hands became hollow,
          fevered my mouth.

Temper the fire,
          coolness shall follow,
Free me from yearning,
          lend me your light!

Love still besets me,
          burning and churning,
Only a strangled
          cry from the core.

Stifle my craving,
          heal what is mangled,
Ease me of passion,
          grant me your joy!


## ELLORA

Pilgrims, you have reached the gate
With your pack of worthless freight.
Leave the garland, leave the flute,
Shreds of solace, shreds of show,
Tints shall fade and sound be mute,
Light and voices cease to flow
On the threshold of Ellora.

High on socles ruby eyes
Glint from hall to portico.
Where the shadows float and nest
Rings of mourning opals glow,
People kneel with muffled cries,
Yearn for darkness, yearn for rest
In the chasms of Ellora.

Cast aside this call and clutch:
When our frenzy is allayed,
Racing of our pulses stayed,
Ivory columns cool to touch,
Altar steps of unhewn stone
Soothe the flame of flesh and bone
In the temples of Ellora.


SACRED LYRE

Are you still concerned with seeking
Outer balm for inner rot,
Filling buckets that are leaking,
Striving for what can be bought?

You are all and all you fashion:
Prayers in enchanted tide
Melt to one with every passion,
Call it God or friend or bride.

Never can an era borrow!
When a storm has cleansed the earth
You shall enter on your morrow,
Turn your eyes with magic force

To the fields within your keeping,
To the throng within your spell:
Land of dawn you once saw sleeping
As an image in a well.

Do not fancy you can capture
More than this: from summer sprays,
From the stars and breathless rapture
One consummate song of praise.


SONGS


OPENING CHORD

Stars are rising
And begin their song,
Stars are setting
And respond with song:

"This, your beauty,
Quickens worlds to course,
Were you mine
I could command their course.

This, your beauty,
Holds me unto death,
And your reign
Is fraught with thrall and death."

"To my beauty
You have given due,
And I vow
That I belong to you."


SONGS I-VI

I

This is a song
For only you,
Of childish fears
And fervent tears.

From dewy lawns it swings
On weightless wings,
And only you
This simple song
Shall move to rue.


II

My question erred
Through windy grey,
As faint as dream,
And you devised
A smile in turn.
A sudden light
From rain and night!
Now May will teem,
And visions rise
Of your hair and eyes!
Day after day
I wait and yearn.


III

Beside the stream
The hazels burst,
The very first!
A twitter sifts
From frosty spray,
A shimmer drifts,
A warming gleam
That shifts and fails.
The field's unsown,
The tree still grey.
Will flowers grace our trails
When spring's full-blown?

284

IV

In morning-dew
You came to see
The cherry tree
In bloom, with me,
And catch the musk
Of early grass.
No dust is here —
The fruit and leaf
Still in the husk.
So young the year
A flower-sheaf!
And southwinds pass.


V

In wintry haze
The freezing tree
Looms bare and high.
In silence raise
Your dream to him
As you go by.
His arms are spread —
More often fling
Him thanks that he
When all is sad
And cold and dim,
Can hope for spring.


VI

Here is the crossroads,
We're at the end.
Day will die soon,
This is the end.

Brief was the going,
Who has grown faint?
Weary for me soon,
Sorrow makes faint.
Hands were ready,
You did not clasp?
Sighs unsteady
You did not grasp?
This road is my road
Which you do not fare.
Tears are flowing,
You do not care.

## SONGS I-III

### I

Far from the noisy wharves
Stretches the sunlit shore,
Washed by the ebbing waves.
Hope flickers down and fails.
Then in the wind-swept sea
Breakers swell up and arch,
Rear to a crest and crash,
Taking the coast by storm
Passion and pain unleashed!
Louder the pounding surf
Hisses on hilly dunes,
Spatters a cloud of foam:
Love that is lost in moan.

### II

My child is home,
The seaweed tangled in his hair,
His gait still rocks
With fears he fought and young delight in quests.

                    The salty spray
Has touched and tinged his cheeks with deeper tan,
                    Fruit early ripe
In savage scents and flame of alien suns.


                    His eyes are grave
With secret things which I shall never know,
                    And faintly veiled
Since out of spring he came into our frost.


                    So rich the bud
That almost shyly I withdrew my gaze,
                    Denied myself
The lips that had already learned to kiss.


                    My arm enfolds
One who no longer moved by me, has grown
                    To other worlds,
My own, and yet how far from me, how far!



III


Love does not value one who feels a lack!
It waits in torment for a single glimpse,
And pours its treasures into thankless hands,
Exalts the flame in which it is consumed.


But be this as it may, my dear, I cloud
Your path to gladness, known to none but you,
And so I bleed and go. A fate revealed
Against my will shall not bewilder you.


But even more, my sweet: Lest any breath
Disturb your buoyance, I shall not return.
And doubly sad I leave, and pain is all
That speaks in me and this unheeded song.


287

## SOUTHERN SHORE: BAY

Often I roved along this very coast
— Like strings of pearls the cities, firm and proud —
For here I longed to play the wedding-host,
And yet a stranger takes the road.

And when I linger on a bridge I know
— Not wiser, only more disconsolate! —
I woo an old and tempting dream and go
Expectantly from gate to gate.

When dancers move with flowers in their hair,
Up in the hall, a swirl of gaudy frocks,
I track the waifs and beggars on the docks,
For loneliness is such despair.


## SOUTHERN SHORE: LAKE

Far is our home, a dark and desert plain
We left behind a range of snow and sleet,
No sound from there that does not call in vain,
This wonderland is still too strange and sweet.

Sharp-contoured pines and gentler olives grow
In gardens where a cool resplendence trails,
And on the smooth and sapphire lake below
Our boat is waiting with its yellow sails

Here in the scent of roses and of balms,
Where even the stern Lord of Endings stands
As if he only came to lavish alms,
And smiles and wanders lightly through the lands.

## SOUTHERN SHORE: DANCERS

The two of you were resting from the dance
Beneath the pines, so young and unconcerned,
A gay abandon in your open glance,
Your strong and graceful bodies taut and burned.

You rose in rhythmic motion, pure and blithe,
Into a plane of golden light you stepped
With slender loins, your shoulders broad and lithe,
And naked as the gods you swerved and leapt.

What urn, what frieze did you desert to pass
All readied for a feast, to life below,
Who kissed and bowed and circled to and fro,
And swung above the silver spangled grass!


## RHINE

Was it not a        beam that broke?
Was the vineyard        not in bloom?
Were not you the        friend for whom
I was searching        since I woke?

Did the river        conjure rain,
Scent of woods        and light of land?
Did a breath of        growth remain?
Shall I follow        tracks in sand?

Bees insist with        humming verve:
"Sacrifice the        old displays,
Dreams of former        nights and days,
Learn to reverence        and serve."

Broad horizons        where a faint
Hope is fused        with early glow!
But above an        arch a saint
Shows a wound of        long ago.

## RAVINE

Have walls of ancient rock been washed and worn
Away in this ravine by lashing hail?
And has a claw or fallen boulder torn
The knotty tree which rooted in the shale?

Is that a stain upon the ground, or here:
Those flakes you see, the greyish patches of
The feathers strewn in every cranny where
A falcon struck and carried off a dove?

Why do you fling yourself among the stones
And grooves, your head, your breast, and shoulders bare?
Why do you wince and call with broken tones
And weep into the earth in wild despair?


## WILD PARK

Misty shadows drip from the beeches,
Glossy grass climbs lustily higher,
Crowds the pond and shallows its reaches.
What a murmur wells from the mire!

Day is quenched in branches and bushes,
Stained with moss a naked and wan
God is framed in the crescent of rushes,
What a sigh has tempted you on!

Light your touch on the granite vases,
Fruit is withered, brittle the bough.
What a wind from infinite spaces,
What a withe has tangled your brow!

And you tremble, verging on dolour,
Guessing at joy you run to the gate.
What a flower has flaunted its colour,
What a beam has blazoned your fate!

Windows where at dusk I once
Looked across the fields with you,
Now are bright with alien light.

There the gate and there the path
Where you stood and did not turn
When you reached the downward bend.

At the curve, the moon again
Lit the pallor of your face,
But it was too late to call.

Dark and silence, sluggish air
Now as then besiege the house.
All delight has left with you.


How the tower glitters from the crags,
Calling up the bliss which summer brought,
And below our faint expectance lags,
Knowing winter came and doors are shut.

Every valley seems to lead us there,
And the gable shines in icy thatch,
But we sadly shun the threshold where
We were banished when we dropped the latch.

Tears and groping never can retrace
Rites that were, or move the bolt. Oh, when
Shall we break the seals, and full of grace
Enter and approach the shrine again,

From the sacred vessel take the host
Which has always healed our every sting?
Shall we see the golden key we lost
In the snow, agleam in grass of spring?

We long to stay and foot the dance with you!
We love the charming valley just as much:
The slanted meadow daubed with many hues,
    Fragrant beneath the morning's touch.

We like to gather blossoms and to skim
The velvet dust from moth and dragonfly,
To make them serve a swift and graceful whim,
    While ripples flicker by.

But over heath and ledges, rough and bare,
An urge impels us to a find in store,
The pointed stones and thorny creepers tear
    Our hands, our feet are sore.

And yet a matchless transport may accrue
To us when on a path beset with dooms,
Close to the chasm, crystalline and blue,
    The magic flower blooms.


SONGS I-III

I

Mourning crape in festive chambers!
Wails of sorrow shrill and float!
But through doleful dirges clambers
Bright and strong a youthful note.

Fields that would not thrive, are covered
With a misty copper hue,
But when on your locks it hovered
It was deepened by your glow.

Come and break apart the dreary
Air in days of weighing pall,
Succour me, the sick and weary,
Pour your light into my fall.

II

"Whenever I approach your house,
I send a prayer up to you
As though you lay within it dead."

When I set foot upon your bridge,
A whisper from the river says
That it was here I saw you first.

And when you chance to cross my path,
My eyes no longer cling — they turn
From you unmoved, without salute,

And greet you only from within,
The way we do when to his last
Repose a stranger passes by.


III

Must you insist on your rights,
Spectre, at dusk and at dawn?
Mingle with all my delights,
Snatch at your tithe of my gain?

Am I still eager to feed
You, who have mined out my core,
Emptied the wine which I bore?
Do I still bask in your greed?

Shall I deny you a part?
Sated with torment you gave,
Shackle you down in a grave?
Hammer a stake through your heart?

## THE FEAST

When you discard your garments, when you cord
Wreaths for your brow, when torches scent the air,
The day no longer weighs you with its care,
You are in bondage to another lord!

When rooms grow wide with shadows, when the lights
Leap from the bowls in green, and red, and blue,
When horns and pipes release you and unite,
You break the chain your will devised for you.

The feast crescendoes to a frenzied tide,
Where kisses stain with blood and singe with fire,
Where all are fused and lost in one desire,
One breath alive in those the god has tried.

But when the dance no longer weds the throng,
When limbs from sweet besieging are unwound,
Then through the darkness wells a mournful sound,
And tears are dropped on garlands worn too long.


## BEYOND

You laid the trowel aside and were content
With what you built, but suddenly you thought
That it was nothing but the fundament
    Of that for which no stone was cut.

You trod the moss and plaited flower and frond,
And spring and autumn gave you of their share,
But when you gazed across to peaks beyond
    You chose to seek your fortunes there.

While you exalted foreign wines, and you
The waxen apples overseas, the ground
Was littered with the fruit your gardens grew,
    And berries withered all around.

And while you listened to the golden brawl
Of bees or to the westwind's haunting sigh,
You very often failed to hear the call
    Of all the sweet that passed you by.


HOMECOMING

Tired pilgrims who are frozen
To our day, you slowly fare
Homeward where no wishes cozen,
Where you rise from old despair.

And you show your spectral counties
To the stranger bowed in pain,
Promise that their gentle bounties
Soon will make him whole again.

None will rue the peace of fasting,
Silence free from hopeless sighs,
And a span of longed-for resting
Will content him as he dies.

But before you enter under
Arches of those calm demesnes
Know: This heart will burst asunder
With the fires it restrains.


From the furrows of the plain
Where the voices drone and flicker
Cruder in the crowds and thicker,
To the hills I stormed again.

From the houses weighed with scent,
From the gardens lush and tumbled,
From the forest black and jumbled,
Up to clearer air I went.

295

Now my head is proud and free.
Are you calling from your hollow?
Will you conjure me to follow?
Will you teach me how to see?

And above the swirl and smoulder,
Fumes and perfumes which I shun,
Floats a magic, greater, older:
You are sovereign and withdrawn.


This is not the realm of light
Where I reigned and where I wooed,
Alien sky and latitude,
Meagre tufts on arid site.

Barren tracts of sand, the bole
Of a twisted tree is sprung
— Thinly webbed with green — among
Puny weeds on wilted knoll.

What a sound is this I hear!
Whisper trailing from the bough,
By your voice I guess you, now
I shall see you, you are near.

I have neither aim nor clue,
None has joy of me or need,
All I know is that you lead,
Even here I follow you.


Forsaken the passion,
The god's incarnation!
A call from the chasm
Now governs creation.

The craving is shallowed,
The fires, the ravage
Are flooded and swallowed
By torrents more savage.

No more let us proffer
The vow that united,
In parting I offer
My lips to the plighted.

Their gesture and glances
Seem almost to fear me,
I shun their advances,
But you are still near me.


## TABLETS


## TO MELCHIOR LECHTER

To your mind, proud and free, and immune to distress,
In the vessel of fate, metal purged of its dross!

To your soul that has bowed realms of dream to its will,
Year by year dazzles us and the world with its fill!

To your life, for the lonely a solace and guide,
Pharos flaming through time in the dark of the tide.


## TO KARL AND HANNA

Though on your quests for beauty you amassed
The gaudy spoils of life in rich variety,
You shall extol one day which glorifies your past
And points with holy finger into times to be.

## TO GUNDOLF

Why probe so much in men who are remote, why read the legends through,
If you yourself can find the words to tell a later age:
You, for a time, were this to me, and I was that to you!
Is this not light and truth beyond what zeal can gauge?


## MEMORY OF BRUSSELS:   PERLS

I think of how your fevered glances met
The fretwork of Saint Gudula ... You drained
The light which warmed the park before it waned,
And down the Treurenberg you dragged your feet.


## GHOSTS:   TO H.

Their eyes, blind to the day, are fixed on graves and broken stone,
They dig the treasure up from tainted tombs. If none
Can save them, they will melt away before they call their own
Gold laughter and the golden light of dawn.


## KAIROS

The day had come, the star was toward,
The gate ajar for you, the lord.
And yet you left the hour unscored!
This star alone could make you lord.


## TO HENRY

Since life has fenced you in with beauty, flood
And chasm need not ever chill your blood.
Attached to none, by everyone adored,
You shun the last encounter — last reward!

298

## GUARDIANSHIP

You wisely locked behind protecting doors
Your comely son, ablaze like burning tinder,
You kept him stainless for his first of whores...
Bare is the house, the grate is filled with cinders.

## JUGGLER

You blind yourself to darken other sight,
Your flames, that seem unending, hiss, and swarm,
And fume, and veer, but never shine and warm.
They send the evil dreams that haunt by night.

## NORDICS

You reach your every goal with steady plod,
When lightning strikes, you too feel beauty, but
You were not made for frenzy! Who is shut
From this, can never know the highest god.

## ERNESTO LUDOVICO: DIE SEPT. MENS. SEPT.

Time passes on, the hours flee, delight has fled.
They come with us and open wide their hands.
Salute to him who smiles on each, from him
Who yields a hundred for a single one.

## IN MEMORIAM ELISABETHAE

Through awful space, and rift from soul to soul, a grief
Unfurls its song and journeys to the empty house,
Evokes the garden and the child who hid in play,
And filled the air with laughter which has died away.
This song can do no more than conjure tears on hands
Supreme in pain — for only they may reach for what
Is gone — and whisper: Is there anything in all
The world more bitter than the death of a young dream?

## TO SABINE

The autumn colours twined the heat
Of summer and its rueful hours
Into a legend, ripe and sweet.
More faintly our desires throbbed
When golden children laughed and sobbed,
And so the season was replete:
A garland wreathed of fruit and flowers.


## TO A JESUIT

Return, O suave and clever fathers, though
With bane and dagger, for your ways outshine
The traitor's who backs equal rights. A mean
Like this is every people's subtlest foe!


## TO VERWEY

We feverishly strained to hear a word
From overseas, as if the war were ours!
So few can brave the never-conquered dragon!

While all the world acclaimed the daring venture,
No one had eyes for silent hands of heroes.
Then came the wretched end! A deal — a yoke!
Masses are worthless now! No hope, no ways
Or weapons of this world can bring relief.


## G. v. V.

Nowhere did your tortured spirit find its tune.
To the farthest cities ceaselessly you travelled,
On to China's gardens, and among the ravelled
Grasses stained with blood, you rest on barren dune.

300

## TO CARL AUGUST KLEIN

Have we not shared alike
      fortunes and visions, courses and aim?
Did we not mingle our blood
      to be brothers in strife?
Was it the will of a star
      that the decade is even the same
Wherein we loosen the old
      bond in the hope of new life?


## TO HANNA WITH A PICTURE

No one but you will ever gauge the pain,
The year of grief, the anguish of the lonely.
This picture is unowned. Take it! The only
Heart here on earth to which I turn again.


## TO ROBERT: I BRIDGE

Water, whirl across the rocks below
Blackened girders of the bridge! Your wild
Tumble soon will steady to a mild
Current in my river's kingly flow!


## II EVENING IN ARLESHEIM

You wait forsaken on a darkening road,
And full of mournful thoughts you doubt and cower,
For you the fruits of earth have grown too sour,
For your sick heart an urge is like a goad.

With poise which we have drawn from dream and daring,
And all the marks which tears and kisses made,
To go together into light and shade!
On all the rest the New Life has no bearing.

## TO UGOLINO

Our minds, which swerve to different zones, divide
Our lives much more than seas with ebb and tide.
But I am grateful for your gentle tears
Across the gap of dreams, and waves, and years.

## TO LOTHAR

Wait till the humid mists no longer bow
The soul that sifts the ashes of the dead.
You mourned the fate of those I loved, and now
I never shall forget the tears you shed.

## TO ERNST

You draw your shades against the morning light
And every wish. You shyly wait and muse,
And your punctilious, faithful hand pursues
Its work contrived of spider-webs and night.

## TO DERLETH

Your valiant thrusts were apt to slay and flay,
And now you press inexorable wants.
But when will you return from ghostly haunts,
Led by a love that strengthens day by day?

In this we are alike within our round:
That unrestrained by house and chattels, we
Alone, wherever we may chance to be,
Can rise and follow when the fanfares sound.

## TO A POET

Behold these buds which deep in your ravine
Autumnal light and gentle showers round,
But only when the fullest sun abounds
Can they unfold their most relucent sheen.

302

## TO ANNA MARIA

"You flaunt your many charms, but lack what fate
Will soon demand of you, what steels and kindles.
The oil within your lamps, O sisters, dwindles
Our offerings, foolish virgins, make us great."

Your ruthless glance implies that we are tares,
Our aims a froth — but sometimes, waspish nun,
Your smile transforms the darkness into sun,
And field and town to marts of magic wares.


## TO A POET

In your green and growing hour
Rays you give and brightest colours,
With foreboding of all dolours,
Though the world is still in flower.


## RHINE: I

Two queenly sisters as their own define
The middle of the inner realm, but from
Aeons of sleep the third true child will come
And raise the crown long buried in the Rhine.


## RHINE: II

And one arose! His mighty trident flails
The spurting waters red with hidden gold!
From barren sameness cliffs and shore unfold,
And living glory springs from lifeless tales.


## RHINE: III

You pour from whirling chasms with the groan
And force of tempests to the Kingly Town,
You rush from Silver Town through Golden Town
To spires reared in consecrate Cologne.

303

## RHINE: IV

You ask me if the land is not aghast
At all the filth and offal it amassed.
Into the cleansing sea I spew afar
The odious scum of reddle, chalk, and tar.

## RHINE: V

This is our land as long as fields are proud
With grain and fruit, the vineyards mount in lustre,
And spires thrust their challenge into cloud,
While in the crannies rose and lilac cluster!

## RHINE: VI

Do not proclaim the Feast, the Kingdom Come,
The new-made wine that brims the new-made bowl,
Until your spirit, obstinate and numb,
Throbs with my fiery blood, my Roman soul!

## MADONNA IN COLOGNE

"When sadly from the west I came, you taught
Me joy, Madonna, on the homeward stretch."
"A people, clear as well as deep, once brought
Me forth: the smiling Virgin with the Vetch."

## PICTURE: ONE OF THE THREE WISE MEN

To you, new Lord, I bring my dues. Now give
Me leave to journey to my native town.
I still am young and light of heart and live
For golden trinkets, for my darling crown.

## NORTHERN PAINTER

We brooded through the night to find the clue
To both your secret and your flaw. You rimmed
Your painted heavens with the residue
Of light around a fallen angel's limbs.


## NORTHERN SCULPTOR

If you could break these chains and cast away
The husk that mars perfection, then you might
Transcend the heavy texture of the clay
And dare to lift your work into the light.


## COLMAR: GRUENEWALD

On earth his limbs endured the hangman's nail,
The hooves of monsters and their fetid hair,
That he might see himself — an instant — smile
Triumphant in a globe of rosy air.


## HEISTERBACH: THE MONK

The triumphs, tales, and towers which determine
Your worth, were only yours because you prayed.
The world of now, a world where prayers fade,
Is chaff before the Lord, and you but vermin.


## HOUSE IN BONN

Before you wage the battle of your star,
I sing of strife and gains on higher stars.
Before you know the bodies on this star,
I shape you dreams among eternal stars.

## WORMS

The world awoke: A distant wind blew treasures
And southern blooms into our northern day.
Then came the frost: disputes and dour measures...
The fairest spring escaped us in dismay.


## WINKEL: THE GRAVE OF GUENDERODE

You were the symbol of a land of lore:
Its aimless flame and moon, its ghostly spark
Were quenched through you beside this very shore...
An empty boat drifts down the Rhine at dark.


## AACHEN: DESECRATORS OF GRAVES

Is this what drives you? Then your crime is less!
Your fear of pitch and sulphur sets you scratching
In sacred tombs. You grope because you guess
That at the gate the end's already hatching.


## HILDESHEIM

Let not the raid on holy places flood
Your hearts with fury for the cold canaille!
The Thousand-Year-Old Rose has — so they say —
In faithful keeping born a golden bud.


## QUEDLINBURG

Niched in the oval arch and massive wall,
The saints and the anointed reel in gales:
We still protect the height although it pales!
There in the east, the sands will mock your call.

306

## MUNICH

O soil, as yet untouched by double bane,
Walls where the spirits still are free to roam!
O town of youth and strength! Our only home
Is where we see Our Lady's spires reign.

## OLD HOUSES IN THE AU

The painted dormers, timbers grey with time,
The shingles conjure worlds that once have been.
To us the village wit's incessant rhyme
Is sorrow sounding on a sleepy green.

## BOZEN: ERWIN'S SHADOW

Voices blurred in the fragrant night, the sheen
Which quivers on the walls, the tremulous
Pulse of the earth — was this accorded us
Because we go where, Erwin, you have been?

## BAMBERG

You, the most alien, sprang — when there was need —
A lawful scion from your people's flank.
Does not this shrine portray you on your steed,
Proud and contending as a kingly Frank?

And carven — neither Ghibelline nor Guelph —
In the imperial chamber, you are shown:
A silent artist who surpassed himself
And waits bemused for God to do his own.

## TRAUSNITZ: CONRADIN'S CASTLE

Here, like your brothers spent in soul, you turned
Away from level land and native stream,
With the impassioned gaze of those who yearn
South to the mountains as to gates of dream.

307

## SISTER CITIES

None will recall our tubas' blaring note
When every nation still will hold sublime
The trace of heroes, gods, who for a time
Ruled in this city, rustic and remote.

And here you threaten from the peak: the last
And lustrous star before the era wanes.
Your foot upon our neck, to be disgraced
By you meant more than any vapid gains.

## SHRINE

How flat the mobs and sounds of many a city ring!
A Holbein painting seems the only living thing.
And this: the death-mask of the head of one
Who like no other spat his scorn at man.

## QUAY

Who can regard this whirl with other thoughts
(The thud of many feet, of hoof and hub)
Than those the emperor had who ordered brought
Ten thousand spiders gathered in a tub.

But tall against the railing stood a youth,
Bare-headed, well above the din, and lost
In looking at the sky, the only truth!
With pallid hand he called and banished ghosts.

## CITY SQUARE

You — whether kings or hoi-polloi — pursue
An idol who transforms your gold to cheap
And common coin. My people, I shall weep
When you atone with bondage, need, and rue.

308

# CENTENARY LINES

## I

Ten thousand perish wordless, one alone,
The founder, gives the name. One sounds the tone
Ten thousand tongues will sing. Each age has only
One god, and only one proclaims his throne.

## II

You too gave up your birthright for a dole.
Soon you will take your precious gains for trash,
Accept as truth a hocus, mad and rash.
What's loose, alas! and runs on naked sole!

## III

A man! A deed! The people and the council plead.
Look not to one who shared your feasts! For one who kept
Beside your slayers many years, or one who slept
Behind your prison bars, may rise and do the deed.

## IV: BATTLE

From far away I saw the flash of war
Such as will soon be rampant at our door.
The group I saw around the flag was small...
And no one else saw anything at all.

## V: UPHEAVALS IN THE EAST

This clash will be a sawdust conflagration,
Unless one man transcends the aimless rage!
But who can fan true fires in a nation
That is a blend of childhood and old age?

309

VI

"Only the most remote can bring renewal!"
The teeming spring resounds with this refrain.
A single wedding cures two ills: dispersal
And too much tasting of a honeyed bane.


TEMPTER I

"Strew out this sand and twice you milk your cows
And thresh your grain, the grape gives double yield.
Now mock your thrifty fathers and carouse."
But wait a year, and all is sear and sealed!

With shrillest of sounds the strings on their lyres grate:
"Straight and yet bent, one and yet none, god and yet brute!"
Dance through the world and through time! A marvel, a fête!
He who can pick out the theme, though, will laugh and be mute!


TEMPTER II

Our sum is not complete, we lack the three,
And want the two to double us, so we
Shall now evoke the four imploringly
From fog and madness, spook and witchery.


CORTEGE OF MASKS

The gods are winding down along the ramp
With him who sows their love and hate, who trailed
Life into death. But first to come and veiled
Is one: the man and mother, with the lamp.

Where once they were conceived, they now must go
To fetch the spark that lights celestial portals.
At every turn of tide they fare below
And bow in service at the feet of mortals.

310

## FEASTS

The common day has blurred the image now,
But here, in times of senselessness and horrors,
They came with torches, wreaths around their brow:
The first procession of the new adorers.


## FOR THE END OF THE SEVENTH RING

Breakers reared and crashed in a turbulent sea,
Wreckage and bodies sank in a rancorous sea.
Later a flicker beneath the siderial gold:
Shores encrusted with pearls, and coral, and gold.


## IDEM: QUESTION

"You, more aloof than kings, whose lordly glances gave
The verdict that his brothers' work was scum,
Who are you, stranger?" "Nothing but the lowly slave
Of one who — with the dawn — is yet to come!"


## IDEM: OUT! OUT!

Out with the witches and the wizards who
Are still abroad! The light is crowding through
The cracks. The house is clean. He only may
Return who dares to shed his sheath by day.


## IDEM

From fallow fields of home these verses sprang,
And grew without a breath from foreign spheres,
What sounded hieratic now appears
As something spoken in a kindred tongue.

## IDEM: TO WACLAW

This book was still a blank at our farewell.
My native soil has fed its every stage.
Now I am glad that on the final page
Still — at the last — your noble shadow fell.


## IDEM

Our parting draught! And though the words you say
Still move, your hands still warm me, yet today
I feel more free than ever, and inured
To friend and foe — prepared for any road.

# THE STAR OF THE COVENANT

## (1913)

## PREFACE TO THE SECOND EDITION OF THE STAR
## OF THE COVENANT

This book was courted by misunderstandings which, though it is easy to see how they arose, were utterly unfounded. It was said that the poet had dealt with actualities of the present rather than with distance and dream, and that he had set out to write a breviary for the people and more especially for the younger generation fighting at the front. But the truth of the matter is this: THE STAR OF THE COVENANT was originally intended for a circle of intimate friends and only the consideration that in our day it is hardly possible to conceal what has been shaped in words, led to the decision to publish as the best means of protection. The torrent of world events which followed immediately upon publication made wider strata emotionally receptive for a volume which might have remained a sealed book for years to come.

# INTROIT

You, always our beginning, end, and middle,
Our song of praise on your terrestrial journey
Now rises to your star, O Lord of Turning!
We saw a darkness laid across the land,
The temple tottered and the inner fires
No longer roused us, gnawed by other fevers
Than those that urged our fathers to the victors,
Serene and poised on thrones unreached and squandered
Our noblest blood in lust for far horizons.
Then you, our own from native stock, appeared
Before us in the naked glow of godhood.
No statue was so fair, no dream so real.
Then out of hallowed hands fulfilment flooded,
And there was light, and all desire died.


You took away the pain of inner schism,
You, who were fusion made incarnate, bringing
The two extremes together: light and frenzy!
To domes above the clouds you were the pleader,
Who wrestled with the spirit, held it fast,
And turned a victim at the given hour.
In spring you loved the river, slim and naked
You clung in its caress, and you were also
The sleeper, sweet among the meadow-grasses
To whom a habitant of heaven leaned.
We celebrated you with palms and roses,
And to your twofold beauty offered homage,
But did not know we knelt before the body
In which the birth of god had come to pass.


You do not know me, but let this be told:
I have not yet begun on words and actions
Earth asks of man, and now the year's at hand
When I shall find another form of being.
I change and still I keep my changeless substance.
I cannot be like you! My choice is made.

So bring the holy branches and the garlands
And carry forth the flawless flame. Farewell!
My step already falls on other paths.
I am already what I willed. In parting
Accept what only one like me can give:
My breath that shall revive your strength and courage,
My kiss that shall be branded in your spirit.


The waters rise, and my unbridled heart
Is roused with passion blazing through millennia,
Which it desires to spend in depths and brightness
And never can discharge to mere reflections.
Its sigh pursues the waves as if it hunted
A creature which escaped and still escapes.
It finds no help until these drops of blood
Have vanished in the loud, unending current.
Then you, the god, emerge before my eyes,
And saturate with you I see you only.
Your earthly vesture, such a slender shrine,
A span which scarcely fills the arm that clasps it,
Snares every thought agog for stars, and conjures
Me here within the day for which I live.


Was time again at zenith? Wells of flame,
"As if a world were just to be created!"
Resplendent peak of noon, yet spectres flitted...
The night with dances round the open fires,
The golden boys with torches and the ivory
Girls bearing garlands! Flutes resounded shrilly,
And storms of kisses lashed us lip to lip.
Then, with the dawn, the spirit caught us close,
And frenzied questions cried for frenzied answers,
Beguiled us into plighting faith and death-vows,
Until in utmost awe we pleaded: Grace us,
O voice and rhythm in our curbless welter,
O crown and consecration of our prayers,
O beam that splits the darkness of our dream!

317

Then stately shadows gathered in the chamber
And climbing curves of fume were shot with flashes.
Reflected bygones quivered: early beings
Of timeless night beside the proud and lovely.
They flowed and flickered on metallic lustres,
They strained and struggled to acquire substance,
Involved us in their torment and grew paler.
How helplessly we waited in their circle!
Where is the hearth ablaze with earthly fires?
Where is the stainless blood that will allay us?
Nebulous vapours, thicken! Mass to bodies!
Dip upward, silver feet, from purple waters!
So through our passioned incantations sounded
The mournful summons for a living kernel.


Resigned I face the riddle that he is
My child, and I the child of my own child,
That Fate commands the great to spring from stuff
Of earth and then, unstained by deed, to fare
Homeward with smiles and sorrow, that her law
Decrees that he who sacrificed his blood
For all and for himself, shall be fulfilled,
And only through his death beget the deed.
The strongest root feeds on eternal night.
You who surround and question me, let this
Suffice: Through him alone I now am yours.
My life was forfeit, yet I was reborn.
Leave the unfathomed, bow your heads with me,
Calling "O saviour!" through the winds of dread.


With you I now grow back through generations,
More close to you in a more secret bond.
I find you in the works of kingly forbears,
You shine in tales of feud and heady venture,
You are the living core — though chastely veiled —
In fervent words of sage and seer. The blood's
Inheritance unweakened through the ages,
Which lords it over lordliest of neighbours:

This is the throbbing flame, the golden tide
You sow in cycles — and the world bears fruit!
And what a day, what hope and what fulfilment,
When you reveal yourself and stand among us,
Heart of the ring, the image born of earth,
The essence of our people's sacred youth.


Who is your god? All that my dreams avowed,
Kin to my vision, beautiful and proud.
He is the force the lap of darkness vented,
The sum of every greatness we were granted,
The deepest source, the inmost blaze — he is
Where I have found the purest form of these.
He flooded every vein with richer teeming
Who first for one was rescue and redeeming.
He filled the gods of old with fresher breath,
And all the words the world has done to death.
The god is veiled in highest consecration,
With rays around he manifests his station,
Embodied in a son whom stars begot
And a new center conjured out of thought.


BOOK ONE


"Since now your tempest, O thunderer, shatters the clouds,
Your winds incite disaster and topple the ramparts,
Is not the stalking of verses a labour unblest?"
"The solemn harp-strings and even the flexible lyre
Utter my will through the rising and falling of time,
Utter the changeless design of the fixed constellations.
And words like these you shall keep in your heart: That no saviour,
No prince can grow on this planet unless the breath
He draws at birth, is suffused with the chanting of seers,
Unless his cradle is rocked in a song of the great."

319

"All your youth sped lightly as a dance,
As the trill of flutes, the call of clarions?"
"Lord, with this I lured your shining children,
Scouted trifling pleasure for your song,
Took the yoke of pilgrimage upon me,
Searched until I found you in their radiance.
Day and night, since I have had a life
Of my own, I did this only: hunted
You on every way and quay."


Now that your seed I carried in distress,
And nourished with myself, and nursed through dangers,
Has risen green and deathless, I have one
More hunger while sweet light is still about me:
To keep the place you chose for me, and even
Though friends applaud, disciples utter praise,
Desist from setting words to hidden rhythms,
And in the fret and clatter of the rabble
Unflinchingly protect your holy secret.


The highest act of grace is that you live
And only reel at each allotted thrust,
Double and split beneath the blows of Fate.
For many are destroyed in first encounters,
The best confront the second: stand and perish.
But you held out! So obdurately armed
That what would crush another leaves you sound:
When near the goal you find one more elect,
You do not waste your strength on impious lunge,
But burn with joy to be the first to serve.


When as a youth you recognized your calling,
You were an outcast walled in clammy air.
Your single self sustained the pain of all.
Then such a cry broke from your lips and mounted
Up to the stars, that earth and heaven flinched.
And stars with greater force intoned their answer
Than ear of man had ever heard before.

It snared and swept you upward: Stay! Who takes
So strange a course has none to guide him, only
What you have helped create can help you, never
Condemn your grief, for you yourself are grief.
Reverse the symbol and reverse the song!

That things we cannot grasp are deeply bedded
In former lives, is the conceit of poets.
Your every work shall match your earliest dream!
From grains of dust you realized the state,
Walked as if led and knew that you were chosen.
"You fought a universe which rose against you,"
Established codes and language, set the norm.
Your labours done, you portioned out your realm
And went serenely on to wider reaches.

Those you gave light to mount the way to you
Know they must not reveal you, and that words
Which might convey you, set before the people,
Are valid for a time and then decay
Unless a new awakener brings renewal.
Before I wring from you my full allotment
I must attempt to solve the one enigma:
How to adjust to space which you have meted,
Perform the task each day demands, and venture
The mating with the vision of tomorrow.

Call it the bolt that struck, the sign that pointed,
This thing which reached me at the given hour,
This germ of life, impalpable yet real!
Call it the spark that spurted out of nothing,
Call it return of circling thought. No word
Can hold it. As a force, a flame it quickens
The image in the world of earth and God.
I am not here to bring what comes once only,
I curve an age that tends to arrow-straightness,
I lead the round and wrest into the ring.

Do words beget the deed, or deeds the word?
In days of old the city called the bard,
And though his limbs were weak his verse aroused
The broken host, and it was he who led
To triumph long delayed. So — with a smile —
Fate interchanges role and stuff. My dream
Turned flesh and ushered into life a form
Shaped of sweet earth. His step is firm: the child
Of deepest passion and transcendent thrall.


I am the One, I am the Two,
I am the womb, I am the sire,
I am the shadow and the true,
I am the faggot and the fire.
I am the bow, I am the shaft,
I am the seer and his prediction,
I am the sheath, I am the haft,
I am abundance and affliction,
I am the victim and the slayer,
I am the symbol and the meaning,
I am the altar and the prayer,
I am an end and a beginning.


The wrath of heaven broke from crimson clouds:
I turn away from nations such as this.
The soul is sick! The deed is dead!
The only ones whose steps I still pursue
With grace, are those who fled in golden triremes
To holy pales, who play my harps, and tender
Their offerings in my temple — and those others,
Still groping for the way, who filled with fervour
Reach out into the setting sun. And all
The rest is night and nothingness


Having all and knowing all, they still complain:
Life is meagre! Want and hunger everywhere!
Lack of fill!

Brimming lofts are under every roof:
Grain that scatters and is stacked anew,
No one takes!
Cellars down in every hall where wines
Dry or ooze away into the sand,
No one drinks!
Tons of gold abandoned in the dust,
Men in tatters brush it with their hems,
No one sees!


The eras which your time that seems so free,
So mild and wise, indicts as dark and savage,
Strove on — at least — through torture, madness, dread,
Through twist, and maze, and murder — on to God.
You traitors are the first to throttle God,
To carve an image, not like him, invent
Endearing names for what is more than monstrous,
And hurl the best you have into its jaws.
You call it your approach and will not check
Your dull and barren speed until all venal
And base alike, instead of God's red blood
The pus of idols circles in your veins.


You build beyond all metes and bounds. What's high
Could be still higher! But no patch or prop
Or new foundation serves. The structure quakes.
And at your wisdom's end you howl to heaven:
"Do what to keep from choking in the rubble,
The spook we shaped from gnawing at our brains?"
But Heaven laughs: "Too late to stop or mend!
Ten thousand must submit to holy madness,
Ten thousand perish in the holy plague,
And tens of thousands in the holy war!


Above the silent town a streak of blood!
And then a storm exploded from the darkness,
And through spasmodic gusts I heard the tramping
Of hosts, first dim then near, the clash of iron.

And proud and threatening rang a thrice divided
Metallic call, and I was overwhelmed
With rage and strength, and yet I felt a shudder
As if a sword sank flat upon my head.
A quicker beat, and faster marched the columns,
And more and more battalions, and the selfsame
Stridor of fanfares. Can this be the last
Tumult the gods have staged above this land?


Speak not of the supreme! While you are flawed
You drag it down to what you think and are.
God is a spectre when your spirit rots.
Speak not of woman! Not until you grasp
Her law: to moan in lust beneath the sharp
And fecund impact of a stronger stuff.
Speak not of simple folk! For none of you
Can guess what governs clod and threshing-floor,
Knows how to mingle, rise, or sink again
And how to knot the ravelled golden fibres.


And one emerged who keen as flash and steel
Revealed abysses and divided camps,
Reversed your Here to fashion out a There,
Who dinned into your heads that you were mad,
With such insistence that his throat was cracked.
And you? The shrewd or dull, the false or true,
You acted as if nothing had occurred.
You hear and gape, you talk, and laugh, and breed.
The warner passed. And now no hand will seize
The spokes: The wheel is hurtling toward the chasm.


"Consider what the blaze will do to scrolls,
To precious images you prize as we."
If they were left to you, your acid drivel
Your morgues for art would ruin them far more
Than wreckage and the lap of Mother Earth.

324

Perhaps that once from even scanter fragments,
Sheltered by rubble, from a broken wall,
Corroded metal, weatherbeaten stone
Or yellowed script life will again be kindled.
The way in which you hoard is sheer decay!


A sunset world, and once again the Lord
Went to the city graced with gates and temples,
And he who came to raze, was poor and mocked.
He knew, no mortared stone may keep its place
If the foundation, if the whole shall stand.
And those who were at odds, though like in purpose,
Countless their busy hands, and big and countless
Their words, though there was need of only one!
A sunset world — they frolicked and they sang,
And all of them looked right, but he looked left.


Fear not the bruise, the gash, the wound, the sprain!
The magic that destroys builds up again.
Each thing is fair and perfect as before,
Yet other breath has slipped into its core.
Whatever has received a name is laid:
A stalk without the pith, a blunted blade,
Those who conformed or longed for what is done.
Bring crown and garland for the Nameless One!


Helpers of yesterday, the judgment nears!
Its pros and cons dissolve all other bonds
And silence former loves and tears of two.
We crossed the bar and you remained behind.
With strength, and skill, and earnest zeal you change
Celestial manna into lethal poppies
And — like the rest — drive toward an evil end,
So that the best among your sons resemble
A pack of mongrels, and the final vestige
Of dream is blotted from your children's brows.

You who must yearn immured in self, who let
Your fancy rove because what's solid irks you,
Stay guiltless in the twilight you exalt,
One move ahead and life becomes a lie.
You are comprised in us, not we in you.
Whatever you achieve hails from the substance
You mock and call unreal, and near the verge
You wait and clamour: "Ecstasy, engulf us!
Embrace us, vast beyond! Break through, O sun,
Solution!" But what comes is only night.


One way alone is left. The time grows short.
The adamant we held eternal, quakes.
But yield what will, that stock which firmly holds
To what it long divined, shall have its say.
The noble are fulfilled when they perfect
Their image, though the price be life itself.
The base live on like larvae, callous to
Perfection, and at last put up with death.
To stars you spun your thoughts and music, now
Probe what is more: the spell of finite form!


You, the extremes: the one from barren snow-drifts
And wave-swept cliffs, the other from the glowing
Wastes of a spectral god, are both at equal
Remove from radiant seas and fields where mortals
Live out their lives and shape themselves and gods.
Fair-haired or dark, the selfsame womb begot you.
Each hates and seeks and does not know his brother,
And always roams and never is fulfilled.


You ride in headlong haste and have no goal.
You ride, a whirlwind, over sea and land.
You ride through men and yearn for one to bind you

326

Who never can be bound, for one to fill you
Who never can be filled, and shun a peace
Where no one will confront you but yourself
From whom you flinch as from your foulest foe,
And your escape? The death you deal yourselves!


You were created for an age of heroes
And dark beginnings — not for later days!
And so you must set out for alien regions.
Your precious blood — a beast's, a child's — will spoil
If not alloyed in realms of grain and wine.
Your ferment works in other stuff than yours.
You light-haired hosts, how often has your god
Done you to death when you had almost won!


Titanic and not wholly shapen forces,
Our era which has marked the faintest rumble,
The frailest swirl of dust within its book,
Heard all, knew all, yet not what really was,
Was deaf to you when under earth you thundered.
It might have held you, saturate with bygones,
And used your heady drive, but it ignored you
Who hovered in the shadow of oblivion.
So back to night you plunge, your strength untapped,
Smouldering sparks around the inner light.


Your gaze is like the eagle's who serenely
Soars toward the sun and only drops to strike.
Your kindred are the men who turned to scourges
And ropes to curb the all-too venal flesh,
Who spurred the flaccid mind with wrath and rigour,
Or Francis, chaste and pure, who crossed the land
And shed on offal his seraphic light,
Bernard who roused the rapture of crusaders.
But you, the tardy champion, found no room
Within the weary Church. Her lap had narrowed.
She could no longer take your earthy strength.

You flicker over ancient walls, a goblin
Athirst for pregnance, crouch beneath the arches
And suck the aftermath of life from ruins.
You touched the fragments of an urn, a kylix,
And what you thought rose palpably before us:
The golden columns hung with garlands, braziers
Of bronze which fumed beside the purple couches,
And intertwined in every form of union
The bodies milk and rose, and brown and copper,
A foot that faltered and then crossed the threshold...
But day was hostile to the throng of shadows,
The spook was gone the coiled and wanton splendours
Of Rome, the harlot who had kings for lovers!


All can be doubted since the one evades!
The spirit blindly struggled from the yoke,
The truant soul became an idle joke,
All can be shouted: thresh on empty blades.
From ferment, tumult, chrysalis, and night
Now wrest the heart engrossed in rage and scorn.
The earth is swept with joy, the deed is born!
The image, free and naked, fronts the light!


BOOK TWO


Render your spirit to rest
Under immaculate clouds,
Drive it to listen and link
Long with the dread of the night,
Till it is tempered and strong,
And you demolish your shell,
No longer silent and numb
When you are roused by the god,
Bound in the breath of your love.

"Release me from the first too facile promise.
Since such a flame was not enough to forge me
Count me among the sluggish souls, I am
Not fit for further rites." — "Do not imagine
That what you do not see does not exist.
There was an evening when I spoke to you
And saw a second face behind your features:
That of the god grew slowly through your own."


On your breast where I can hear your heart beat,
Let me lay my mouth to suck the festered
Sores of former fevers as a healing
Stone upon a wound extracts the venom.
When my hand takes yours a current runs
Through your body, and you move untrammelled.
Sigh no more that turbid fumes which foul
Dreams have bred torment your rallied spirit
Over and again. They flare disbanded
In the conflagration of this passion.


"Come and shackle me, the sombre,
And destroy me in my madness!
You will profit, I shall prosper."
"Curb your rage, give me your hand!
You shall bear another bondage,
Pace another path to gladness.
Sun shall reign and overtide you,
Break the spell which holds you bound."


Sacred night which he allotted,
Let me stay within your shadow.
Not until I drain your rapture,
And perfect what you have founded,
Shall the day impose its burdens.
Only light which he has shown me
Shall invest with warmth and clearness.

He is radiance! When he blazes,
Do not turn your head from stainless
Light, where on a crystal summit
We can laugh at what's below.
He is darkness, and he sweeps us
Into surges where we tremble
Blind and frenzied. Can you fathom
Where through you, he ushers me?


When to your mouth my mouth is pressed in yearning,
Your inner breath impels my every heart-beat,
And then I loose the arms which hold me clasped,
Release your body, fountain of my fires,
And draw away from you with bended forehead,
It is because I feel my flesh confront me:
In pasts too far and dark for thought to gauge,
With you I sprang from the same stem of kings.


This circle which is mine and yours and ours,
Add to its fill and we shall be fulfilled.
When you have spent yourself you feel the richer,
The ring we narrowed widens, you are solely
My own, and this enhances all for me.
See how this day of radiance breaks through barriers,
Comprises what has been and what will come.


"You came to me from years of perfect plenty,
And gave at will as you have always given.
I do not yield myself for what is rationed,
I am the outset always wanting all."
"But you shall be my life and more than rapture,
And bliss and blaze as long as fate exacts it,
Be everything to me, my inmost heart,
And such a cycle is eternity."

Put away what pained and tried,
Rebel in the soul is routed,
No one but the god shall guide.
Now the savage dream is flouted
Where in you my self had died.
For a greater force directed
How in you I be perfected.


Not he who lost or never had should weep,
But he who is unworthy of his wealth
Because he hoards it. You have found the rod
That jerks where healing waters wait to rise
And lap of darkness prisons veins of gold.
Do not recoil and ask: Must it be I?
Nor thrust the charm your reason does not grasp
Defiantly aside. But help and know
Delight while in your hand the wand obeys.


Not aware of what I wanted
I divined my growth and ferment,
Like a tree that buds and branches.
I was locked in husks of heavy
Sleep until a breath awoke me.
Come, my helper, let me strengthen,
Only you can guess my stresses.
Free me from my wintry bondage,
Let me thaw, and stir, and quicken!


You have received and you have given
In keeping with our law.
You will not lose nor make for losses
Until the ring is closed.
Then do not reach for goals and gladness,
For more than we have had.

A noble spirit is not wanton
With vintage of the god.
Live in the shade of consummation
Aware of its demands,
And praise the final force which never
Will dash you to the depths.


Since I am twined in you with every fibre
I wish I could unfold a fairer fulness
To multiply the gift I have to offer.
Destroy me! Let me drink your flame! I freely
Gave up my freedom for your keeping. Every
Ambition shall dissolve and every bond
Break in the service of this love, save one
Of even subtler power: sacred awe.


What more have I to give? I let you mould me
Like clay between your palms, I tune my thinking
To match the rhythm of your heart. Your marrow
In me will shape me gently toward your image.
Your eyes, your steps direct my course, your colour
Has dyed the fabric of my dream and only
Through you I find the words to form my prayer,
It is your breath that brims my praise of planets.


What happened that I almost am a stranger
To my own self, the same yet something more!
Who loved and valued me still does, my comrades
Still wait for me with fair constraint. All that
I had is still my own: delights of summer,
Audacious dreams, the touch of tender lips.
My blood is running with a bolder rhythm!
While I denied and stinted, I was needy,
But since I gave myself, my self is mine!

You tell me it is much you take as yours
All that is mine, and yet you have not said
What really is: You share my every hour,
Your wishes have the weight of a command.
I must protect you when you head for danger,
And bear the blow intended for your hurt.
I vouch for you with all your flaws, I shoulder
The load you found too heavy and cast off.
And it is I who weep the tears your spirit
Should wring from you — the tears you never weep.


The secret pain which racked me is uncovered:
When driven by the storm of youth I found you,
The elder who accepted me, I felt
That I should rather suffer any sorrow
Than let a bond like this grow slack or break.
The burning force which masters me informs
Me when to cede or stay, and that my status
Will shift as gently as the sliding seasons,
Yet everything involve a bond with you.
Already I have changed my place in silence.


As one, who walked the cliffy ledge unscathed,
Looks back and knows he cannot cross again
Now that he sees the danger of each step,
So you recoil from what you dared when I
Put all my self into your hands! Had they
Been weak or frail, I should have been destroyed.
Now yield to this unyielding law and heed
The form in which I carry out its bidding,
For stuff the soul is made of, must decay
Unless the dark surrender is renewed.


The seed calls in the furrow: From the plot
Of dark and ferment everything must spring.
Do not condemn the dread in which you cling,

Be not afraid of so much night. The lot
Of those who carry is beset with sorrow.
But I foresee the gladness of a morrow
When sun will shine on what we both begot.


Over miracles I mused
In the lower shafts of wisdom.
Did the vision which enthralled me,
Did the god who lit my being
Come from unimagined summits?
Was it I myself that bore him?
Pray, my soul, and shun reflection!
Are there miracles to equal
What has marked and filled this year?
Have I not from out its orbit
Snatched a star into our confines
By the power of my love?


When I left the land of rapture,
Bloom and fruit of lavish regions,
Here at home in frail and golden-
Green and brittle spring I saw you
Sprung from earth among the flowers,
Standing naked, free of trappings,
Up against the white of birches,
You, a god of now and nearness!
Eyes alight and still unshadowed,
Knees and shoulders of a shepherd,
Strong and firm your palms and fingers,
You, a god of dawn-beginnings!


Is this the boy of oldest legend,
Who came in later times with rosy
And tender girlish limbs? With wanton
Wreaths in his locks, with coaxing eyes?
Now he is slim and taut. He takes
And does not ask, is unadorned.

334

The lust for venture lights his glances,
His kiss is brief and burning — after
His sacred seed is sown he urges
Relentlessly to risk and toil.


When gracious peace and freedom come the paean
Again shall rise to all celestial powers,
And lovers, light of heart, will sport in meadows
And woods, and sip the cup of sweet abandon.
I still must curb the rapture we are granted...
When you divine me in my true vocation
And recognize the rank I am accorded,
The day will dawn that brings you my surrender.


Before the evening when you shared my goblet
Of wine and drank to us among the hills
We left the river, climbing to the heights.
And all at once the grassy green of heaven
Grew limpid blue like southern bays. A halo
Of gold transformed the trees and roofs to dwellings
Of the immortals. Timeless flash of Now,
When landscape turns to spirit, dream to substance.
We trembled in a moment of consummate
Delight that held and crowned our whole existence
And put an end to envy for the longed-for
Sea of the gods, the radiant island-sea.


Give thanks to him who chose and guided us
To do tomorrow's deed and fall as victims
In praise of stars, my brother in the fight!
You thirst for glory and I covet rest.
No give and take can mitigate the fires
Which you have roused in me, and the same power
Which holds would crush me. No togetherness
But blood we shed together will release me.

O quiet of the last night in your arms,
Before the signal calls me to oblivion!
O peerless joy of magic dawn! To conquer
With God and you, with you to welcome death!


The drunken Lord of Autumn said: "Before
You try to find my twin in these terrains
As one embodied, as a separate self,
— A hope too unrestrained, a wish too daring —
Savour this fruit and taste this cup of wine.
The common plant is sweeter there than here,
And grows more lush than in your native soil.
The choicest of the choice thrives only here."


I do not know if I have duly praised you,
You the incarnate, you the uncreated.
I know one only: He is many-shapen,
And grows and craves to be destroyed, and quickens
Again in freshened flame. First he is single,
Then fills his many forms, and each with equal
And yet with other majesty, whenever
He reascends from purifying night.


Some teach that this is earthly, that eternal,
Another: I am want and you abundance.
We tell how earthly stuff can be eternal,
And one man's want another man's abundance.
Unconscious of its dawn and dusk is beauty,
The deathless spirit snatches what is mortal,
It shapes, it keeps alive and heightens beauty,
And with empyreal power makes immortal.
A body that is fair incites my blood,
I, who am spirit, clasp it with enchantment,
And changed in works of spirit and of blood,
It is my own and changeless in enchantment.

Where are the pearls, the tears of tender
Lament? The roses, couch of ease?
The game of wooing and surrender?
The scent is rank, the splendour flees.
Atone with stern and silent rite —
The month of growth, the dawn is breaking,
The secret bud, a chaste awaking,
A crisper breath, a cooler light.


BOOK THREE


What light has touched the morning earth with wonder
As on the first of dawns? The wind is sated
With the astounded song of wakened worlds.
The timeless mountains seem to change their shape,
And flowers nod as in the days of childhood.
The river laps against the shore and drowns
The dust of ages with a wash of silver.
Is this a state of grace? Creation trembles,
And everyone who walks the road is ringed
With majesty which he is unaware of.
Across the land a wealth of sun is flooded,
And all who move within its beams are blessed.


This, the realm of spirit, mirrors
My domain with grove and grange!
Each is born again and given
Other form. His home and country
Dim to legend, and the rites
Of the message, of the blessing
Change your kindred, name, and station.
Father, mother are no more.
From the sons who have been chosen
I elect my lords of earth.

Who ever circled the flame
Always shall follow the flame.
No matter how he may rove,
Reached by the rays he will not
Wander too far from the goal.
But when he loses their light,
Tricked by a gleam of his own,
Broken from bond of the core
He will be scattered in space.


The nobility you long for
Does not hail from crown and scutcheon.
Through their glances men of every
Rank betray their venal fancies
And their raw and ribald prying.
Sons of rare distinction grow from
Anywhere among the people,
And you will discern your kindred
By their frank and fervent eyes.


With the women of an alien
Kind you shall not taint your bodies.
Patience! Peacocks are for monkeys!
Near the lake Veleda governs,
Teaches girls forgotten knowledge,
Woman's most intrinsic secret.
Versed in laws of world-beginnings
She will join you to the ripened
Wombs avowed to bear your children.


Grey and golden drifts of twilight
Thread the garden with their croon.
And bemused, a spectre brushes
Summer cobwebs from her forehead.
Wistful cadence! Through the windows
Shreds of music coax and beckon,
Sap the soul with sweetness. Hasten!

338

All of this is autumn song,
And the voice in you wants neither
Potions nor a faded sheen.


Your friend conducted you. With him you crossed
The sacred threshold for the consummation.
Roused to the core you knelt in silent fervour,
Surrendered to the One, the All-Comprising.
Old doubts dissolved, your life grew meaningful.
You rose in exultation and not only
Your features, but your body burned with radiance.
A loving heart can fathom every creature,
An eager heart storm every height, and holy
And plain the common workaday begins.


You have avowed with eyes that span the world,
And sacrificed with wreathed and wind-blown hair,
Vying in body with the swiftest, lithest.
Unblessed are they who jeer the bond which holds you,
Who fix you with their stare and rather suffer
The chains they forged than welcome a deliverer.
Their doubting is not freedom but distortion,
Constraint, and lassitude. Faith is the vigour
Of blood, the strength of full and fair existence.


Under changeless constellations
Peoples shift from dawn to darkness,
Spirit ripens, spirit withers,
Sleep is tantamount to waking.
Wash of ebb and tide erases
Even proudest earthly unions.
But this knowledge does not weigh us,
For our year gives us our frontier,
Flame within the ring our fire,
Tending it our aim and joy.

Now we no longer haunt the tract
Of sterile land, the forest greyed
In blighting wind, and furrows cracked
With drought, the shrivelled weed and blade.
Fresh islands rise in secret, girded
With bloom, on hills a fountain broke:
The new commandment you have worded,
New generations you evoke.


The new commandments for the new are these:
The old may revel in their store of riches,
The distant thunder does not reach their ears.
But brand as slaves the young who in this era
Can lull their hearts with melting strains and toy
With chains of roses on the brink of chasms.
Spew out the morsel seasoned with decay
And mask the dagger in a sheaf of laurel,
Tuned to the coming war in pace and song.


What you have met with, clasps you like a ring
Of steel. If madness swept you and you wake
And cannot face the dawn unflinchingly,
Run on your sword: the chosen death of heroes!
If — in some trifling thing — you harmed an equal,
Leave him in silence and atone with deeds
Before returning. You have not the right
To soil his honour and your own and redden
Your brother's brow with shame. For it is vile
To ask to be forgiven, to forgive!


Fate wills it that your foe is never reared
Outside yourself, your want is what creates him.
His function is to parry thrust with thrust.
He is a hybrid, tricks and foils, but whets
Your blade and quickens your essential powers,
Brings needed poisons with his loathsome deeds.

340

So challenge the aggressors from without:
Block us! You cannot wilt the word that blooms!
Hear us! You favour it, and yet it blooms!
Kill us! Whatever blooms, will brim with blooms!


One knowledge like for all implies a hoax!
For knowledge has three forms: the one that grows
From blind divinings of the throng, from seed
And stuff into alert and active sons.
The schools and books of ages give the second,
Only initiates pass into the third.
Three rungs for those who know — and none but fools
Try to dispense with that of birth and flesh.
The other, just as strong, is grasp and vision,
But only he the god knew, knows the last.


The spirit that is always male has shaped
The world we know. The woman's gift is substance,
No less a shrine to bow to! Woman bears
The beast, but men and women hail from man.
Your rib produced her, she is good and evil.
Eschew her secret! Hers the inner circle!
In council she is lawless and nefarious.
As in the Book of Books, so the Anointed
Proclaims at every era's turn: "My mission
Is to dissolve the works of woman."


If a recluse should accost you,
One of those who muse in deserts,
Gaunt with matted hair, and counsel:
— Calling this the peak of wisdom —
"Keep to one that stands for all things
To prepare for Nothing." Answer:
"He whose love was never squandered
Never need repent of earthly
Fulness, nor reject the body."

"Break the seal which keeps us silent,
Let us read the rune to hungry
Crowds who cry their want aloud!"
"Do not blunder like the dullards
Who demand solution only
To pollute the rune, divest it
Of its power, scratch it under,
And become more needy. No one
But the master sets the day."


If men of now mistake you, men who blink,
You say, but do not gaze, who jerk and quiver
But do not feel, how then when many rise
To tempt and dazzle: "Come, we are the way!"
Then my bequest shall serve: I gave you eyes
That see in lieu of brains that dupe. His body
And face will show you the elect. Before
The seventh year, when light begins to break
In us, he grows into the mould of kingship,
The kiss of coronation on his brow.


Head off the unprepared and shut the gate.
Souls that are blind can be destroyed by knowledge.
It lives secure in image, tone, and rhythm,
And dealt from mouth to mouth conveys a message
Whose depths no one alive today can probe.
The first oath postulates what calls for silence,
And, still restrained by awe, we dare not name
The cherished forbear who divined so clearly
What you envisage now and shall envisage.


So far the secret lore may be discovered
More than the sum of parts the total counts.
And through the circle new élan is ushered
So that the strength of every member mounts.

And from this source of love which never shallows
Each tyro-templer will, in turn, attain
A greater force which tides into his fellows
And washes back into the ring again.


You are the cornerstone, and I acclaim you
For how you face yourselves, and me, and others,
Fulfill your tasks and urge to faithful hearts.
You are the vassals, bearers of the realm
As utterly and veiled as other stars,
Before or after, show the trends of earth.
Eschew a swifter growth of greater power:
The crowning number holds all odds, what works
Within it soon will work the whole, and what
You do not grasp today can never be.


He grows immune who was allowed to probe
The depths, and for the common good transmits
The spell of rite and image. If he brings
Nothing but tokens, he annuls himself
And them: He saw too much, yet lacked an eye!
No one who found true wisdom ever tells.
For men would be convulsed and numbed with terror,
The blood and semen of the most intrepid
Would freeze, their limbs would fail if they were faced
With monstrous otherness reared up in menace.


The rapture of the wakening! When you turned
To leave, and up above my roof I saw
A golden star which signed to me, the first
To be transmuted wholly by the spirit,
You granted me the right to put a question.
I hesitated first, and then refused:
"Who lived the utmost needs no clues: If we
Could grasp you, we should be your equals. You
Gave me enough to change the course of planets:
The single foot of solid ground I stand on."

343

I took the praise the schools awarded,
They held me worthy of their honours...
The time for guilelessness is gone.
Then insight dawned: to know while knowing
That which can be acquired is cheap.
Only the wisdom which the god confers,
Makes wise! With you I pass through sacred
Terrains and toward the sacred goal.
I sense accord in bloom and wilting,
And joy in all I live and do.


Who would desire a different you, when with
A smile you droop your head and slowly swerve,
Too full a flower on a stem too fragile.
Who would begrudge you gentle air and sun!
And yet I say that you must face the day
When salutary tempest sweeps the last
Remains of ashes from your golden hair.
"Do not condemn a weaker one who left you.
Remember how you once indulged me, seeing
Me as a light-haired wonder — nothing more."


Do not dissect too much what no one knows!
The symbols life has traced cannot be read!
The wild swan which you wounded in the wing
And tended in your yard awhile, reminded
You — so you said — of infinitely distant
Yet kindred substance you had crushed within him.
He wasted, never grateful for your kindness
And never vexed, but when his end had come,
His breaking eyes expressed reproach that you
Had forced him to invade an alien circle.


You hung your head, both diffident and young.
I guessed where books had failed you. Whether flesh
Or spirit shall prevail, the tenor of
The hour prompts. A living hand must point
What's axle and what's wheel, what shifts, what stands.

344

Once at a feast, the lord we feasted flung
His spell on you. The frenzy of his flame,
Deluge of long-restrained delight, submerged
More than the spirit. Late, when haltingly
You came to where I lay, the flesh was silent.


Friend and teacher, dictum, counsel
Did not help me on my way,
But you grasped the bitter need of
Youth, and vouched for me until
Precious growth of those imperilled
Years had strengthened for the clash.
So to you I pledged my being.
Bid me go from pole to pole!
Let me throttle those who hate you,
Take my blood to wage your work!


Now you may venture from the inner space,
The cell which holds the nucleus of powers
And life unborn. Before you lies the land.
The rung you reached is written in your eyes
And in your form your kind of future daring.
Your ways divide, your purpose is the same.
Within your veins the wine of love runs triple.
The fair today will be the strong tomorrow,
Who throve because the wakener leaned and knew them,
Gave them his strength, transformed them with his smile.


After the field was won, the battle ended,
When furrows reached for seed again, and crowned
With leaves the troops and crews were homeward bound,
From fairest shores the sound of fête ascended.
And flanked by flute and clarion, glittering
With every colour, caught in dance and cadence,
Imbued and ringed with fruit- and flower-fragrance,
The paean rises, an eternal spring.

## CLOSING CHORUS

God has put his path before us,
God has linked us to his land,
God has called us to his combat,
God has ringed us with his wreath.
God has quelled our heart with quiet,
God has steeled our breast with strength,
God has grooved our brows with anger,
God has leased our lips with love.
God has graced us with his dower,
God has swept us with his blaze,
God has locked us in his power,
God has blessed us with his praise.

# THE KINGDOM COME

## (1928)

## PREFACE TO THE FIRST EDITION OF THE KINGDOM COME

This volume comprises all the poems written after the completion of THE STAR OF THE COVENANT. Many appeared in the *Blätter für die Kunst* (1914-1919). "The War" and "The Poet in Times of Confusion" together with two other poems, were published as separate pamphlets. "Goethe's Last Night in Italy" which opens a new series, dates back to 1908.

# GOETHE'S LAST NIGHT IN ITALY

What a ray has reached us from southerly seas?
Over there two pines with their sombre pinions
Spread through the night's everlasting blue and between them
Silver and luminous, single and tranquil, a star.
Two I see emerge from the grove, on a lawn
Circled with shrubs advance toward the image of marble.
Shining as they who are clasped as they pledge their faith.
Great through the power of mystical rites, their heads
Lift with the promise of rule and radiance. Astounded
Spaces bright with the bliss of eternity listen
Long to their paean which tenuous winds carry out
Over the slumbering land and the sibilant surf.

Parting claws at my heart — farewell to the sacred
Soil where first I saw creatures moving in light.
And through the broken columns the dance of the blessed.
I whom you dubbed "the heart of the people" and called
"Truest of heirs" felt poor and deprived and I trembled.
Starting afresh as a child here I grew to a man.
Through the mist I can hear your censorious voices:
"Lotus of Hellas deadened his love for his country."
Oh, could you fathom my words, for no wiser befit you:
Over the mountains you still shall continue to lavish
Not only drops of your kingliest blood, but a torrent.
This be your share and your task until you are freed.

Fate denied you the lot of more fortunate stems
Who were accorded a seer at the dawn of their eras,
One who was born as a son, not a grandson of Gaia,
Sensing the secrets in strata of earth and beyond them,
Who was a guest in the halls of celestials and there
Stole for his people a spark of empyreal flame,
So that their years are not wholly entangled in error.
One who went forth to the gorge where the terrible Mothers
Sit at the roots of the undermost regions as watchers,
Forced them to yield to him, while they struggled and screamed,
Wrested from them the magic he needs for his spells.
You had no helper like this, and I am not he.

Once — I remember — we rode on the Rhine, our ship
Gallant with flags, to the vineyards of neighbouring shores.
Feathery blue of the autumn sky transfigured
Meadows, the oaks on the hill, the white-washed houses.
They were loading the last of the harvested clusters.
Naked, gaudy with gold and fluttering ribbons,
Revelling vintagers twined the vats with their garlands
Echoes of song and laughter! The must full of fragrance!
Crowds of Bacchantes with scarlet vines in their hair,
Stormed up the road by the river, glowing and green.
There at the empire's limits: the Roman wall,
First I divined the soil from which I was sprung.


And yet where I lived was your land of longing and music.
In your cathedrals I worshipped with reverent prayers,
Till from the nebulous dimness, fretwork, and turrets,
Crying in torment, my spirit reached out for the sun.
Now I bring you one of the life-giving beams,
But in my heart I must hide the more passionate fires,
Lest they destroy while confusion still reigns in your minds.
Open your soul to this beam! Do not think it too tepid!
And I shall scatter you quartzes, and simples, and metals,
Colourful sequence suggesting now nothing, now all,
Till you have learned to see and can fathom the magic —
Norm of the gods — which lurks in bodies and things.


Long will the learned among you refuse to acknowledge
Tiding of gladness. They fondle their billowing beards,
Point their fingers at mould-spotted volumes, and clamour:
"Foe of our fatherland, prophet of gods that are false!"
Ah, when the circle of time is closed, for a thousand
Years the refractory necks and the carefully reasoning
Minds of your rulers and sages again will follow
Indigent bands of the frenzied who fled from their countries.
They will believe in the wildest of miracle-legends,
Taste with their sense the body and blood of a saviour,
Then for another millennium kneel in the dust,
Bowed to a boy whom you have enthroned as a god...


352

Where do you lure and lead me, illustrious two?
Are these the shadows of yearning, lovely and bitter?
Pillared courts I see with trees and fountains,
Groups of the young and the old in action and leisure,
Measure and strength I had fancied were only allied to
Attic sublimeness, and sound to the vigour and sweetness
From an Aeolian mouth. Instead I encounter
Sons my people bore, and the tongue of my people
Rings in my ear. Delight overwhelms me, the promise
Marble and roses held out to me, now is fulfilled.
What a tremor is loosed from inviolate space!
What a ray has reached me from southerly seas!


HYPERION

> "A sign was enough
> For those who yearned, and so the gods,
> Since time began, gave signs and were silent."


I

Where, O my brothers, my people,
Was it a far-away region
Where I was nurtured?
That though I drink of our vintage,
Live on the grain of our country,
Still I am alien!
Just as the son in his proud
Dreams is remote from his younger
Half-brothers, knowing
Even in laughter and games that
He is aloof, that his father
Must have been better.
You who are snared in reflection,
Melted away into music,
Lag in your labours,
Wailing, alas! by what waters,
Weeping, alas! by what willows,
And for what pleasures!

You who are yielding, yet brutal,
You cannot master the lovely
Steps of a dancer.
Shying from fruitful communion,
Lonely though friend is with friend,
You who need mirrors!


II


Kindred to you is my core,
           children of island and sea,
You who linked action with grace,
           art with sublimeness and fused
Charm of Ionia with stern
           Spartan command and restraint.
Who led the chorus in youth
           shaped the heroic in age,
He who was lord of the feast
           guided his country in stress.
Temples and games joined the tribes
           zealously vying in deeds.
No later wisdom has brought
           more than the founders of then.
Ships which have sailed on these seas,
           people who passed on these shores!
Here, as an era grew old
           down to the cypresses walked
With the most kingly of youths
           one who had mastered his times.
Darlings of Fortune, your hand
           conquered whatever it touched,
Rendered the grandson intact
           all that his fathers had stored.
You who made patterns for men
           formed them in flesh and in bronze,
You who in frenzy and poise
           dared to give birth to our gods.
Thousands lament in despair
           that this was destined to fall,

That by implacable law
              life is the killer of life,
That at the Syrian's decree
              beauty was plunged into night.


## III

I journeyed home: Such floods of flowers never
Had welcomed me before, and in the fields
And groves I sensed the pulse of sleeping powers.
I saw the spell on valley, hill, and stream,
Saw you, my brothers, heir to sunny morrows.
Your eyes, still chaste, are tranquil pools of dream.
In time you will be moulded by your yearning.
My anguish reaches out for rest. And yet
A gracious promise of the gods is granted

The suppliant who will not pace the realm.
I shall be earth, the very grave for heroes,
Which fervent sons invoke to be fulfilled.
"They bring the second era. Love engendered
The world and Love shall kindle it again."
I spoke the magic and I drew the circle.
Before I drown in night a vision sweeps
Me upward: Soon the god will set his weightless
Foot on my cherished land — the flame made flesh.


## THE CHILDREN OF THE SEA

### I

Once I revered you as my host — then shunned you.
Is this the vengeance for my long evasion,
That waves with changing contours guide my fancy,
Convoy me on this portion of my way?
When you appeared in dismal streets you brought
Us joy and torment and you seemed a wonder
Hailing from bays as he, the nearest, dearest,
From woods beside the sea where beads of amber
Once drifted from an undiscovered world.

The most remote, forbidden dream is wreathed
Around your stubborn, northern brow and lights
Your tranquil eye, a well of shade, because
The child was shifted by his destiny
From dusk of rocking ships to magic ports.
Though free of care you seem to drag a chain,
Elude us and yet strengthen our belief
That those with hair as blond as light still squander
Their priceless blood in sweet and senseless spending.
A sailor's luck and hunger for adventure
Sweep you, the potent spell in days of fervour,
Beyond our ken and to the furthest sea.


II


A land of bloom! The favour of immortals
Shines on the shores they chose, and only smoke
Betrays the crater gorged with inner fires.
O fair and glowing son of earth, approach
The bronzes of a Golden Age, the gods'
Own messenger, whose knees compel our homage
And — unabashed — the temple by the waters.
Devoid of wish and plea the mind adores,
And like the lord of life and death you tether
The soul with subtle threads, and merely lifting
Your long, black lashes, startle and arouse
Whenever you appear. How wan the morning!
Is there a film in fragile domes of blue,
A tarnish on the sated blue of waves,
A menace muttered through the organ tones?
Do longings we are versed in, cloud the coasts
Of rapture and forgetfulness? Not they!
The sun is still the same, the brilliant air,
The limpid calm on days of sacrifice.
Only your eyes, less bright today, have darkened
The fathomless abode of gods: the sea.

III

Awaited guest who often at our door
Called us for fleeting walks in autumn winds,
Whose soft metallic laugh and questions were
A balm to winter's night — who after years
Of care confronts us supple, fair, and free,
Upon his fresh young lips the sacred loathing
And lovely greed that stamp the sons of gods!
You too were nurtured to the sough of surges,
On blessed shores where men are not enslaved
By toil and need, and where as yet no breath
Of sleepless lust afflicts with languid sleep.
From tiers of rising foothills rimmed with white
A moving flood of green, a candid sail
Gleam through the silver lace of olive branches,
And in the dark the cliff resounds with song
Of deathless passion locked in deathless grief.
And after you have dealt delight, unknowing,
More kin to us through common rites of life,
Your quest begins, and wrested from our keeping
— Greater in force — you leave your noble harbour
To seek what other land, what other sea?


IV: ECHO

The sea resounds, on every coast the lustre,
The rising and the ebbing of the surf,
The flakes of curdled foam, the screaming birds
O children of the Sea whose early dreams
Divine the bliss of ever young horizons,
Want and abundance, action and repose,
The waters sing for you — your praises surge
Within the hollow shell the sea abandoned,
The shell a boy holds to his ear, and listens,
And gazes out into the salty wind.

357

For you the song, and now you live in us,
Unfathomed, cool-eyed, as if just forsaking
The lap of waters and yet unaware
How close the end! What alien shimmer masks
Your head with smiles of smooth malignant oceans?
No god can help you steer an even course.
The wave that bore you washes you like flotsam
And in the west still glistens with your hair.


On azure shores the gentle midday murmur
Of sun-enveloped seas evokes your face
In palpable and luring loveliness.
You stand among the throngs with sombre eyes,
Your cheek suffused with summer, and are equal
To those we name with awe who, bridled only
By strength within them, lived erect, and light,
And radiant as the body of the Foamborn.


But you the sea has cast from south to north,
You, the amazing blend of fire and ice,
Of sudden zest for strife and flaccid pauses.
Why cling to us, you ending of this age,
Choose us along with others for your whims?
You feel the drive of wish or wave, but soon
Your soul will have exhausted every pale,
And moan and stray, too frail for love or faith.


The ring is closed. The sea-god circles cliff
And island with his song, he flings a spell
And links the course of destinies with waters
That press and thrust and throng, or plead and glide,
Are almost quelled but gather for return...
Now, scourged beneath the longed-for storm, the tide
Engulfs what moulders, and the current snatches
You too! And yet your souls remain and sound
Within the hollow shell the sea abandoned,
The shell a boy holds to his ear, and listens,
And gazes out into the salty wind.

358

# THE WAR

              ... a mind imbued
With shame for others or itself grows strange,
And well may find that what you say is crude.

But do not listen, nor have lies derange
Your tale. Your vision shall be manifest,
And let him scratch himself who has the mange.

Although the sounds you utter may molest
When tasted first, once they have been absorbed
The food which they provide is of the best.

DANTE, DIVINE COMEDY, PARADISE XVII


As jungle beasts, which slink away or snarl
At one another in their greed to rend,
Seek company and huddle in a flock
When forests are ablaze, or mountains quake,
So in our country, split to factions, foes
United at the cry of war. A breath
Not felt before, a breath of union floated
From rank to rank, and a confused divining
Of what was now to come. The people, seized
By throb of changing worlds, one little instant
Forgot the glut and gauds of coward years
And saw themselves majestic in their need.

They journeyed to the hermit on the hill:
"Does this stupendous fate still leave you calm?"
He said: These shudders were your best response.
What grips you now — I knew it long ago!
Long have I sweated blood of anguish while
They played and played with fire. I exhausted
My tears before and I have none today.
The thing was almost done and no one saw,
The worst is yet to be and no one sees.
You yield to pressure goading from without...
These are the beacons only, not the tidings.
The struggle, as you wage it, is not mine.

359

The seer is never thanked, he meets with scorn
And stones when he foretells disaster, fury
And stones when it arrives. The crimes unnumbered
Which all ascribe to force or luck, the hidden
Descent of man to larva call for penance!
What are the slaughtered multitudes to him,
If life itself is slain! He cannot splutter
Of native virtue and of Latin malice.
Here whining women, old and sated burghers
Are more at fault than bayonets and guns
Of adversaries, for our sons' and grandsons'
Dismembered bodies, for their glassy eyes!

His charge is praise and blame, amends and prayer.
He loves and serves upon his way, with blessings
Dispatched the youngest of those dear to him.
They do not march for catchwords, but themselves.
They know what drives, what renders them immune!
His dread goes deeper, for he feels the powers
Are more than fable. Who can grasp his plea:
You, who on reeking corpses swing the broadsword,
May you preserve us from too light an ending
And from the worst, the blood-betrayal! Races
Committing this will wholly be uprooted
Unless their best is used to halt the doom.

You shall not cheer. No rise will mark the end,
But only downfalls, many and inglorious.
Monsters of lead and iron, tubes and rods
Escape their maker's hand and rage unruly.
Who saw his comrade crushed to pulp and fragments,
Who lived the life of vermin in the broken
And desecrated earth, must laugh with hatred
At speeches once heroic, now deceitful.
The ancient god of battles is no more.
And in the tumult fevered worlds are sickening
Toward death. The only ichors that are sacred
Are those which, still unstained, are spent in floods.

Where is the man who stands for all? And where is
The only word that holds on Judgment Day?
Monarchs with pasteboard crowns and foolish gestures,
Lawyers, and scribes, and traders — froth and chaff!
Even in firm and charted limits: turmoil!
Then threat of chaos. From a modest house
In suburbs of the greyest of our towns,
Supported by his cane, a plain, forgotten
Old man appeared and solved the hour's riddle.
He saved what they — God knows! — with pompous slogans
Had driven to the chasm's brink: the realm,
But from the fouler foe he cannot succour.


"Have you no eye for sacrifice unmeasured,
For strength of unity?" These also flourish
Across the border. In nefarious eras
Offerings are useless, duties dim and dull.
Crowds have their value, but they shape no symbols,
Are aimless and forgetful. Only sages
Want reasons. People drool of charity,
Humaneness — and embark on monstrous slaughter.
On spittle of the basest wooing follows
The slime of vile affront, and what's at odds
Would fawn with fond caresses if the future
Made manifest its terror to their eyes.


This bloated mask is spirit? Blooms so frail
Spring from another soil. The withered cant
Of zenith and a resurrection savours
Of rotted fruit. The old will not be young
When they return! Who speaks of truth and errs
In basic truth is maddest of the mad.
The wily say: a lesson for the future!
That will be different, though, and those who face it
Must learn to change, to grow the inner eye.
Not one who summons now and thinks he governs,
Know that he gropes about in doom, and no one
Can see the palest flicker of a dawn.

Less strange that millions die than that more millions
Still dare to live! Whose rhythm is his era's
Will see the present only as a spook.
A childish fool finds comfort in: You did it!
No! All and none — so reads the final verdict.
A cheating fool pretends: This time the kingdom
Of peace is near. But when reprieves are over,
Your ankles and your knees again shall wade
In must the Master trod. But then a race
Will spring to life whose gaze does not dissemble,
Who know their fate and will not turn to stone
For fear of pitiless Gorgonian law.


In neither camp a single thought, a glimmer
Of what's at stake. Here, only greed to traffic
Where others came before, to be converted
To that which one reviles and not acknowledge
That when its gods have died a people dies.
And there they boast of old prestige, of splendour
And culture, while they want to sprawl in comfort,
In gains — and in the lap of clearest judgment
They do not even guess that those they slighted
Destroy what has been ripening for destruction,
And that, perhaps, a "hate and scorn of mankind"
Will usher in salvation yet once more.


But let the song not end in curse! Some ears
Aldready grasp my praise of stuff and stem,
Of seed and fruit. And many hands already
Are stretched toward me when I proclaim: O land
Too beautiful for alien feet to ravage,
Where groves are harps for winds, where in the osiers
A flute resounds, and where the dream still lives
Although your heirs incessantly deny it,
And where the radiant Mother of Caucasians,
Divided now and rampant, first accorded
Her face unveiled, O land, still saturate
With so much promise that you cannot fail!

Now youth calls up the gods, both the eternal
And the returning when their day is rounded.
The king of storms gives him of clear horizons
The scepter and delays the Longest Winter.
Who hung upon the Tree of Weal cast off
The pallor of pale souls and vies in frenzy
With him they rent. Subtly Apollo turns
To Balder. For a while there will be night,
And not the East will bring the light! The war
Was solved on stars: who shelters the palladium
Within his land is victor, and who changes
Himself at will is lord of times to come.


THE POET IN TIMES OF CONFUSION
TO THE MEMORY OF COUNT BERNHARD UXKULL

In placid times they say the poet is
A wingéd child who sings his tender dreams
And showers beauty on a busy world.
But when abuses swell into a storm,
And Destiny pounds at the door his verses
Ring like a pick on ore and are misheard.
When all are blinded he, the only seer,
Unveils the coming doom in vain, and though
The cries of a Cassandra fill the house,
The frantic rabble sees one thing alone:
The horse, the horse, and rushes to its death.
A prophet may foretell the anger of
The tribal god, the trot of Assur's thousands
Which drag the chosen people into bondage,
The clever council has more sure report,
Derides the warner, shuts him in a cell.
And when the Holy City is besieged
Burghers and warriors jostle in confusion,
Within the lords and priests have bloody quarrels
For broomsticks, while without the stoutest bulwark
Is falling, he is silent and he sighs.

But when the victor rides, and loots, and burns,
And saddles man and woman with his yoke,
Then some in foaming rage reject their guilt
And charge the fault to other hands, and some
Weary with hunger, struggle for the crust
The shameless conqueror throws, and numb themselves
With bawdy mirth, and lick the foot that downed them.
He stays aloof, the only one who feels
The utter wretchedness, the utter shame.

Go to the peaks once more, go to your spirits,
And bring a better solace to relieve us
Of this affliction, clamours an old man.
What boots a voice from skies when no one listens
To simple sense? What boots the talk of spirit
When there is not a single urge in common
Save fight for food? When every guild reproaches
The other and upholds its flimsy craft
Although it foundered, looks for help in increase
Of darling gadgets? When the wisest babble
Of new construction built on ancient vices,
And counsel: Shrink to worms so that the thunder
May spare you and the lightning fail to strike!
The living of this epoch who have wandered
Through long distress will always burn their incense
To every promise of the lying idols
That hurl them into serfdom and destruction.
For they forgot their noblest inner law
And what allows them to survive, rejected
Faith in a lord and need of an atoner,
And want to dodge their destiny with guile.
Still harsher ploughs must break those clods to furrows,
Still denser vapours must oppress the air,
And not a glint of blue will pierce the darkness
And fall upon the people of our era,
Until all those who speak a common tongue
Join hands, and arm against corruption, tear
The faded tatters of their flags, regardless
Of red or blue or black, and think of nothing
Except another Vespers — day and night!

But in a mournful age it is the poet
Who keeps the marrow sound, the germ alive.
He stirs the holy flame that leaps across
And shapes the flesh in which to burn, discovers
The truth of tidings which our fathers gave:
That those elected to the highest goal
Begin by passing through the waste, that once
The heart of Europe shall redeem the earth.
And when the final hope has almost perished
In sternest grief, his eyes already see
A light to come. Unstained by venal mobs,
By threadbare minds and follies steeped in poison,
A younger generation rises toward him,
The youths who, steeled by years of galling pressure,
Again have honest standards for the probe
Of men and things, who — fair and grave and proud —
In alien worlds accept themselves for what
They are, avoid the rocks of brazen boasting
And the morass of would-be brotherhood,
Spat out the lifeless, stale, and base, and from
Their consecrated dreams, and deeds, and sorrows
Begot the only one who can restore.
He breaks the chains and sweeps aside the rubble,
He scourges home the lost to lasting law,
Where lord is lord again, the great is great
And where integrity returns. He fastens
The true device upon the nation's banner.
Through tempests and the dread fanfares of dawning
He leads his tried and faithful to the work
Of sober day and founds the Kingdom Come.


## TO A YOUNG LEADER IN THE FIRST WORLD WAR

When to your country you came   home from the desolate field,
Whole out of shattering hail,   trenches in billows of dust,
Chastely your words seemed to flow   as of a service enjoined.
From the most daring of rides,   from the most agonized toils
Proud rose your shoulders and free   bearing a weight even then:
Fate of your squadron.

Action and rapid command   lay in the lift of your hand,
Gentle and pondering eyes   watched for a danger in wait,
All of your being exhaled   power and calm and poise,
So that the older suppressed   that he was secretly moved,
When the slim form of a boy,   looming light and erect,
Swung from the saddle.

Dice in the conflict were cast   otherwise than you had dreamed,
When the disintegrate host   turned from the weapons of war.
Sadly you faced me as though   after a sumptuous fête
Workaday soberly dawns,   empty of shining rewards,
And with tears you deplored   rare and significant years
Utterly wasted.

You, though, should not ape the crowd,   always a plaything of whims,
Branding as rubbish today   what in the past they extolled,
Razing a milestone that tripped   feet no more sure of the way.
Suddenly all were at one,   marched to the gates of success,
Fell under onerous yoke.   Meaning is hidden in this,
Meaning within you.

All that has ripened in you   while you won honours in war,
Never can pass from your grasp,   arms you for struggles to come.
And as you walked at my side   avid for counsel and help,
Evening which paled in the sky   haloed your fluttering hair,
Haloed your temples with light.   First it ringed you with rays
And then it crowned you!


SIGNS


*


M.

        "Now, after centuries the only
        Instant has come that sets us free!
        Now all the chains at last are broken,
        The earth is cloven, and a half-god
        Mounts from the chasm, young and beautiful."

366

One came from the fields and toward the gate.
Carmine fires broke along the peaks,
Lifeless air and ashen heavens weighed
On the walls as though before a quake.
Everyone was lapped in deepest sleep,
He was roused and all his body shook:
"Lord, have I construed your signs aright?"
Down the answer chimed: "The time is full!

Three stood in a room and were afraid,
Joined their hands to form a ring, and fixed
Each the others with ecstatic eyes:
"We are here to meet your hour, Lord!
If you choose us as your messengers,
Give us strength to bear the load of joy,
For we witnessed the eternal child
Rise incarnate from chaotic night."

Seven on a hill surveyed the land,
Ruins smouldered, mildew greyed the grass.
"Through the realm we have diffused your breath,
In the furrow we have sown your seed,
Lord, a second time you shift the lots,
Though the drouth which you decree be long,
We shall wait, the keepers of your height,
Die serene for we have seen your light.."


PRAYERS

I

When I recalled those avenues of April,
The light around us, waiting for your glances,
The evening saturate with purple darkness
And life that quickened us with its enchantment
Until in vaults of night it ebbed to prayer,
It seemed to me the dream my blood had nourished
Was only a mirage of poise and power,
That I had hardly even grasped the tremors
We felt before your fair and fervent nearness,

And that my song was pale to what had happened
As to a thing its shadow on the water.
But now I know a single mouth can never
Extol the consummation of what sages
And seers foretold since first our verses flowed.
And now I face the many noble foreheads
Which unaware caught something of your splendour
And so exalt your being through their beauty.
Resigned, a worker who has done his portion,
I shall not sound my dirges any longer,
I must submit since you have proved the stronger.


II

In wild confusion and the sad expectance
Of words that tell of ruins, tears, and summons
Which come from graves — where shall I find a refuge
To celebrate the fête of earth in freedom?
I feared that, walled in clouds of frost and rigour,
I trusted less profoundly in the presage,
And that the zeal which goads my days, no longer
Impregnates stubborn matter with my fire,
That left without the torch of wanted guidance
I stumbled backward into utter darkness.
But from the mountains comes a wind, a deluge
Of blue and brightness floods the greying gardens,
The planes of shadow swim in tints of nacre,
And silver as the south the mild resplendence
Of early dusk is laid on arch and tower
As in the spring when you appeared before me.
I tremble with the hope that soon a portal
Will echo with the steps I long have yearned for,
As if you walked — in other incarnation —
Through streets your presence granted consecration.

## III

No one has ever known delight so perfect
That he was given sojourn in its radiance,
It only lasts in that it dawns and darkens.
I bow my head above the sombre waters
To probe the depths again, to find the image
Other, yet always you, and draw it upward.
The most profound of rites calls for renewal
And so makes permanent the fleeting moment.
Then let me pay the law of life my homage
By seizing every joy as fuel for rapture.
Since dulness threatens us when we are stagnant
Our spirit often bursts beyond its borders.
It textures dreams from luminous beginnings,
And follows move by move the endless sequence
Of madcap ventures to the latest eras,
Hails an imagined day with exultation,
And hovers spellbound in uncharted levels.
And then again it reaches out through mazes
Toward a fixed star, your star, for constant praises
And toward a stay among siderial phases.


## BURG FALKENSTEIN

## TO ERNST

To the forested summit
            I climbed at your side,
Where the rough-cornered bastion
            holds a circular tower,
And from a weatherworn fissure
            springs a vigorous tree.
Here lies the Pagan Wall,
            there the stones of the fort,
Tier on tier toward the lowland
            slant the boroughs and hills
To our river that shines
            far off and eternal.

My hand pointed downward:
                    "Look! The inscrutable face
Of this ponderous stronghold
                    fronting full toward the blue,
And the fair-watered valley.
                    They conjure the dream
Of inviolate childhood
                    which quickened me once
With the exquisite shudder
                    in peaceful beginnings,
With the voice of the woods
                    and smoke from the hearth at dusk."


Gravely you answered:
                    "So stupendous a thing,
Magic, has other roots,
                    does not take nature's course,
Does not flit with the wraith
                    over mouldering walls,
Does not breathe from the branches,
                    eerie phantoms of dark.
Lost forever the age
                    of untroubled delight.
Gone is our forefathers' soul,
                    gone with the flutes of the shepherds.


Here a people, a past:
                    toil that verges on thrall,
Rarely at peace with themselves,
                    joyless all they have done.
Who so long have not felt
                    a more generous urge.
Clogged with knowledge they lack
                    lightness, the gift of the gods.
Where they founded their homes
                    they are stifled and hemmed,
All too often their songs
                    turn into dirges."

"But I am struck by a note
                    clear on the somnolent air,
Broken the old string but stretched
                    taut was already the new.
Alien as yet to the ear
                    golden the sound is released
— Canons our fathers ordained,
                    prophecies pledged by our god —
Rises from nacreous straits,
                    flows over undulant fields,
Cities with traffic and haze,
                    pierces the wintery heart.


Over the glaciers and peaks
                    on to the cedars and groves,
Down to the luminous gulf,
                    purged of chatter and din
Vibrates the powerful tone
                    born of a metal more pure.
With the procession of shades
                    legends return to the north,
Tales of orgies and blood,
                    tales of glory and glow:
Splendour our emperors shed,
                    storms our battalions unbound."




SECRET GERMANY

Let me stand at your verge,
Chasm, and not be dismayed!

Where irrepressible greed has
Trampled down every inch of
Earth from equator to pole and
Shamelessly wielded relentless
Glare and mastery over
Every nook of the world,

Where in the smothering cells of
Hideous houses, madness
Just has found what will poison
All horizons tomorrow:
Even shepherds in yurtas,
Even nomads in wastes —

Where no more in a stony
Forest valley the she-wolf
— Rugged nurse! — suckles boy twins,
And neither untrodden islands,
Nor a garden of virgins
Dawn to foster the Great,

There in the sorest of trials
Powers below pondered gravely,
Gracious celestials gave their
Ultimate secret: They altered
Laws over matter and founded
Space — a new space in the old...

Once down by the southern
Sea I lay on a boulder,
Wrung as lately my kin
Spirit, when breaking through
Olives, the Spook of Noon
With goaten foot flicked me:

"Now that your eyes grew discerning,
Go and find in your sacred
Land primordial soil,
Slumbering lap of fill,
And regions as pathless and dark
As the densest of jungles."

Pinions of sunny dream,
Carry me close to the depth!

They told me of one who from rock-ridden coast
An instant had seen the Olympian gods
In heavens which split with the light of the dawn,
Whereat his soul was flooded with dread.
He shunned the board where his friends were grouped
And plunged into riotous waters.

In the town where the trivia from everywhere
Are posted on pillars and patches of wall
For people to gape at and hasten on,
No one had eyes for the greater event:
Uncanny through tottering structures and streets
The dangerous prowl of the demon!

In winter he stood in the candle-lit hall,
His shimmering shoulder hidden in folds,
The flame on his cheek in the leaves of a wreath.
The god concealed from the stare of fools,
In clear-scented warmth of the winds of spring,
Set foot on flowering courses.

The Listener who knew every person and thing,
Played ball with the stars in a rapturous reel,
The hunter unhunted, yet here he avowed
With stammering lips, his apostle-like form
Transfixed in the gleam of the opaline globe:
"This passes my grasp, I am silenced."

Then forth from the region of order and peace,
Through sulphurous night a tempest unloosed
The clash and the clamour of savage wars,
The smoulder of worlds in the throes of the end.
And crumbling terrains and shadows unleashed
The silver hooves of the chargers.

I came upon him of the pale-golden hair
Who smilingly lavished serene repose
Wherever he went. He was hailed by us all
The darling of Fortune, but late he confessed
His vigour was drained to give strength to a friend,
His life a sequence of offerings.

I loved him who — my blood in his veins —
Had sung the song only less than the best,
Who idly shattered his lute when he failed
To gain a treasure he once divined,
Who merged with anonymous throngs and bowed
A forehead destined for laurels.

Throughout the country, on roads and in squares,
Wherever I was on the watch, I asked
Omniscient Rumour with hundreds of eyes:
"Have you ever heard of the like?" And he
— Though loth to be startled — replied: "I heard
Of much — but this is unheard-of!"


Let me mount to your height,
Summit, and not be destroyed!

Who then, who of you brothers
Doubts, unshocked by the warning,
That what most you acclaim, what
Most you value today is
Rank as leaves in the fall-wind,
Doomed to perdition and death!

Only what consecrate earth
Cradles in sheltering sleep
Long in the innermost grooves,
Far from acquisitive hands,
Marvels this day cannot grasp
Are rife with the fate of tomorrow.

# HE WHO WAS HANGED

**THE QUESTIONER**

I cut you from the noose! Now will you answer?

**THE HANGED**

When through the hue and cry of all the town
They dragged me to the gates with maledictions,
I saw in every one who cast a stone,
Who scornfully had spread his arms akimbo,
Who stretched his finger out above the shoulder
Of him who stood in front, and gaped, and glowered,
That one of my defects was ripe in him,
But narrowed in or hedged about with fear.
And when I reached the gallows and the elders
Regarded me with grim contempt and pity,
I only laughed: Have you not guessed how much
You need the sinner you have flouted? Virtue
Which I transgressed could never beam so brightly
— However real — within your eyes and those
Of honest girls and wives, had I not trespassed!
And when the rope around my neck was tightened,
I gloated on a triumph I foresaw:
For as a victor I shall yoke your minds,
Dug under as I am, and in your litter
Live as a hero one extols in song,
A god! And now, before you even dreamed it,
I curve this rigid crossbar to a wheel.


# MAN AND FAUN

**MAN**

The narrow stream — and here a waterfall!
But what is this that hangs a shaggy leg
From cushioned mosses dripping on the rock?
A thick and curly pate and — look! A horn!

Though I have hunted far on wooded mountains,
I never yet have met his like. Stand still!
The way is blocked. And do not try to hide!
In limpid waves I see a goaten foot.

FAUN

Your find will pleasure neither you nor me.

MAN

Through ancient tales I learned of creatures kin
To you, but did not know that even now
Such useless, ugly monsters still survive.

FAUN

When you have driven off the last of us,
Your search for noble quarry will be vain,
The gnawing beasts and worms will be your prey.
And when you have explored the densest thickets
The drouth will take what most you need: the well!

MAN

You, of a baser stuff, would tutor me?
We slew the hydra, giant, dragon, griffin,
And cleared the wilderness that bore no fruit.
Where marshes spread, the wheaten acre sways,
Our docile cattle browse in sappy fields,
Estates and cities rise and shining gardens,
And woods enough are left for stag and doe.
We lifted treasures from the sea and earth,
The columns cry our victories to heaven.
What do you want, you relic of the jungle?
Our tracks alone are dogged by law and light.

FAUN

You are mere man, and where your wisdom flounders
Our own begins. You only see the brink
When you have suffered for the step beyond.
When harvests ripen, when your cattle thrive,
When sacred branches yield you grapes and olives,
You think this only comes through your devising.
The earths that drowse in dumb, primeval darkness
Do not decay! If ever they were joined
They sunder when a link escapes the ring.
Your rule is right for your appointed time.
But now away with you! You saw the faun!
The worst in store, you do not know: Your mind,
That can do much, will lose itself in cloud,
And rend apart its bond with clod and creature.
You will no longer grasp the cyclic change:
Loathing and lust, monotony and flux,
And dust and blaze, and death and being born.


MAN

Who tells you this? The gods shall be our sponsors!


FAUN

We never speak of them. You claim they helped you,
O fools, in person. Without go-betweens
They never came to you. You dawn, you die —
Whose thing you are in truth, you never learn.


MAN

Soon you will have no room for shameless sport.


FAUN

Soon you will pray to him you curse today.

## MAN

You poisonous monster with the crooked mouth,
Misshapen, yet enough like us to keep
My lifted missile from destroying you.

## FAUN

Beasts are devoid of shame and men of thanks.
With all that you contrive you never learn
What most you need, but we in silence serve.
One thing: In slaying us you slay yourselves.
Where we have trailed our shag the milk will spurt,
Where we withhold our hooves no blade will grow.
If only mind of men had reigned, your kind
And all you do would long ago be done.
Your field would be infertile, dry your brake...
Only by magic life is kept awake.

## THE LORD AND THE CENTURION

## CENTURION

I know, Lord, that your words exhale eternal life,
That for the children of your house you come with bread,
And yet do not begrudge the stranger fallen crumbs.
So ease my tortured soul!

## THE LORD

                    Wherein, Philippos? Speak!

## CENTURION

Those miracles for which they praise you, are they true?

378

## THE LORD

Child who has need of them, child whom they sting with gall.
Before the throng they came to pass and faith gave help.
The blind man saw, the lame took up his bed and walked,
The water turned to wine. But what are they to you,
Since you are not of those who feel them in themselves?

## CENTURION

You never teach the wise, but poorest of the poor,
The fishers, tollmen, too untutored for your light.

## THE LORD

The bright and dull alike besiege our Father's throne
At times the wisdom men possess is dust and chaff.
The world cannot be saved except through kindled blood.

## CENTURION

From early youth I served the ever valid law
You also have enjoined to win the realm of God.
I listened long to orators of great renown,
And on my journeys learned the mysteries of him
Who is the sun — they never may be told! — and of
The "Mothers" and "The Three" whom island folk revere.
I joined the naked hermits near the sources of the Nile...
The essence was the same. Have you a different creed?

## THE LORD

You give your own reply in that you seek me out.

## CENTURION

Great one, I plead! You know: in sacred bounds, before
We are allowed to see the highest, we are shown
That only he who leads the dance unites with God.
You never trod nor taught it. Are the rites then wrong?

379

## THE LORD

You err, not they. The love-feast done, I led the dance
For those with me. But words are void where thought is vast.
They only need my inner blaze and not my core.
The banner of the Son shall triumph over worlds,
For aeons men shall gaze upon his sign before
One comes who sees the bond fulfilled: the dancing Christ.

## CENTURION

But tell me, Master: Do you bring the final reign?

## THE LORD

Your mind will be confused whether I speak or not.

## CENTURION

Take me. I kneel! Why should I not belong to you?

## THE LORD

Because your watered lymph cannot endure the strength of God.
What you can have you now have had. Get up and go!

## THE BURNING OF THE TEMPLE

### THE PRIESTS: THE ELDEST, FIRST, SECOND, AND THIRD, THE FOURTH AND FIFTH AS MESSENGERS

## THE ELDEST

Why must I live to see that in the outskirts,
Where wall meets city, they are tearing up
The stones and sowing grass.

380

THE FIRST

                              Do you remember
— Twelve years ago — how when the drought befell us,
Our king crept through his gardens, old and witless,
And leaned above the earth? With pallid hands
He broke the arid soil to plant a straggle
Of roots.

THE SECOND

                    And all is quaking, all is lost
Since we were vanquished in the Scarlet Field
Where — turned to flee — our prince and leader fell.
Since giants came upon us, and the castle,
The throne are His.

THE FIRST

                         What we have built through decades
He topples in a day.

THE THIRD

                         But checks his warriors!
And even now the stolid throng is almost
Content.

THE FIRST

                    They yield to any sword, if only
They have their meagre rations and may watch
Their betters founder...

THE SECOND

                         And the crumbling peerage
Thinks he will never fall.

THE THIRD

                    He's just, they rumour.

THE ELDEST

I think: too cool for hate!

THE FIRST

                    To merchants who
Exhorted him to moderate the taxes
Which speed their ruin he dispatched this answer:
"Who cannot live beneath my rule must perish."

THE SECOND

And to the wailing women who implored him
That food be given to their new-born children,
He made reply: "If wenches drop their young
Upon the streets, their brood were better stifled."

THE FIRST

And how he thrust aside our fervent plea
To save our shrine! But with the vicious zealots
Who — laxly spared — have always scorned our law
And state — with them he came to terms and claims:
"You are not fit to heal your country's foulness.
What use are gods that cannot help you? Volumes
And images that fail to rouse? Be grateful
To one who helps you cast them off!"

THE THIRD

                    His words
Are simple and direct and not like ours.
They strike like lightning, suffer no retort.

THE FIRST

No one can tell his age or name, and no one
Has seen him with his helmet off. A breath
Of power circles him but, like a beggar's,
His wants are few. He lives among his men,
A common soldier, yet they vie to serve him.

## THE THIRD

He listens, but rejects all flattery.

## THE FIRST

He prays, they say, before an unhewn stone.

## THE SECOND

His form is lithe, his cheeks are young, but ageless
His mouth and brow.

## THE FIRST

               His host addresses him
As "Lord," his mother calls him "son," his friend
— When none is present — with a sound like "Ili."
He dubbed himself "the Scourge of God."

## THE THIRD

                                 Since Clelio
Died he has grown austere and even grim.

## THE FIRST

The best of all his men, his sword in battle,
His only friend surrendered to the glitter
Of gold and to the bright hair of our daughters,
And in the council duped his lord — who felt it!
Three days he did not speak, then summoned him:
"Your sorrow cannot shrive you for my sorrow
Cannot be measured! Do you still recall
The proudest evening in our years of conquest,
When both of us contested for the wreath?
We made a promise then that each should grant
The other one demand, nor ask for reasons.
You had yours long ago, my own is: Sentence
Yourself, lest I be forced to sentence you."
And Clelio kissed the hand which had condemned him,
And was dismissed, and rushed upon his sword.

## THE SECOND

It almost seemed as if his yoke was lighter
When, with her vulture's eye and mannish mouth,
The crone was still beside his chair. He exiled
Her to a convent near the woods, but gave her
Escort and honours and the consolation
That he would always be where she could find him.

## THE FIRST

To her reproach that she had been his comrade
And counselor from childhood on, he answered:
"A woman may have suffrage in the times
Of tents and trails, but in the palace age
She spells the fall of rule." Before she left him,
They claim she tried to tempt him with this tale:
"You were a babe in arms when in our flight
Before your uncle's henchmen, all in haste,
We climbed with Phrixos over icy mountains.
Then suddenly a pair of wolves attacked us,
Our faithful guard stabbed one, but with the second
He could not cope. I laid you on the beast
Whose flesh still held its warmth, and ran to aid.
And so, along with milk, you tasted blood.
I carried you for hours from the narrow
Valley we lived in, to the rocky peaks,
That you might see the sun. You owe your fortune
And all your prowess to those early rays."
He answered: "Mother, you have always willed
My happiness, but now you plot my ruin."
And sent her off!

## THE SECOND

                        Is he a mortal man!

## THE ELDEST

While here you weigh the destiny of strangers
Our own is jeopardized. This lofty house
With statues of the gods, with sacred tablets

384

And writings, precious gifts of many forebears,
Which we have guarded to this day and hour,
Is threatened with destruction. All the rites
Have been performed, our fathers' customs honoured.
We have done all that we can do ourselves.
And now Eternal Powers must lend their favour.

## THE SECOND

Our princess in her lovely youth, not he,
Was meant to govern us. She nobly chose
To do this heavy errand in our stead.
Now she is with him he may feel compassion.

## THE FIRST

How many gladly would have cast away
Goods, life, and honour for her slightest gesture!
Now she must cross a hostile threshold — pleading!

## THE ELDEST

Protectors of these precincts, give her aid!
The hour nears that renders us our sentence.

## THE FOURTH (entering)

This is the message: With a trumpet blast,
As though she were a queen, he had her bidden
And ushered to the throne, then asked her wish.
She told him warmly both what you had prompted
And what she felt herself: that it would heighten
His fame to spare the marvels of the temple.
He only made the same reply which once
He meted out to us. Her train alleges
His features were suffused with terrible light.
"I have been sent with torch and steel that you
Grow hard and not that I grow soft. You cannot
Appraise your needs. If, in your fall, you will not
Give up what saps you more and more, then I
Must wrest you from its grip. This is the law."

With brimming eyes which would have thawed the coldest
And with the gracious smile which even quickened
Old men to tremble she began once more:
"How could I dare to argue law with you?
But majesty has one celestial gift
To offer when all else is forfeit: Mercy!"
He hesitated for a single breath,
Surveyed her gravely with his chaste, barbarian
Unclouded eyes, and answered: "Majesty
Should spare the weak, but never when the plan
Of fate is thwarted as it would be here.
Shall I indulge your wish at such a price?
What bends me now would break me on the morrow."
Before his gaze she dropped her lids, and shaken
With anguish glided through the hall and back
Again, together with her faithful women
She chose to leave a world which had denied
Her honour's due, a world that now is poor.


THE ELDEST

When those we name with awe and cannot grasp
Deserted us, you were our shield, and we
Stood firm in stress through you alone, but now
That you no longer breathe the air we breathe,
Our brittle hope is shards. Pamfilia,
You, the most exquisite, most perfect flower
Of all our stem, here, now, before the others
I cleanse you of the loathsome rumour that
You loved him since he galloped through the gate.
Your brave and faithful heart could not endure
That the barbarian witnessed your abandon
To tears and to entreaties.


THE PRIESTS

                       She has done
What we must do hereafter.

THE FIFTH (entering)

        Save yourselves!
The halls are thick with smoke, from every corner
The fire flares and soars.

THE PRIESTS

        The temple's burning!

THE ELDEST

It burns and half a thousand years must pass
Before it finds another resurrection.

### VERSES FOR THE LIVING

"Why at the crossroads wonder and wait?"
"Ought I go to the left or the right?"
"Love has called you, follow the voice!
Dawned has the year which determines your fate,
It is the first that the man makes his choice."


While a tremor still holds us,
While a shadow still broods
Balking the probe of your reason,
What I ask of you is
That you yield to the song
Of which you are the soul.


Let the wash of the moon-
Dappled river submerge
You by shivering reeds.
Shed what has governed your day,
All that covers you, all
Sham is shattered and drowned.
Stirred and stricken you rise
Between me and the night.
What this hand now enjoins,
What is wrung from these lips
Bears witness to what you are worth.

Prize the treasure you were given,
It will never slip your fingers,
But you cannot weigh it fully
Till you know how it was granted,
When, with whom you have to share it,
And when you possess unchallenged.


This is what must still be done:
See the steps your glance comprised
As a miracle within.

What you think fulfilment, though
You may call it kin to gods,
Is an outset sheathed in light.

Good and great and precious things
Gain — when one thing more accrues —
Double depths, unique delight.


Love, indeed, cannot be gauged,
And to measure yours were heinous,
Great the deed it did with greatness!
But there are degrees of awe.
What occurred is past belief!
Can you even it that my
Awe is more profound than yours?


If by yourself you cannot see
A light will dawn on you, the day
That I absolve him from his vow
Who rants to you of being free.

If my doubt perhaps offends
Wait! A little time will tell.
I have much to make amends:
All I own is yours as well.

Riddles flicker old and new,
Now you cannot read the rune
Which you shall decipher soon...
Bow and give them all their due.

My hand pleads and threatens. Today
You were as I wished, if you could
Tomorrow be still as you should...
What vistas, beloved, and what joy!

A.

I

It was your voice I heard, but not your soul.
A year our course must lead through storm and sleet,
Each heart must tremble with the other's beat.
Now that you know — will you still brave the goal?

II

With grace and pride you govern in your round,
And do not suffer if it springs a flaw.
I am not free when I transgress my law,
I do not know I love until I sound.

All that the day demands you do aright,
But what you lack is awe of destiny,
And so that advent made me pensively
Give up for you what promised me delight.

III

You savoured all the sweets of life: no bliss
Or frenzied dream to which you were a stranger,
Do not demur that now your fate is this:
The other part true life comprises: danger!

B.

I

By night we walk in step along the gate,
No want nor force will open it. My one
Request to you, beloved, is: watch and wait
With me until we hear the call within.


II

You know the inner world, you understand
I cannot chain you in the reach of day.
You cannot gain me with the speech of day,
The heavy wind of dreams must first descend.

They change and dye each thing in space and time,
So we may see the form that is its own,
So by its proper name it may be known...
But yours the mouth that causes all to chime.


III

This hour shall afford you certainty.
The thoughts it brought were neither great nor rare,
And from our lips the words came haltingly.
And yet the inner space was charged, and there
You heard a heart that augured ecstasy.


W.

I

Could you not, should you not let
Arms you confided in
Lift you across the only
Threshold that offers and thank them,
Impious child of this age?

Ignorant child of this age,
Who will later invest
You with the power to break
Open the door when you toil
Vainly with lacerate fingers?

II

You chose and think that you may choose again,
But only once the easy way is plain,
That you will take the hard is to be doubted,
You dream of solace, and what comes is pain.

III

We face the rim of fate with equal rue:
"Our joy was great — can we attain this too?"
If you mean those who hope to win what's rare
Without an effort — then there is no heir!

P.

You long have craved to head for seas and shores,
To know the world with jeopardies and wars.
Unconsecrate you hunt for life and so
It sends you back with not a thing to show.

The highest grace which man receives from fate
Was held in store for you, was at your gate.
You did not see, you always will be blind.
You did not feel, a child unto the end.

G. R. H.

Your foot still roots in clods of yester-year,
Your poise and gesture burgeon from the new,
And far into a world of sunrise you
Fling out your arm whose greeting finds me here.

391

27

## H. M.

How wise is he who from the noisy mart
To brush and plectrum silently retires,
But wiser who — though master of his art —
At times regards it wrong to finger lyres.


## L.

### I

A great achievement does not need display,
But burning impulse craves to be expressed.
For days I set myself a single quest:
To find a word for our unwonted way.

### II

Constant waiting draws a sneer,
Constant hoping is amiss,
And the greatest secret this:
God of gods the Now and Here.


## F. W.

Let Fate extinguish nations with her bolt,
Impregnable, you brave the rudest jolt.
God weighs alike the wars within and out,
Where there are men like you they win the bout.


## J.

Your untouched flesh took confidence from me,
And up your spirit rose from fog and sea.
I clasp you, tempered now and sound again,
And gird myself with strength from your domain.

392

E.

I saw you, perfect in your flowering year,
Our lives were merged, our days a fiery chain...
Perhaps you once will change and bloom again
Should southwind sweep you over your frontier.


R...

He ranks the highest whom the god has let
Advance beyond the threshold here on earth,
Not much beneath who — knowing this — is yet
Content to serve wherever he is set.


S...

"Can summer not be spent more wisely," you objected
When with the swimmers' merriment incognito I vied.
Let me avoid the poet's lot, who at the ford reflected
So long upon the boys' conundrum that he died.


A. VERWEY

I
A poet, always eager to make clear
Where true and false in wild pursuing veer,
Must expiate with silence many a year.

II
You spoke from your soul:
"I found unsurpassed
Companions at last."
But years took their toll,
You write hard and fast
And day after day
To drive them away.

III

"Here is the rift, I can believe no longer!"
What? What you hide or what you frankly say?
Believe that sterile worlds again will blossom,
For poets, poet nothing else should count!


IV

You and none but you
Know, *van buiten*, through
These terrains alone
Ageless realms shine on.
Search through multitudes,
Ask if others caught
Your exalted thought.
Then your wrath will flee,
Miss the mark and be
Brief as brothers' feuds.


V

Do you recall that years ago you told me
With resignation "I have reached the end."
But then you quickened with a quicker current,
For all the spirits alien to your soul
Were loosed and broke into your narrow home.
Though you remained yourself, you were renewed.
And now with lavish phrases you are trying
To gloss your sorrow that I need not say
As you yourself must say: I am alone,
I am the very last among my people.


M.

In thinning mist of early morning hours
Your garden wakened to the happy twitter
Of many birds, where once you loved the litter
Of tangled branches and luxuriant flowers.

And sultry sorcery kept you surrounded
With garnet walls as steep as precipices,
Until your eyes, wide-open and astounded,
Slowly attuned to cool and boundless spaces.

And spurred from grey of dawn to fullest splendour,
The slave of dreams into a comrade grew.
He wanders at my side, serene and tender,
And gently laves his childish face in dew.


THE DANCER

The garden wavers with the roundelay
Of children, and the dusk subdues their rhyme,
They swing in circles, then in pairs they sally
And to the same refrain disband and rally,
How gayly, hand in little hand, they sway,
But one invents the moves and marks the time.

How light the legs that leap and whirl with him,
How lithe and swift the hips that bound and rest.
His hair floats on the dark with trembling shimmer,
He is the lodestar in a maze of glimmer,
He is the heart of youth with all its dream,
He is the heart of youth with all its zest.


B. v. ST.

I

In streets where gods have walked through summer blaze,
We often mused, and mourned the traces of
The princely child who died.

What do we gain from triumphs, wit, and strength,
From brave defense in lowlands soaked with blood,
If majesty has vanished!

The upstart finds himself in empty halls,
His gardens will be sterile once the old
And sacred tree is felled.

What gain in ease and equal rights for all
— Granted that these are more than guileless dreams —
When graciousness has vanished!


II

Imperishable charm of come and go
In streets where fate unwound — and with us you
In full and fairest flower.

That was your time of lordly rule and we
Adored you while the people even claimed
Their prince was resurrected.


## HEAVEN

"Come with me to the mystic who convinces us so well
Of true hereafters and of false terrestrial gleams."
"I have been there! Before he said a single word, I knew
His heaven is an evil jest and nothing more."


## THE KEY

"I listened to your words. Nobody else can show me
The world like you, now I myself shall see and test it!"
"The alpha of all wisdom is the key: with it
You may unlock the world. Your way is wrong.
Search seven years and go to every teacher,
You will return less wise than you are now."

## BODY AND SOUL

"The Sage has taught," you said, "the body's beauty
Weighs lighter than the soul's." But soul and body
Express one thing in flux. The state grew weak,
The burgher dull and brash, then the Divine
Devised the soul for therapy and succour . . .
Not long ago you sketched a former friend:
His eyes, once bright, had dimmed, his noble forehead
Seemed narrower, and his young lips were dry.
Was it his soul you pictured or his body?


## THE TEACHER OF WISDOM

"For thirty years you delivered your lectures to thousands."
"Who backs you now?" "Not one or two, but the entire world!"
"Then surely, O teacher, you better had kept the doors bolted,
Since you have worked for nothing save a worthless word."


## EDUCATOR

"The wonted way has missed the goal, now we shall try!
Two failures! But a third attempt may score success!"
"You should not act until your heart is sure it knows,
In your profession to experiment is crime!"


## TEACHING

"I want to learn from you. What is your charge?"
"Let me have access to your secret being,
So that your inner beauty may unfold.
I am your destined teacher if I love.
Your core must burn, it matters not for whom.
You are my destined pupil if you love."

## DISCIPLES' DOUBT

"He who circled in your orbit,
Can he bear to break away?"

"Some give only transient service,
Treason comes from festered blood."

"He who sat at such a banquet,
Can he ever be destroyed?"

"Some have drunk the wine of living,
Others eaten of their death."

"Love and only love you taught us,
Yet your call is often harsh!"

"Peace is what I have accorded
These, but those I bring the sword."


## VERSES FOR THE DEAD

When men of the future are purged of dishonour,
Their shoulders released from the shackles of bondage,
Their vitals alive with the hunger for virtue,
Then flashes of blood will illumine the millions
Of graves of the fallen, then thundering armies
Will ride over clouds, and the terror of terrors,
The third of the tempests will sweep through the country:
                              The dead are returning.

When men of this nation no longer are cowards,
Or weaklings, but feel their vocation and mission,
Their hearts will decipher in untold disaster
A message from heaven, their hands will be lifted,
Their lips will be tuned to the homage of honour,
The flag of the king, the legitimate symbol,
Will fly through the dawn and be lowered in praise to
                              The highest of heroes!

398

## HEINRICH F.

Your daring mind that fanned your fiery core
Comprised the near and distant in its zone,
Like an adventurer who walks a shore
No foot has trod and claims it for his own.

Blithe as a child, a bird, bewitched and proud,
You left us, friend, your fate was in your eye,
And you — away before you said goodbye —
Were first to fall, the gallant flag your shroud.


## WALTER W.

Their mournful dance whose lightness was pretended!
The puffs of dainty satin, pink and frilled!
They were the last whose lives were linked and filled.
This was my world — it was — but now is ended.

Where can we find a footing, where a prop?
The hinges creak and all the rafters crumble,
Soon in the brittle house the flames will tumble,
What shall we do? How can we help or stop?

I found the longed-for door, I dreamed of wonder,
Implored and knocked — no words or wits availed.
I cannot bear to see the prize I failed
To capture — so the wave shall wash me under.


## WOLFGANG

Before you solved the riddle of this year
Into the next you dexterously crossed,
Where pleasures bound to comfort you appear...
But you, too clever, know what you have lost.

You look at me — what word shall I devise
To speed you? Can I find no stronger spell?
Drive out the sadness lurking in your eyes,
Or, rider, this will be your last farewell!


NORBERT

You lived a monkish life with books and felt
Distaste for tools of war, but once you knew
The rough, confining cloth, the soldier's belt,
You scorned the safety which was offered you.

You seemed too spent to fight, too overbred,
But grazed by winds from worlds without a name,
Like any lusty youth you stormed ahead
And fell, dispersed in air, and earth, and flame.


BALDUIN

The poise with which you rode across the square,
Your eyes which, on that day, were filled with glory,
The way you stood and paced the thoroughfare —
Is like a dream, is even now a story.


BALDUIN

But for what did we lay down our lovely mantle,
Shed the sheath of tender flesh among the flowers?
So that you might raze our pillared houses,
Set your idols on the ruins of our temples?
                          Oh, I
Know how long our dead have yearned for Lethe,
How they famish for the drop that brings forgetting.

400

Was it this for which the radiance of the jewelled
Crown was dimmed? Has darkness brimmed our shining vessels,
That you, rebels, might pollute the vital essence,
And, though beggars, sell the foe your kin and children?
                                   See with
What desire to level shores they hasten
And allay their thirsty lips with sombre waters.


Do not bring us wreaths or harass us with statues!
Do not take the ashes back to soil you tainted,
For the plains on which we fell we call our homeland,
And our mother holy earth that offers refuge.
                                   Oh, though
Deep the draught, our staring eyes are wild with anguish,
And our foreheads grooved with awful accusation.


## VICTOR AND ADALBERT


V: Across our sunlit days among the hills
   A shadow seemed to fall. We ousted it
   With joy. But tell me now: Why are you sad?


A: While everyone is feeding idle hopes,
   I feel the threat of chaos and despair
   Draw closer and refuse to be engulfed.


V: We muster greater strength with greater dangers.


A: Dangers I braved to long! Enough of war
   And murder! Now that I am sound again
   I have begun to think, and know that this
   Is madness doomed to end in madness, know
   That in the coming battle I shall be
   The first to fall. I rather go unbid.

V: That would be flight, and flight is base!

A:                                                          For one
   Who hoards his life as I have never done.

V: Forestall the gods! That would be sacrilege!

A: These very gods of yours have changed my vision.

V: Were I to name the many who will mourn you,
   And suffer from an act they cannot grasp,
   I should be silenced by your weightier word.
   But you are consecrate! Who can accord you
   The leave to go?

A:                         It is my consecration
   Which drives me to obey my law and shrink from
   Whatever might subtract from what I am.
   To fall in blind haphazardness no longer
   Befits me, nor to lead a slowly fading
   Existence in an era of decay.
   If we remain, we rot. If now we loosen
   Our hold on earth and go with pride and valour,
   We shall continue in our lighted courses
   As young as stars in their eternal glory.

V: My friend, did you say "our"? Then let me say:
   Though you infused me with your stronger strength,
   I cannot feel as you, and so your Must
   Is not my own. I slept or watched beside you
   Serene through this enchanted spring. But sometimes,
   Since we were last together, thinner substance
   Than air surrounded us, our pulses beat
   With something that had not the weight of blood.

A: I will not beg you and I dare not force you.
   If you ignore my plea, or rather Fate's,
   I know your lips will pale before the grasses
   Have time to yellow. Do you see me tremble?
   I shudder with the thought that this could be.

402

V: How can those hours blazing with abundance
   And marvels cede to fears!

A:                          This is the turning!

V: Through sallow twilight looms the ghostly peak
   Where now the witches dance. If you must utter
   Such reckless words, then wait until the new moon.

A: Faced with the grave, you play with childish fancies
   The demon in me stamps as silly spook.
   And yet you guess the savage goad which prods me.

V: And would you go, though I do not?

A:                                     I must.

V: If long and sunny mornings spent together,
   If radiant evenings in the valley, full
   Of tranquil joy while worlds were split asunder,
   Were not too much of happiness for mortals,
   And call for penance now — I cannot tell.
   If not another need than that which moves us
   Enjoins the sombre deed, I do not know.
   The gods have given me no sign, but I
   Believe in all that holds for you and keep
   The vow we made when we were adolescent
   And often have repeated since. I cannot
   Live on without you, impious though it be.
   So if you choose the gate of dark, obeying
   Your destiny in this, then take me too!

### THE SONG

> Whatever word and thought I still can frame,
> What I still love — the features are the same.

What a venturesome foot
Flits through the garden of fay:
Our grandmothers' innermost kingdom?

What a riot of sound
Pours from a silvery horn
Through slumbering thickets of legend?

What a breath from beyond,
Born of yesterday's grief,
Invades and fondles the spirit?


THE SONG

A boy once roamed into the woods,
His cheek was smooth and bright,
He lost his way in woods of fay
And was not home by night.

The village folk turned out and searched
From dawn till day was sped,
But since they found no trace of him
They gave him up as dead.

Now after seven years had passed
One morning it befell
That he was seen beyond the green
And heading toward the well.

They asked him who he was and stared,
His face seemed strange and dim.
His parents both were gone, and no
One else remembered him.

"A while ago I lost the path
And walked in woods of fay,
I came in time to feast with them,
But soon was sent away.

The people there are white as snow
And they have golden locks,
These are their words for sun and moon,
For valleys, hills, and brooks."

404

They laughed: "This early in the day
He can't be full of wine!"
They said that he was mad and made
Him keeper of their kine.

So every day he fared afield
And sat upon a stone,
And late into the night he sang,
They left him quite alone.

And only children heard his song
And often sat beside,
They sang it far into the years,
Long after he had died.


SAILOR'S SONG

YVOS FAREWELL TO JOLANDA

You wait in vain!    Though he is gone
And lies at rest    where no one shall
Discover him,    my blood has cooled,
I go aboard    and far from you.

When strangled down    the cliff he sank,
The joy I thought    so near was fled.
You guess at much    but not the whole:
I am not yours,    the wild wave calls.

Your tears will flow    when late at night
The message comes    I am at sea,
My ship my friend    until in work
On foreign strand    my course is run.

We all are base,    may you stay pure!
Soon you will sigh,    and wind a wreath
Around the shrine    on rocky shore,
And pray for your    and for my soul.

The brooding earth decrees below:
Though free as fish and fowls of air,
Wherein you cling you do not know.

A later mouth may once reveal:
You too have taken of our share,
You too have tasted of our meal.

Yours was a vision fair and new,
But time grew old, none lives today,
If one will come who sees it too

In years untold — you cannot say.


SEA SONG

When on the verge the fiery ball
Dips downward in reluctant fall,
I linger on the dunes and yearn
For one I cherish to return.

This time of day is dull at home,
The flower wilts in salty foam,
And no one seeks the last, lone door
And her who came from alien shore.

A fair-haired child now passes by
With naked limbs and cloudless eye.
Singing and skipping as he nears,
He skirts the boat and disappears.

I watch him come, I watch him go,
He never speaks to me, and though
My lips are silent, just to see
Him for an instant gladdens me.

My hearth is warm, my roof is tight,
And yet it harbours no delight.
The rents in every net are sewed
And room and kitchen well bestowed.

I wait, I sit upon the sand,
My temple pulses in my hand,
For if the blond child stays away,
What use to me the livelong day!


## THE FOOLISH PILGRIMESS

Where the highway from the hills
Turns abruptly toward the stream,
And the furrows climb the crest
Where the pregnant woman once
Asked my help to lift her hay-load,

There beside the road a girl
Lay as though she had been felled
By fatigue — with tangled hair
And bedraggled skirt. I bent
Down to her and helped her up.

Sadly thanking me, she said
With her hand against her brow:
"Often have I passed you by,
Nothing but my luckless fall
Caused your eyes to rest upon me.

When we meet again, I shall
Wear a finer frock, and though
Even this will fail to please,
You will look at me because
Once you raised me from the ground."


## THE LAST OF THE FAITHFUL

While he is kept on foreign shores,
My native land seems dim to me.
I feel I am a stranger here
Because my king is banished.

407

I do not live for joys and feasts
Like others, and I only wait
These many springs, these many falls,
Because my king may call me.

And if he never should return
Nor summon me to serve him there,
My only thought and aim to die
When he, my king, is dying.


## THE WORD

I carried to my country's shore
Marvels and dreams, and waited for

The tall and twilit norn to tell
The names she found within the well.

Then I could grasp them, they were mine,
And here I see them bloom and shine...

Once I had made a happy haul
And won a rich and fragile jewel.

She peered and pondered: "Nothing lies
Below," she said, "to match your prize."

At this it glided from my hand
And never graced my native land.

And so I sadly came to see:
Without the word no thing can be.


## THE CUPS

This is a cup of gold
Gorged with wine beyond price,
Each has the right to a taste.

That is of wood and it holds
Three stones cut into dice,
Each has the right to a cast.

This, when caught in the hand,
Shows us what destiny
Grants to an unmoved heart.

That conveys the command
No one can shift or foresee:
What is my part, what is your part.


## THE LIGHT

We grieve when you deprive us of your favour
And turn to others who are given more
On evenings when your essence weaves a savour
Around our spirit yearning to adore.

We should be fools to let our hatred touch you,
When often with your blaze you threaten blight,
We should be children if we tried to clutch you —
Because you shine for every one, sweet light!


Through deepest rest
Of ordered day
A glance has flashed
That rouses to alarm
Undreamed the tranquil soul.

Just as on heights
The moveless tree
Looms firm and proud,
And late a tempest bends
It downward to the ground.

Just as the tide
With strident sound,
With savage lunge,
Once more into the long
Abandoned sea-shell thrusts.


You like a flame, unflawed and slender,
You flower sprung from Crown and Spear,
You like the morning, light and tender,
You like a spring, withdrawn and clear,

Companion me in sunny meadows,
Encompass me in evening haze,
And where I go, you shine through shadows,
You cool of wind, you breath of blaze.

You are my thought and my desire,
The air I breathe with you is blent,
From every draught I drink your fire,
And you I kiss in every scent.

You like the morning, light and tender,
You flower sprung from Crown and Spear,
You like a flame, unflawed and slender,
You like a spring, withdrawn and clear.

# THE LADY'S PRAYING

A Legend in the Manner of the Old Masters of Cologne.
Dedicated in Homage to the Lord of the Castle of Rheinstein.

This poem should be presented through tableaux. The descriptive passages serve
as stage directions, while the direct discourse is either recited by the characters
or spoken in the background in an even, passionless voice.

The characters are:

> The lady
> He with the falcon
> He with the griffin (an apparition)
> A priest
> A messenger
> Maid servants

There is no change of scene. After the fifth tableau the curtain falls for a
brief intermission.

The consecrated beads slip through her fingers,
Ringless and half concealed in calabar
With which the sleeves are furred. She kneels enveloped
From head to foot in black and rigid folds
Before the desk designed for her devotions.
The lady's praying.

    Slanted rays descend
Upon her from the arched and pointed window
With lozenged panes, where Mary floats in green
And crimson, yellow sheen around her hair,
The rich and radiant dyes of other worlds.

Down in the court a clash of weapons breaks
The spell of awe which silences the watchers.
Maid servants cross the corridors on tiptoe:
"The two who vie in homage to our lady
— Her lord was treacherously slain, none knows
By whom, while he was hunting in the forest —
Ride at each other in the lists, so one
May prove that his was not the guilt and win
the favor she has promised to the victor."

413

She prays, and through her prayer seems to hear
Him with the falcon speak:

                "I lean to laughter
And love the company of merry spirits
Who cannot do without me. When the guard
Lets down the bridge at my approach, he claims
That gloom is now about to leave these halls.
The village girls caress my very words,
And at my lute the women burn with fervor.
Who ever saw me walk forbidden ways
Alone, with furtive eyes which children shun!"


He with the griffin:

             "Weigh my blameless life,
The testimony of my glorious scars!
Before my lord was king I crossed the Alps
With him and shed my blood in his campaigns.
I fought to succour the oppressed and with
My name the people learned to couple honour.
My lance subdued the Moors, I even saw
The hill on which Our Lord hung on the cross."


A crashing blow, a pause and utter silence,
Then loud acclaim and mutter of dissent
Invade the lady's prayer. She listens, lifts
Her head and trembles, bends again to kiss
The bead which holds the sacred splinter, hurries
To greet the victor whose resounding tread
Already fills the hall.

               Her eyes are bright,
And with the hand she yields as graciously
As mourning widow may, she indicates
That God's decision tallies with her own,
And the young knight sinks down upon his knee.

         ***

414

"The clamour of the feast had scarcely died
And those who witnessed our delight dispersed
When off my husband rode to savage bouts
With angry words for me on his return.
I sit alone beside the hearth and spin,
Or from the terrace gaze into the river
And, as I weep about this present sorrow
I think of all the bitter trials and dreary
Distress which clouded years that should be fair.


Long, Reverend Father, did I strive to follow
Your counsel and surrender to my lot.
My candles burn before a host of shrines,
My chests are drained of treasure. Fearlessly
I cross the thresholds of the sick and yet
The day I first was forced to hear his rage
Intensified my suffering to despair.
And in the agony of empty nights
I am obsessed by a nefarious thought..."


"O daughter, do not try the highest Judge
Unerring as the stars within their course,
For only now that Satan and his tribe
Have come to lord it in your heart, does true
Disaster reign supreme, but you must strive
To curb the rebel flesh and cast him out
— No matter how he balks — by pleading for
The intercession of your patron saints."


A rider gallops up the path:

                    "My lord
Gave me a message for his lady, that
The noble monk before the city of
The seven bridges made him see the light,
And too impatient of delay to bid
Adieu, he now is spurring toward the grave
Of Christ, the templar's cross upon his shoulder."

The rider storms into the court, dismounts,
Looks down the passages and through the hall,
Sees that the door which leads into the chapel
Was left ajar. He flings it wide and pauses,
Then gently swings it to again and puts
His finger to his lips:

"The Lady's Praying!"

*From the* PRIMER

## DRAWINGS IN GREY (1889)

### PEACE

Evening flutters about me on soundless wings,
Day with its vehement swirl is done,
Its gross and ravening prod and drive.
In aimless profusion my thoughts
Rushed, and tumbled out their abundance,
And one devoured the other.
I sighed: Will the time ever come when I
Can pause over this and muse on that?
Evening is here — a span of silence
Unfretted. I am alone,
And now I have an excess of hours,
But I stand riveted and my eyes
Are drawn to the magnet of the lantern
Outside, emitting vague rays
Against the black mirror of night.
No longer will I think — I cannot.
I only want to bend my knees,
Think of nothing — almost pray.


### YELLOW ROSE

In an ambience undulating with tepid odours
And silvered to an artificial day
She breathed. A yellow radiance poured around her
All sheathed in yellow satin.
Only when her lips curl to a dying smile
And her breast and shoulder stir ever so slightly,
One divines the contours of form.
Mystic goddess from the Ganges, the Brahmaputra!
You seemed a thing of wax, without a soul
Until you suddenly lifted
Your long-lashed lids, weary of languor.

417

## THE IMAGE

I wake at night in a spasm of fear...
Enormous clouds confront me with their darkness,
Are torn alternately and merged to masses,
And while a multitude of shadows
I cannot see although I feel them,
Impel my mouth to burn and tremble,
The image seeks me out.
Today I found it — one of many.
An instant of profound emotion
And it forsook me pierced with longings.
Then I forgot it. Even dreams
Could not evoke it from oblivion.
Claiming revenge and demanding its due,
It rose through the terror of night
Once more to play the powerful intruder.


## PRIESTS

When the mist dissolves they hasten away
With the day which unravels its filmy skein,
Both bear unmistakable traces
Of joys indulged beyond measure —
Marked by gestures that quickly betray
Insane embraces and kisses.
Priests who have given their bodies as offerings
— Unbridled by wisdom or knowledge —
To orgies that shatter and slay.
Their foreheads are mirrors for lust
With that indisputable ugliness
Which spells the majesty of vice.
But both are justified,
For both still have
The poise and gait of youth.
Beneath her long-drawn brows
Unquenched desires still are burning.
His lips are still curved with
The smile of the blessed.

## VENOM OF NIGHT

I have returned. A bell nearby
With long and sonorous chimes dismisses
The day that has grown old.
Wearily I lie down but I cannot sleep
Alone with my dreams.
And I see myself as a boy
Who does not know the fruits of savage lust,
And not disfiguring furrows,
Nor eyes of sinister fires —
Whose childish cheeks still have
Their untouched bloom.
A boy — the boyhood years are done —
Still caught in the spell
Of freshness and youth
Through the breath of candles
And odour of incense.
And then I hoped to find
Her who is wise and vicious
In ruses of destruction,
To run with open arms
Into my ruin,
To love like a madman,
To blight myself wholly,
And then to yield to death.


## A SUNRISE

And now on the sombre hearth
Of heaven, after a night
Of wintry cold the sun
Again is kindled.
It climbs and casts the quiet shimmer
Of early rays.
With the clouds that skim around it
And mirror its brightness,
It sparsely illumines
The morning greyness.

Swiftly it gains in strength
And seized and sears
Curtains of colour
That venture too closely.
And then the whole
Horizon fills with grey
Impenetrable mist.
Warmth and light deepen and glow
Until at last the clouds, the mist,
All are devoured in flares
Of boundless conflagration,
And without alien substance,
Only through inner powers
The disk discharges flame.


CHANGE

When first I saw her she did not please me:
She has no trace of beauty
Except for her black, her deep black hair.
One day my lips caressed it only an instant,
And I was greatly pleased with her hair
And also her hand...
She has no trace of beauty
Except for her hair and — yes — her delicate hand.
One day I clasped it a little more closely
And I was greatly pleased with her hand
And also her mouth.
Today there is nothing about her
That does not please me greatly,
That does not fire my adoration.


TO A SLAVE-GIRL

Since the divine goal now has vanished,
And a transient flame transfigures
An image made of clay,

420

Since animate shades of the beautiful
Gathered long and guarded well
Demand an offering once despised,
I shall say to her: Be silent!
Lest sweet address and antiphon
Of speech be desecrated,
And shabby and meaningless words
Destroy our counterfeit heaven
And add disgust to the absence
Of holiness — I shall say:
Never open your lips
Except for sighs and kisses...
Be silent as I shall be silent.


## IN THE PICTURE GALLERY

In a world of colours I wanted
To shed the dust of common day.
I entered as you left, and the moment I saw you
Your brow revealed an unexpected wisdom,
Your eyes conveyed profound discernment.
With what delight I should have walked beside you
Throught the spacious halls, contemptuous of
The stolid stare, the foolish laughter
And idle remarks of the masses around us.
How I desired to force those many contours
Together to a wall of the elect!
Why did you leave? You did not notice me.
I roam about incapable of pleasure.
In the copious outpour
Of flesh and blue and green
I cannot find your face.

# A CHILD'S CALENDAR

Our memory of Epiphany and the weeks that followed yield little more than the exotic sight of the Three Wise Men with their gold, frankincense and myrrh, and then the sleigh rides across the frozen river, now one with the level shores. Round Candlemas there was much talk of longer light and the hope of winter's ending. Early in the morning we went to see the wax consecrated. The next day candles were held up before us, and we received a blessing. The carnival at which we wore strange and many-coloured disguises, showed us a topsy-turvy world with men changed into women and human beings into beasts. At dawn, when it was still quite dark, children who carried round loaves speared on tall poles, ushered in Shrove Tuesday. On Ash Wednesday we went up to the altar where the priest dipped his fingers in ashes to sign our foreheads with the Cross. After Mid-Lent-Sunday we watched the farmers start their work in the fields again, and when the sun rose in the trees we sat in a clump of willows, loosened the bark from the shoots by beating them for a long time, and cut notches for flutes and pipes. The swallows returned and the storks. Holy Week came: Altars were stripped, the organ stood silent. The sound of wooden clappers took the place of bells and chimes. On Good Friday we followed the priest and the acolytes and threw ourselves down in the choir to kiss the Cross now laid on the floor. The dusk resounded with the age-old lament over the destruction of the sacred city. Then came Saturday when the Cross was unveiled and Easter heralded with jubilant trumpets. On White Sunday anthems from the tower wakened us early. We went out to see a train of small brides and grooms going forth to partake of the Lord's fare for the first time. They were pale with fear and awe, and this was the only day in the year when even the most stolid among the children were touched with beauty.

End of April we took to the hills and meadows again. Our mother taught us the names and virtues of flowers and herbs, and we were shown the place, high up and hard to get to, where the rare plant dittany grows whose cup brims with white flame by night. Toward evening, in Mary's month, we went to the chapel with wreaths and masses of lilacs to adorn the image of the Queen of Heaven. Here we were taught the two attitudes of prayer: the one with fingers intertwined and lowered to express submission and gratitude, the other with fingers close, tips touching and lifted in praise and supplication. On Corpus Christi a vast procession accompanied the monstrance as it was borne through festive streets, flower-strewn and fragrant with

423

incense, and in the Te Deum our high voices merged with the deeper notes of the men.

Pentecost marked the beginning of summer. The woods and the banks of the river were again alive with song. We carried wine uphill in big stone jugs, were told to cool it in the brook, and then settled down to a merry meal in a round clearing between the spruces. On Saint John's Day we went from house to house to collect kindling and logs. The wood was then loaded on carts, built into great pyres on the hilltops, and lit when it grew dark. We liked to thrust our naked arms through the tongues of fire. During the harvest we went into the fields when the heat of day was over and wove wreaths out of cornflowers. Someone showed us how to make little princesses from poppies turned upside down. There we once heard the reapers sing a song about Woden and did not know why we were suddenly awestruck and afraid. It did not occur to us until much later that it was because a god dethroned thousands of years ago was still remembered, while one of today was already being forgotten. Toward the middle of August we followed while the image of the patron saint of our city was carried aloft on a platform from the church to the chapel on the mountain. He wore a mantle of purple velvet, over his shoulders hung the first clusters of ripening grapes. We had put on pilgrim's cloaks trimmed with scallop shells, and each of us held a staff and a bottle of water. But the row of Sundays from Pentecost until Advent brought little change in our year and they have already paled in our memory. In between came Trinity Sunday — on which sleepwalkers are born and those who foresee the future — the harvesting of the grapes and All Saints' Day, the last festival before the onslaught of fog and cold. During Advent we needed lanterns to go to early Mass when the hymn *Rorate caeli desuper...* was sung, and long weeks were filled with the expectancy of coming Christmas.

# HÖLDERLIN

## A Eulogy

But where gold is more profuse than clear-running water
Of springs, and more than ominous the wrath in the heavens,
Once between day and dark
Something of truth will be granted.
Seal it in symbols three, but
Even left unsaid, O Guileless Ones,
It still will persist and be changeless.

\*\*\*

Before the streams cascaded from the mountains,
And groves and cities grew on the banks of rivers,
A thunder pealed as He
Created a law without fault
And formed the sounds that are faultless.

\*\*\*

Now Nature has awakened with a clang of arms,
And from the zenith down to chasms Rapture
Begetter of all, is reborn from holy chaos, as once,
And brims with a deluge of life
Compelled by immutable canon.

\*\*\*

The temple-columns stand
Forsaken in days of despair, yet even without name
The god is within them, and all that is sacred
The offering-bowls, the vessels vowed in thanks are
Entombed by the earth where a foe cannot find them.

\*\*\*

The age of games, when secret and unseen the
Acclaimed, the hero, sat with poets, watched the wrestlers
And smiled his acclaim at the gravely-playful children.
It was, it is a loving without end.

\*\*\*

For many things a sage or friend with
Eyes that never betray may draw out of darkness, but only
The advent of a god can renew the earth
And sea and heaven with radiance.

* * *

Someone always serves as a link between mortals and Him,
Apparent rung by rung, a
Celestial descending.

* * *

But when celestials are dragged into common day
And miracles shorn of wonder, when the
Titanic princes plunder the gifts of
Their mother, a more sovereign rises and aids her.

Hölderlin


It is something of a miracle when a poet, forgotten for generations or at best considered a sensitive dreamer of things past, suddenly assumes his rightful role of seer for his people. The Sibylline book, long under lock and key because no one could read it, has now become common property and an unknown world full of secrets and tidings unfolds before our astonished eyes. The danger this may involve appears less formidable when one remembers that — now as always — what is not felt cannot be understood, and that imminence of the hour of destiny justifies a deviation from reverent silence.

Hölderlin's early writings are rooted in the century of Goethe. His later work, most of which was unavailable or unelucidated up to now, establishes him as the progenitor of another lineage. The masters of classicism were unable to evaluate the best he had to give because they were still faced with the difficult task of extricating themselves and their people from barbaric confusion and conflicting urges which barred the way to Hellenic clarity. In painting and sculpture they knew and admired only what Apollo embodied, or rather what they could conjecture from copies in which the original vigour had been smoothed away. They would have ignored the flute-playing girl or the youth with the scales of the so-called "thrones." It is true that they had mastered the Greek tragic poets, but Pindar was read only in part and now-and-then, and in Plato they saw a mere propounder of ideas. What Dionysos and Orpheus stood for was still buried in oblivion. It was Hölderlin who unearthed it. He needed neither guide-posts nor directions; his inner eye showed him the way. He was the lightning that cleft the sky and confronted us with overwhelming counterparts such as Herakles-Christ. Even today his boldest visions and syntheses force us to bow our heads and drop our hands. There was much talk of the amiable idealist and sonorous lute-player, but never of the intrepid messenger who evoked the idea of a community other than any in existence. Nor did they speak of the confident explorer who probed into the sources of language — for him not mere cultural equipment but his native element — and rescued the life-giving word from its dilemma between factual description and destructive analysis.

Those to whom the era of enlightenment had bequeathed a feeling for nature and a love of reason, called him a stranger on earth, forgetting that their much vaunted experience is vain and superfluous for one who has a covenant with the gods and with Destiny. We are little concerned with the arduous career of his prime or the course of an old man's illness, for we are sound enough to know that the Daimon works in pales beyond those of health and of reason.

Not that his torn and tortured life is intended as a model for a new society — more is at stake! He is what he called himself: a tomb and a temple to which future generations will bring their wreaths. Not that his mystic and volcanic rhythms are intended as a model for the apprentice to poetry — more is at stake! In that he broke up and re-concentrated traditional words and their patterns he gave a new youth to language and thus to the soul. His unambiguous predictions which cannot be pried apart make him the pivot of Germany's immediate future and the prophet of a new god.

Printed in the USA
CPSIA information can be obtained
at www.ICGtesting.com
LVHW090814090724
784925LV00001B/4

9 781469 657868